BUSINESS HISTORY OF INDIA

BUSINESS HISTORY OF INDIA

Editors

Chittabrata Palit

Pranjal Kumar Bhattacharya

KALPAZ PUBLICATIONS

Delhi- 110002

Business History of India

Rs. 690

ISBN : 81-7835-497-7

Published in 2006 in India by
Kalpaz Publications
C-30, Satyawati Nagar
Delhi-110052
email : kalpaz@hotmail.com

Laser Type Setting by: Mega Graphics, Delhi
Printed at: Salasar Imaging System, Delhi

Contents

Preface

Business history of India - a top priority area of historical research was the subject of a National Seminar held by the Department of History, Jadavpur University in March 2002. This was an exploration into the business heritage of India through the ages to find out India's moorings in material development. India has been believed as a religious and spiritual nation without any roots in material culture. It is necessary to establish that India had both sacred and secular traditions intertwined in its historical past.

The papers presented in the seminar and included in this volume argue this aspect. There are one or two existing volumes in the field but this will be a welcome addition to this growing literature. The funds for the seminar came from Jadavpur University Higher Education Department, Govt. of West Bengal and ICHR, New Delhi. We wish to thank all these funding agencies.

Our special thanks are due to all the participants in the seminar who have finally contributed their articles to the volume. We wish also to thank Sri Ajay Jain of Monohar Publishers and Distributors L.T.D. for undertaking to publish the volume.

Editors

Introduction

Business history of India is now a thrust area of historical research in view of its importance in the life of a nation like India. In western perspective, India was viewed as a country given to spiritualism and philosophy, art and letters. Its material development and pursuit of science, technology and business were systematically ignored in western treatises on the subject. In fact, India was identified as the sacred and the secular in contrast was considered the staple of western culture. The motive behind this dualistic approach might have been prompted by the colonial hangover which perceived India as a producer of raw materials only and the mother country as the industrial manufacturer. India's commercial and industrial heritage was ignored and even suppressed to keep up the industrial domination of Britain. As a consequence not only business and industry withered away but also the history of such enterprises. In free India, histories of science and technology and business and industry are now being written to restore our heritage of natural activities to inspire national reconstruction. Such consideration led to the holding of a national seminar on Indian business by the department of History, Jadavpur University in March 2002. Many important papers surveying the growth of Indian business through the ages were presented in this seminar. These papers are now gathered for producing a composite business history of India.

In the ancient section, the opening paper by H. P. Ray raises some methodological issues to study business in ancient India. She queries the western view that the Asian merchants carried on peddling trade whereas Europe indulged in an institutionally superior organised company trade which led to its later economic triumph over Indian business. She tries to show that it was Europe which tried to adjust to Indian conditions to survive against equally efficient Indian trading ventures. The role of the state in controlling trading activity 'situated in overall agrarian milieu' has also been questioned by her. She has argued that the state had in many ways patronised trade instead of holding a monopoly. So also had religion and religious establishments nurtured trade. The state and the religious texts had also evolved a code of conduct for business including gifts, barter and trade. She urges at the end of her essay to produce deeply researched studies to establish the above facts instead of celebrating business heritage in loosely done compendiums.

Her fillip is well taken by Nupur Dasgupta in the next essay on the exploration of the smritis in search of a legal and moral code of conduct for commercial enterprises. Dasgupta delves deep into the subject starting from Arthashastra, Manusamhita and a host of smritis and other literary Buddhist texts. She matches the literary sources with epigraphic evidence between the second century BC and seventh century AD. She is able to prove that the state and community codes and laws prescribed suitable codes of conduct for free flow of business. All kinds of business transactions viz., gifts, barter and trade, sale and purchase, sellers liability, stock-in-trade, allocation of shares and insurance of seafaring commerce are brought under the purview of these codes. Then she turns to the guilds and their operations mainly drawing from Arthashastra and some smrities. Early Indian business was not unrestricted as a modern business enterprise. But still there was legal support for Indian business and business communities. There was, after all, no religious or moral tabu on business nor state law to thwart it. Business ethic was what was enforced. Dasgupta has really demonstrated the immense importance and possibilities of the subject.

Suchandra Ghosh in her next paper, Business in early Bengal of the Pre-Gupta phase uses a numismatic approach to establish a history of mercantile and commercial activity and a market network. Coin as an exchange medium can open up the history of the market, its customers and articles of trade. She has correctly remarked that coins are invaluable source for a proper understanding of the economic history especially the business history of the given period. From this source, she states with conviction that metal money in Bengal cannot be pushed beyond 3rd century BC when copper coin and punch-marked silver coin become available. According to her, seals being often stamped and inscribed are generally dependable trade and administrative documents. The legends written in Bramhi-kharoshthi mixed scripts are also important documents. The availability of Kushana coins and Satavahana coins in Bengal shows the extensive trade through Bengal from North India to South India. Bengal was participant in coastal trade network and middle category vessels were in operation in eastern bay and deltaic areas of Bengal for transportation of commodities like grain, textiles, spices and horse. For these items, Bengal imported silver and gold from Burma, Maldives and even China. This paper is also a pointer to new horizons of business history through the studies of coins.

We pass on to the late medieval and early modern period with Ruby Maloni's paper on the Seventeenth Century Merchant Capital : The case study of Surat. She digs out valuable materials from factory records, Mughal records and Gujrati Business manuscripts to make her case study of Surat as a flourishing port in pre-colonial India. Surat, according to her, was the unquestioned capital of external trade in the western Indian ocean. In the trading world of the Indian ocean, Indian merchants and Indian products were dominant. Gujrati traders organised direct voices with their shipping and capital. Prominent merchants like Virji Vora, Haji Zahid Beg, Hari Vaisya and Abdul Ghafur dominated the commercial scene in Surat. It declined only when the British occupied Bombay and established their sway in the region. Businessmen began to desert Surat and flocked to Bombay the new commercial capital of the western coast.

We turn from the western coast to the east. S. J. Stephen explores the business world of middlemen and merchants in The French Commercial enterprises in Pondicherry between 1674 and 1741. Stephen shows that the Mudaliar family for three generations served the French company in Pondicherry as their 'Dewan'. From 1702, it was the turn of the Pillais, to act as the chief broker till 1724. They were the middlemen between the buyers and suppliers of textiles. Apart from these brokers, there were merchants like the chetty family, who also held a monopoly on the textile trade. The French heavily depended on them for supply of capital. One merchant Narasu by name, was appointed as the chief merchant by the French.

His commercial activity was not restricted to textiles only, he was also engaged in rice trade. He had a share in minting 'Pagodas' and was also functioning as a money-changer. He floated a joint-stock company of twenty five local merchants, but this company did not last long, due to inner opposition. But the tradition of joint-stock company continued. Stephen mentions one Sunku Rama, a famous Chetty merchant in Pondicherry. The other famous Indian merchant was Sunku Seshachalee Chetty, who also had extensive trade with the French, till 1741. There were other prominent merchants too, who had connection with the French company, but were not dominated by them. The Komalli Chettys showed a considerable capacity to resist the French pressure and establish full control over textile trade. But they also began to move to Madras, with the decline of the French and the rise of the British East India Company. Aniruddha Ray explores the role of two Indian brokers of the French East India Company in Eastern India in the first half of 18th century. He shows how the French East India Company at Chandernagore and Patna were abjectly dependent on Indranarayan Choudhuri, the broker at Chandernagore and Deepchand at Patna for loan and procurement of goods for exports. These two established a wide range of commercial practices under the French umbrella. Both became millionaires and were in full control over the entire affairs of the French at these two places. Both were partners of Dupleix's private trade. With the fall of the French Company however, their fortune also declined. Their business operations have been detailed in this paper with the help of French sources for the first time. As a contrast against this compradorial trade Rila Mukherjee builds up the story of the Nawab's of the same period from Nizamat papers, British and French factory records, travellers, accounts etc. She demonstrates how internal and external trade of Bengal shifted from Dhaka to Murshidabad and Nawab's patronage led to the development of commercial agriculture and tràde in foodgrains, cotton and silk. A whole network of bazars and ganjs sprang up with Kasimbazar as the entrepot of such business. The importance of this new network of bazar, ganj and bandar was that it was completely under indigenous control. While the Nawabs were successful in garnering the agrarian resources of Bengal Subah by means of controlling the distributive network of grain and essential staff, they failed to develop an articulative commercial policy centring around the silk production of Kasimbazar. The English East India Company established its control over the up-country riverine network and access to the sea port of Calcutta. Thus Bengal's internal trade was controlled by the Nawabi network while the export trade through Calcutta came to be monopolised by the English. In the domestic sector, the rise of market towns or ganjs, golas bazars and haats was promoted by the Nawabs by directly establishing such commercial establishments or by patronising private enterprise under the zamindars. She also traces the decline of the East Bengal ports and their takeover by the Europeans and the rise of Calcutta as the supreme port of the Subah under the English.

Balai Barui gives a vivid account of Bengal salt merchants in the second half of 18th century who rose from the indigenous tradition of golas and ganjs. These Bengali merchants continued to thrive even after the East India Company had set up a monopoly over salt trade. The competition of European private traders could not affect their business effectively. There followed a period of collaboration with the Europeans whereby many salt merchants became their banians. The contractors and sub-contractors had their different modes of business unknown to the Europeans and formed their sub-monopolies over salt. Leading merchants among them were Pal Chaudhuris of Ranaghat, Deys of Serampore, Motilals of Bowbazar, etc. They frequently combined their business operations by caste solidarity.

Smriti Kumar Sarkar goes further back in the pre-colonial era to trace indigenous entrepreneurship of artisans in north and south India. His study of weavers and black-smiths particularly of south India is highly interesting. He has given a few case-studies of artisans-turned great merchants like the Pramaniks of Calcutta, Gurudas Das of Nabadwip, Barmans of Matiary and Kanai Das of Sonamukhi, all in Bengal who evolved from the status of artisans into merchants themselves illustrating the potential of capitalist development.

The colonial period was generally stifling for indigenous business, but even under the Company's monopoly some Bengali banians found their escape routes in trade with American merchants in the Indian Ocean. One such family of American merchants were the Browns of Providence about whom Ranjan Chakraborty writes in his next paper. As East India merchants they brought their bullion to purchase Indian silk, cotton, spices and condiments. Their ships visited Calcutta, Bombay and Madras and contracted Indian merchants like Ram Dulal Dey, his nephews Asutosh Dey and Promatha Dey, Rajendra Dutta and Kalidas Dutta and Raj Krishna and Radhakrishna Mitra. With their help it was possible to bypass the Company's monopoly and run a parallel trade favouring enterprise. These Indo-American ventures were on the basis of partnership, without the prejudice of a white club which helped the growth of Indian business well into the 19th century till the British authorities thwarted it by one way free trade.

But colonial rule could not altogether throttle swadeshi enterprise. Amit Bhattacharyya sketches the evolution of swadeshi economic thought in Bengal in the late 19th and early 20th centuries which sustained swadeshi economic enterprise. The thoughts of Dadabhai Naoroji, M. G. Ranade, William Digby, R. C. Dutt are well known in this respect. They have argued how the arm of political conquest ruined agriculture and industries by crippling effects of drain of wealth. He then discusses the thoughts of Sakharam Ganesh Deuskar, Rabindranath Tagore, Ramendra Sundar Trivedi, Jogindranath Sarkar, Prafulla Chandra Ray, Surendranath Tagore, Jogesh Chandra Ghosh, Gananath Sen and others.

These thinkers inspired the establishment of the Bengal National Chamber of Commerce in 1887. Chittabrata Palit in his following paper revives the Bengali business tradition of 19th century with reference to Ram Dulal De, Dwarkanath Tagore, Motilal Seal, Ram Gopal Ghosh, etc. He shows how some of the later entrepreneurs like Digambar Mitra, Durga Charan Laha, and Bholanath Chandra failed in their business enterprise due to colonial stranglehold. Bholanath Chandra in his Mukherjee's Magazine had pleaded for establishment of a National Chamber of Commerce which ultimately took shape in 1887 through the collaboration of Bengali and Marwari communities. The National Chamber fought many notable cases against the government in its long career. It fought against the unequal tariff on salt trade in the 1890s, against unequal freight and license fees levied on steam navigation on the Bengal rivers in the first two decades of the 20th century, ban on women labour in collieries in the 1920s and the use of buffalo carts for transportation of goods in the same periods with some success but the efforts of the National Chamber were badly compromised. Marwaris led by G. D. Birla established the Indian Chamber of Commerce in 1925 and carried out compradorial alliance with the British companies till the Second World War. But after the war, some of the swadeshi enterprises still survived and new ones like Anandabazar Patrika and Hindusthan Insurance Company came to prominence. Palit argues that Bengali business heritage spans more than three hundred years though chequered. It is a story of continuity which is now spearheaded by entrepreneurs like the Peerless Group, Development Consultants and Sahara India.

In the last essay, Pranjal Kumar Bhattacharyya traces the transition of the Marwaris from petty traders and Compradorial merchants into nationalist industrialists of independent India. Before the Second World War and soon after they had started investing their profit into important industries like jute, coal, cement, cotton, paper, metal, etc. Jalans, Birlas, Singhanias, Khaitans and Bajajs led the way. They became the national bourgeoisie and the backbone of the Indian National Congress. This business history of India is a collaborative effort to highlight the main trends of Indian business from trade to industry written by a number of experts. It presents unity in diversity - the saga of a viable and vibrant Indian business enterprise.

In a microstudy of the Marwaris of North Bengal, Narayan Saha has given his investigative analysis of their migration and settlement, family and business network. As migrants, Marwaris cooperated with each other and always moved as a community in their struggle for survival and pursuit of prosperity. Saha has got into the gut feelings of the Marwaris in this indepth study.

List of Contributors

1. **Himangshu Prabha Ray** : Professor of History.
   Jawaharlal Nehru University,
   New Delhi

2. **Nupur Dasgupta** : Reader in History,
   Jdavpur University,
   Kolkata.

3. **Suchandra Ghosh** : Lecturer in Ancient Indian History,
   Calcutta University,
   Kolkata.

4. **Ruby Maloni** : Reader in History,
   University of Mumbai,
   Mumbai.

5. **S. Jeyaseela Stephen** : Professor of History,
   Visva Bharati University,
   Santiniketan.

6. **Anirudh Ray** : Former Professor of Islamic
   History and Culture,
   Calcutta University,
   Kolkata.

7. **Rila Mukherjee** : Reader in History, Jadavpur
   University, Kolkata.

8. **Balai Chandra Barui** : Professor of History,
   Kalyani University,
   West Bengal.

9. Smriti Kumar Sarkar	:	Professor of History, Kalyani University, West Bengal.
10. Ranjan Chakraborti	:	Professor of History, Jadavpur University, Kolkata.
11. Amit Bhattacharya	:	Professor of History, Jadavpur University, Kolkamta.
12. Chittabrata Palit	:	Professor of History, Jadavpur University, Kolkata.
13. Prinjal Kumar	:	Professor of History, Bhattachary Jadavpur University, Kolkata.

1

Business in the Ancient Period Some Methodological Issues

Himangshu Prabha Ray

It is not often that seminars focus on themes and discuss these across the different periods of Indian History. In this regard the concept of the present seminar on "Indian Business : Pre-Colonial & Colonial Perspectives" is indeed laudable. One way of addressing the topic would be to present an overview of historical developments related to business and trade in the ancient period. As I will show in my paper, this approach is the more commonly followed tendency. A second would be to focus on specific issues, which may help in understanding the complexity and diversity of mercantile practices in the ancient period in order to comprehend the nature of change in the colonial period. I will adopt the second approach. The objective of my paper then is to review some of the important trends that have emerged in historical writing on the subject, particularly with reference to the study of ancient Indian history.

I

The first question that needs to be addressed is the definition of terms such as business and trade and the extent to which these may be termed synonyms. One view would contrast the peddling trade of Asian merchants with the institutionally superior organisation of the European companies, which was, it is claimed, in part responsible for their success. Another would, however, argue that the Asian trading ventures were no less economically efficient than those of the European counterpart were. Can one then propose a separation between trade, which may better represent transactions in the ancient and medieval periods in contrast to the complexity of business as it developed in the modern period?[1] The issue is further complicated by the fact that the "older notion that the European 'impact' (now decried as a value-loaded word) changed indigenous commercial institutions quite significantly has been strongly refuted, and all modern historians are agreed that it was the European who adapted to the indigenous commercial institutions and practices".[2] There was constant balancing that the Europeans had to contend with, in order to reconcile the interests of the state-regulated European trading companies with what was termed 'Asian trade' that was largely in private European hands.[3] Perhaps a more effective option between these two opposing trends would be to analyse traditional forms of mercantile operation in the pre-colonial period and to assess their contribution through a variety of factors. Obviously there can be no uniform pattern in the extent to which these may have been transformed or survived intact after contact with European powers either chronologically or spatially.

A second factor that is crucial to a study of traditional mercantile operations in the ancient period is interaction between trading communities and the state. In the writing of Ancient Indian History the study of trade and exchange networks has largely been seen as controlled by the state. It has been argued that trading networks evolved around the middle of the first millennium BC in north India as a result of agrarian expansion and the availability of a surplus.[4] Secondly, the Mauryan State is created with initiating integration of parts of peninsular India into the trading systems of the north. The period from AD 600 to 1200 was marked by an increase in the number of land grants to brahmanas by the rulers leading to a major shift in the material culture, which became rooted to the rural agrarian economy. This agrarian expansion resulted in the growth of a rural economy and the emergence of rural and locality-level trade centres.[5]

These trends continue to be repeated as evident from a recently edited volume on *Trade in Early India*, which reiterates that trading activity was controlled by the state and "situated in an overall agrarian milieu".[6] This is in spite of the fact that Prof. B. N. Mukherjee has raised the question of applicability of terms such as the 'state' in the ancient and medieval periods, especially since the concept of the state evolved in a political sense only in 16th century Europe.

He argues that "in the field of Indian historiography, the legends and theories which pass as indicating the origin of the state, are really concerned with speculations about the beginnings of kingship".[7] Thus the interaction between political control and trading activity in the ancient period needs to be re-defined.[8] It is also time that the study of trade was unhinged from an agrarian milieu and located within the wider domain of cities, changing consumption patterns, the dynamics of economic transactions and transformations in institutional systems that supported and allowed diversification and expansion.

It is also important that studies on trade and trading activity in ancient India should incorporate data from a variety of sources and by no means restrict themselves only to inscriptions. A comparative study of the Jain literary sources with the data from inscriptions of Gujarat and Rajasthan indicates several significant contrasts. Maritime trade and seafaring activity is referred to primarily in the texts dated between the eighth to eleventh centuries AD. These contain several references to long-distance trade and merchant communities, but the stories are invariably set in Kausambi and Hastinapura and the primary objective is the propagation of a moral code of conduct. The second phase of literary activity dated between the twelfth to fifteenth centuries AD was marked by the composition of plays and epic poems eulogising prominent merchant families. The inscriptions, on the other hand, provide valuable details regarding the lineage of the merchants, their elaborate family genealogies and the extensive geographical spread of their business operations, but contain few references to their overseas trading ventures (Sharma, 1996).

Another issue that requires greater attention is the role of religion in providing identity, establishing networks and the fact that traders and scholars often combined journeys undertaken in their personal interest with pilgrimage to holy places and shrines. I have argued elsewhere that the attitude of Buddhism towards seafaring activity is unlike that of its contemporary religions, especially its approach in adopting the notion of a saviour from the dangers encountered at sea.[9] It is not to be suggested that adherents of Buddhism dominated maritime activity in the ancient period. Instead there are references to a range of communities involved, owing affiliation to a variety of religions, such as Hinduism and Jainism.

A fourth issue that one must contend with is the appropriateness of studying Indian Business as a discontinuous activity within the boundaries of the subcontinent, since there is evidence for several overlapping networks that transcended national boundaries into the larger Indian Ocean world and which continued already established maritime traditions. These ranged from movements of merchant groups involved in the exchange and trade of a range of commodities to contact between the carriers and boat building and seafaring groups along the littoral and travel by religious functionaries. The mobility of the merchants enabled them to migrate and shift their areas of operation to newer regions and ports. For example, the merchants of Siraf and Sohar shifted to the ports of Qais and other regions after the decline of trade in the upper Gulf. This mobility also meant that merchants were often stationed on foreign shores and there are several references in literature and inscriptions to groups categorised as outsiders. On account of the complexity of economic transactions in the ancient period, determining religious identities of maritime networks, i.e. Muslim trading system and national affiliations, such as Indo-Roman trade is a task fraught with difficulties.

In the writing of ancient Indian history, ceramics have been used most frequently to demarcate trade networks and often to establish the identity of the groups involved in trade. While the former objective may be well founded, the validity of information on identity of trading groups based on pottery types needs to be questioned. Wheeler identified so-called 'foreign pottery' during his excavations at the site of Arikamedu on the east-coast of India. He used these ceramic finds to endorse not only the nature of trade, i.e., Roman, but also the ethnicity of the users and hence suggested an Indo-Roman trading station at the site.[10] More significantly, he unwittingly started a trend for the study and interpretation of ceramics that has proved surprisingly tenacious. Indeed a recent publication titled, *A Source book of Indian Civilization* refers to the existence of foreign settlements on the east coast of India, especially those of Roman sailors and merchants at Arikamedu. The evidence for these settlements according to the editor is based on finds of pottery fragments of Rouletted Ware from the site, which "arrived in India around 2nd century BC."[11]

The commodities involved in maritime trade in the western Indian Ocean may be divided into various broad categories such as aromatics, medicines, dyes and spices; foodstuffs, wood and textiles; gems and ornaments; metals; and plant and animal products. These categories find mention in a range of textual sources from the first century AD *Periplus Maris Erythraei* to the Geniza documents of the 11th to 13th centuries, Chinese accounts and medieval Arab writings.[12]

Gold, silver and copper were the main traded metals, exchanged both as currency and bullion. Though sources of copper and lead are available in the subcontinent, the *Periplus* refers to the import of copper, tin and lead to Kane (section 28), Barygaza (section 49) and Muziris (section 56) on the west coast. This is repeated in the Geniza documents, which refer to trade in metals from south India and regular export of iron and steel, brass and bronze vessels. In return copper, tin and bronze vessels were imported into the south where new ones were created and old ones repaired.

These commodities were exchanged through a complex diversity of transactions including gifts, barter and trade. There are several references in the *Periplus* to presents given to the ruling classes, for example, wine and grain in considerable quantity imported into the region of the Barbaroi in east Africa was "not for trade but as an expenditure for the goodwill of the Barbaroi" (section 17). Muza offered a good roadstead for mooring and a market for a wide variety of merchandise. To the king and governor were given horses and pack mules, gold-ware, embossed silverware and expensive clothing (section 24). Similarly in the region of Barygaza or Bharuch on the west coast of India, for the king was imported slave musicians, beautiful girls as concubines, fine wine, expensive clothing with no adornment, and choice unguent (section 49).

This practice is alluded to in the later period as well when the governor of Sohar sent a variety of gifts to the Caliph in AD 917 to solicit his help against the Qarmathians. These included a talking myna bird from India, several monkeys from Indonesia and an ant as large as a cat from Africa and a number of giant serpents. "These exotic gifts clearly made a great impression on contemporaries since different items are recorded by no fewer than four independent writers". Thus no single medium of exchange was adequate to cover the diversity of transactions mentioned.

II

With these remarks, one should move on to a discussion of some of the more recent works, which discuss data from the ancient period within a broader canvas. There are at least two major publications that present a history of Indian Business from the ancient period to contemporary times. One of these is an edited volume sponsored by FICCI titled, *Footprints of Enterprise* : *Indian Business Through the Ages* (Oxford University Press, 1999). The other is a study by P.N. Agarwala under the title *A Comprehensive History of Business in India from 3000 BC to 2000 AD* (Tata McGraw Hill Publishing Company Limited, 2001). Both these volumes attempt a chronological narrative of Indian Business and highlight the domination of British business interests in the last half of the 18th century. The objective is to stress that this transformation of the East India Company into the colonial state was largely to the detriment of Indian business enterprise. While these accounts are useful compendiums they end up as celebratory narratives tracing the beginnings of the Indian business heritage to the Harappan period. Perhaps it is time to introduce rigour in the subject and to focus on merchant communities and the complexity of interactions in specific historical and regional contexts.

Kanakalatha Mukund in her study titled *The Trading World of the Tamil Merchant* (Orient Longman, 1999) attempts "to piece together a composite picture of mercantile activity and organisation" in the Coromandel starting from the early centuries of the Christian era to the 18th century. Her study is based on the hypothesis that merchants in the

Coromandel had evolved over the centuries into a distinct class of merchant capitalists, with a conscious perception of their identity both as an economic and as a social class. Thus she uses data from the ancient period far more creatively than the two works mentioned earlier. She traces the evolution of trading as a specialised function as distinct from production and the development of a hierarchy of markets, which integrated the economy both spatially and functionally. There is clear evidence for the establishment of new institutions and changes in the trading structure over time. Much of the discussion on the ancient period is however, compressed in two chapters, but could form the basis of further investigations linking the pre-colonial with the colonial.

Other approaches that historians of ancient India could use profitably are field studies, which "explore the process by which social, cultural and economic processes are woven together into webs of trade".[13] These empirical studies highlight three network systems that are particularly characteristic of the functioning of business communities in western India. The first is the kinship system, which helps in regulating the internal working of business groups. The second is the circulation of credit, which determines interaction between different social groups and different branches of activity in the production and marketing process. The third network system concerns the territorial links amongst and between mercantile groups.

Writings on World History have often used data from South Asia for comparative studies and a recent addition to the list is the book by Philip Curtin titled *The World and the West : The European Challenge and the Overseas Response in the Age of Empire*, Cambridge University Press, 2000. The objective of the book is to assess the contribution of technology in changing human society from 1700s onwards and to emphasis the dominant position of the West in this development on a global scale. The author achieves this through case studies of particular problems relating to a range of diverse non-Western societies. One theme that is relevant to this discussion is that of maritime technology, which the author suggests was fundamental to the entire colonial exercise. The aim is to re-examine the superior technology of the European watercraft as envisaged by the author.

The author divides human history into three periods : pre-agricultural age; agricultural age; and industrial age. As the author argues, there is no doubt that with the development of the industrial age, 'Western' societies played a central role in world history. In earlier centuries the most important modes of cultural contact were commercial. Between about 1425 and 1525, European mariners revolutionized human ability to travel by sea and return. This maritime revolution gave Europeans significant military advantage and this mobility of sea-power made it possible for the Europeans to build trading post empires and enclaves at a time when they were still inferior militarily on land. These trading enclaves were no threat to major Asian powers, but they were the entering-wedge from which territorial empires were to spread in later centuries. The period from 1870 to 1900 was the central period of European military superiority based on the new weapons.[14]

An issue that is relevant to the debate is the nature of the European vessels during the early voyages to the Indian Ocean. Major innovations in hull design and rigging took place in Western Europe from the 12th to 15th centuries, which transformed the earlier unwieldy water vessels into those capable of transoceanic voyages. In spite of the improvements, the craft utilised by merchants and explorers for travel to Asia continued to be of modest dimensions, shallow-keeled and rather primitively rigged. In the 16th and 17th centuries there was a greater use of Asian boatyards by Europeans for shipbuilding and a majority of these yards werc located on the west coast of India at Goa, Cochin, Calicut, Bassein and Daman and at centres in Gujarat and Kathiawar.[15] The reason for this was that production and labour costs were much lower in India as compared to Europe.

In addition to these, other vessels involved in Indian Ocean trade were termed 'country ships' and a majority of these were built in India and owned by Europeans.[16] For example, twenty country crafts were built in the mud dock at Mazagon at Bombay from 1800 to 1833 and the Europeans owned fourteen of these. These privately owned merchant vessels traded along the Indian and Malay coasts to Sumatra, China, the Persian Gulf, the Red Sea and East Africa. These vessels, nonetheless had to obtain the Company's licence and be registered at the port of Bombay, but it is difficult to quantify the number of craft that complied with this regulation. Armed to varying degrees, when required, the country craft were also used for transporting troops.

Another category of vessels plying the Indian Ocean were the Gujarati vessels owned by diverse communities such as the Sidi Muslims or Koli Hindus, which called at ports such as Porbundar and Bhaunagar on the west coast. Built of teak, these ships were very different from European vessels, both in the methods of construction adopted and the materials used. European visitors to the Indian Ocean marvelled at the longevity of the ships built at Surat. These lasted "much longer than European ships, even a century, because they were so solidly built, the planks in their bottom and sides being let into one another in the nature of rabbet work".[17] Nor was size a constraint, as Gujarati vessels were built of 1000 tons and upwards.

There were several segments in the maritime network of the Indian Ocean in the 18th and 19th centuries. From September to April, there were regular coastal voyages between the ports of the Malabar coast and Bombay and these brought timber, pepper, coconuts, coir and some rice to the latter. In addition were annual voyages from Bombay to China and these vessels invariably carried raw cotton. This trade was almost entirely in the hands of private merchants both Europeans and Indians as also employees of the East India Company in their private capacity.

In the first three decades of the 19th century several modifications were introduced in the country ships largely because of transformation in the nature of trade as well as political changes in the Indian Ocean region. The primary export commodity cotton gave way to increasing demand for opium from China. To be able to maintain the competitive edge, the generally smaller and faster Bengal 'opium clipper' evolved. But by the middle of the 19th century, the country ships built in India could no longer compete with European vessels. "The new trade from England relied on increasingly more sophisticated European banking systems and the involvement in time of money markets worldwide. In this field, Indian merchants found it hard to compete".[18]

III

In the final section, it may be pertinent to present a comparative approach based on recent studies of the Mediterranean region. The most influential in this regard has been Fernand Braudel's path breaking study, which opens with an unambiguously Romantic assertion of his passionate love for the Mediterranean. Following from this is his attempt at writing total history in which the deciding geographical forces are the sea, the climate and the surrounding landscape.[19] The influence of the Braudelian paradigm on Indian historians has been significant, especially in the writings of K.N. Chaudhuri[20] and R. Chakravarti,[21] but has been critiqued in the more recent study of Horden and Purcell.[22]

Horden and Purcell in their 750-page work raise an important question regarding Braudel's selective use of 16th century documents for his study on the Mediterranean and the unity of space and continuities over time that he assumes rather than establishes. The overarching influence of geography over the destiny of man denigrates conscious behaviour and the impact of man on the environment. Besides the abstract notion of unity of the sea has to be contrasted with a visual ordering of geography as is evident from chains of beacons or signal stations used by Greeks and Romans as part of their networks of communication and for conveying messages. "The chains of perceptibility created by looking from one vantage point to the next served both to express the relationship of individual localities to one another and to make sense of the wider world."[23] In the contest of the sea this was even more important since it was the coastal features along the shore and the visibility of sea-marks that defined the sailing world in antiquity and created a distinctive maritime milieu. This maritime milieu created coastal enclaves, which dominated communication both across the ocean as well as with the hinterland.

The history of ancient commerce has often revolved around long-distance networks in high value goods as opposed to the small movements along the coast. This dualism does not take into account the fact that archaeological data and the Cairo Geniza papers dated between 11th and 13th centuries indicate that trade in staples was much more voluminous than that mentioned in literary sources and that this short-distance connectivity added to the interdependence of the micro-regions of the Ocean. "High and low commerce are inextricable, and the former is best seen as depending on the latter, arising out of it, declining into it, in overlapping phases of what might be labelled intensification and abatement".[24]

The geography of religion showing the constellation of religious sanctuaries provides a further dimension to connectivity across the seas and challenges the somewhat linear view of development of religions as generally accepted by historians. This geography includes not only religious structures such as mosques and temples, but also holy burials or tombs, sacred trees, springs and rural cult spots. Individual physical features such as mountains were not only easily visible from the sea, but were also associated with religious veneration. It is also important to recognise that almost every holy spot has been associated with more than one religion, be it Buddhism, Jainism, Hinduism, Islam or Christianity. Secondly local shrines and cult spots linked the village to the town and located these within a larger religious geography. Practices such as that of pilgrimage provided wider connectivity through movements of groups and communities.

"Both Islam and Christianity are geographical religions. They might be said to have expressed the layout of the world religiously in three principal ways : through a sense of the boundaries beyond which the faithful are no longer found; through the relationship of the narrative of the religious system and its locations to the wider world of the faithful; and through the subsequent establishment and maintenance of certres of devotion replicating the original holy places".[25] Given this complexity of the religious geography any discussion of an Islamic or Hindu landscape as done by Chaudhuri remains problematic.

It is also necessary to highlight the dual role sometimes played by pilgrims and a case in point is that of the Gosains or trading pilgrims. Gosains are said to have been major carriers of coral and pearls from the south-eastern coast of India into the foothills of Nepal. In a painting now in the Bodelain Library in Oxford three sanyasis are shown carrying shoulder poles with wicker baskets. An inscription at the back describes them as coming from Caussia or Kasia, a province on the Nepal border and states that they travelled to the south-east coast of India to buy corals and pearls.

As a group they first appear in historical sources in the 15th –16th centuries as followers of Caitanya (1485-1534) and in Bengal, they continued to retain their Vaisnavite affiliation. Elsewhere in the subcontinent, from the 18th century onwards, the Gosains also included members of the Saivite order. They obtained coral, pearls and spices during pilgrimage to the seacoast and exchanged these for gold dust, musk and yak tails on return to Nepal and Tibet. Facilitating their participation in trading activities was a network of *mathas* or monasteries extending from Nepal to south India, which provided halting places on the way. In addition Gosains travelled in armed groups for protection and this, together with their religious status, allowed them to wield considerable political power at the local level.[26]

In conclusion, the diversity and complexity of transactions involved in a study of traditional forms of mercantile operations is evident from an analysis of data in the ancient period. What is required is an understanding of the structures of trade, particularly within the parameters of law and banking functions. These were in turn subject to variations and changes within the larger world of land routes and maritime transportation networks. The religious landscape influenced the trading system in several ways from moulding cultural preferences and choices to active participation. Religious shrines were both consumers of a variety of commodities used in ritual, as well as important locales for trading activity as indicated by shops and markets within or in the vicinity of temple premises. The building of new temples stimulated economic growth thereby transforming both the geographic and social landscapes of the region. [27] At the same time there are several instances of a differential tax on commodities required for religious purposes. More importantly, of course, several commodities such as textiles were imbued with multiple meanings and were both items of common consumption as well as products for elite and religious requirements. The organisation of trade as it evolved both spatially and chronologically is important, but more so is its resilience and ability to overcome challenges. It is this multi-pronged approach that would make a study of Trade and Business in the ancient period more meaningful to historians.

Notes and References

1. Denys Lombard & Jean Aubin edited, *Asian Merchants and Businessmen in the Indian Ocean and the China* Sea, Oxford University Press, 2000, p. vii.

2. Kanakalatha Mukund, *The Trading World of the Indian Merchant*, Orient Longman, 1999, p. 7.

3. Lakshmi Subramanian edited, *The French East India Company and the Trade of the Indian Ocean : A Collection of Essays by Indrani Ray*, Munshiram Manoharlal Publishers Pvt. Ltd., 1999.

4. Instead of being consumed in Vedic sacrifices, this surplus was invested in trading ventures as a consequence of the preaching of the heterodox sects of Buddhism and Jainism resulting in an unprecedented expansion of trading ventures in the Early Historical period. Professor R.S. Sharma in his pioneering work titled *Material Culture and Social Formations in Ancient India* (1983), proposed that the generation of a surplus provided the basis for the emergence of a state and trade and towns played an important role in the distribution of the surplus. "Our study keeps a rather plain evolutionary framework, based on the findings of Marx, Engels and Morgan, and enriched by the generalizations of Gordon Childe and other investigators, who have explored archaeology, anthropology and sociology more or less on the lines of historical materialism" (RS Sharma, *Material Culture*

and Social Formations in Ancient India, Macmillan 1983, p. xix).

5. Ranabir Chakravarti edited, *Trade in Early India*, Oxford University Press, 2001, pp. 80-81.

6. *Ibid*, p. 95.

7. B.N. Mukherjee, *Reflections on Trends in Indian Historiography, Indian History Congress, 61st session*, Calcutta, 2001.

8. A study of the archaeological data and inscriptions indicates that the expansion of trading activity in the Deccan in the Early Historical period resulted not from direct intervention of the Mauryan state, but at the initiative of trading groups. Merchants and guilds exploited the mineral resources of the Deccan, but there is little to suggest the economic integration of the Deccan within the Mauryan State. Similarly there is no evidence to indicate the control of the Mauryan State over the routes or even of a communication network between Pataliputra and the southern provinces that would have made effective military control possible. A significant point that should be mentioned here is that many of the Early Historical routes in peninsular India follow networks established in the earlier Iron Age Megalithic period. H.P. Ray, *The Winds of Change*, Oxford University Press, 1994, Chapter II.

9. H.P. Ray, *The Winds of Change*, Oxford University Press, 1994, p. 153-154.

10. REM Wheeler, A. Ghosh and Krishna Deva, *Arikamedu: and Indo-Roman Trading Station on the East Coast of India, Ancient India*, 2, 1946, pp. 17-124.

11. B.D. Chattopadhyay edited, *A Sourcebook of Indian Civilization*, Orient Longman, 2000, p. 610.

12. L. Casson, *The Periplus Maris Erythraei*, Princeton, 1989, pp. 39-44. M. Tampoe, *Maritime Trade between China and the West*, BAR International Series 555, 1989, pp. 131-153.

13. Philippe Cadene and Denis Vidal edited, *Webs of Trade : Dynamics of Business Communities in Western India*, Manohar, 1997.

14. Philip Curtin titled *The World and the West : The European Challenge and the Overseas Response in the Age of*

Empire, Cambridge University Press, 2000, pp. 3-4, 36.

15. S. Arasaratnam, *Maritime India in the Seventeenth Century*, Oxford University Press, 1994, p. 248.

16. Anne Bulley, *The Bombay Country Ships : 1790-1833*, Curzon Press, 2000.

17. *Ibid.*, p. 27.

18. *Ibid.*, p. 243.

19. F. Braudel, *The Mediterranean and the Mediterranean World in the Age of Philip II*, 2 volumes, Paris, 1949.

20. K.N. Chaudhuri, *Trade and Civilisation in the Indian Ocean : An Economic History from the Rise of Islam to 1750*, Cambridge University Press, 1985. K.N. Chaudhuri, *Asia Before Europe : Economy and Civilisation of the Indian Ocean from the Rise of Islam to 1750*, Cambridge University Press, 1990.

21. R. Chakravarti, *Trade and Traders in Early India*, Manohar Publishers, 2002, pp. 114-115.

22. Peregrine Horden and Nicholas Purcell, *The Corrupting Sea : A Study of Mediterranean History*, Blackwell, 2000.

23. *Ibid.*, p. 125.

24. *Ibid.*, p. 151.

25. *Ibid.*, p. 457.

26. Clarke.

27. Cynthia Talbot, *Pre-colonial India in Practice : Society, Region and Identity in Medieval Andhra* (New Delhi, Oxford University Press, 2001), p. 87.

"Moreover, temples offered arenas for the formation of new sociopolitical identities and the patronage of specific temples was often motivated by such factors. The paronage of temples can hence be viewed as both a symptom and a cause of the dynamism of medieval Andhra society : it both reflected ongoing processes and helped shape further evolution."

2

A Leaf from the Smritis : In Memory of the First Tentative Ventures into Legal and Commercial Enterprises

Nupur Dasgupta

Working on the early history of commerce in India, I chanced upon the evidences, both of archaeological and literary nature. What was found to be lacking was a social perception of this very important aspect of ancient socio-economic life. It seemed as if the entire gamut of early Indian trade operated within epigraphic references to guilds, which either donated grants to religious organizations or themselves received grants from several donors with the stipulation to maintain some religious beneficiaries. Or, if viewed from the literature, the picture that looms large is of merchants, dressed up in resplendent attires visiting the attractions in town. The practical business of the professionals in commerce does not emerge in an institutional format, although abundant references to guilds and the fact of their association with town and village administrations hint at this development. I turned first to the *Arthasastra* of *Kautilya* and then to the *Smritis* in search of a more realistic and practical picture and came upon volumes of evidence that produced a somewhat more focussed illustration of early Indian commercial enterprise. I have rendered this article into a tribute to those un-named scribes of old, whose efforts led to the compendiums on juridical literature being collated as well as those intrepid entrepreneurs who traversed a greater part of the ancient world under all natural and man-made conditions, in pursuit of fortune. The scribes had done the daunting task of collating the major customs and turning them into, what for want of a better and acceptable term, I call 'proto-legal' codes, practised in the contemporary courts of judiciary. The merchants, from hawker to the rich banker, have handed down a heritage that would make us fortunate if followed in the right, relevant spirit in this age of globalization.

Let us begin with the colonial administration. The India Act., re-codified in 1956, closely followed the U.K. Companies Act, 1948. But since then the company legislation in the U.K. has grown in quantity and intricacy. In U.K., amendments of the Act till 1985 kept pace with these developments. On the other hand, in India the Companies Act of 1956 which was founded on the report of the Company Law Committee (Bhaba Committee) and which placed considerable reliance on the U.K. Act of 1948, has been amended on more than fifteen occasions till 1988 and further still in 1991. This evolutionary picture of the Indian Companies Act reflects the changing business scenario in the contemporary Indian and global context. Indian business is continuing on dynamic lines, especially in the recently emerging context of globalization of the world economy.

It might be pointed out that a spurt of commercial activity on a global scale has been observed in the history of early India. The external trade of India between the 1st century AD and 5th century AD may not be described as 'business' in the modern sense but exchange economy. A look at the references to the ancient guilds and the regulations laid down in the contemporary juridical literature as well as epigraphic records lend this assumption historicity. The volume of proto-legal regulations included directives on contract, debt, investment and profit in the context of early historical and early medieval India. The *Dharmasastras* and the *Smritis* discuss the subjects in increasing volume between the 2nd and 3rd centuries AD in the *Manusmriti*; and the *Visnusmriti, Yajnavalkyasmriti, Narada* and *Brishapati* between the 4th and the 6th centuries AD. Interestingly enough, this chronology fits in with the timeframe of what is known in history as the "Indo-Roman Trade", followed by the Persian and the South seas trade operations. The term Indo-Roman trade popularly signifies the long activity of commercial contacts between the eastern Mediterranean shores and Constantinople on the one hand and South-East Asia, China on the other, in which the Indian merchants had played a significant role. Historians have been voluble on this phenomenon and leave very little ground for questions on the evident growth of external commerce from India. Various comments from H.G. Rawlinson throw light on the issue : "In Antioch, Palmyra, and Alexandria, Indian and Greek merchants and men of letters met to freely exchange ideas."[1] The importance of the Kushanas in the Mediterranean and West Asian map is evident in the following comment, "From the time of Mark Antony to that of Justinian, i.e. from 30 BC to AD 550, their political importance as allies against the Parthians and Sasanians, and their commercial importance as controllers of one of the main trade-routes between the East and the West, made the friendship of the Kushanas and other dynasties who held the Indus valley and Gandhara of the highest value to Rome." The greater orbit of the trade is illustrated in the statement that, "Meanwhile a brisk trade was springing up between the great mart at Alexandria and the coast of Malabar."[2] Similarly the evidence for Indian trading enterprise extending into the South-East Asian world is positively abundant. Alastair Lamb writes on this in the same volume with Rawlinson in 1975,"There is archaeological evidence from both India and South–East Asia to suggest that it was the stimulus of demand in the West which set Indians sailing in significant numbers across the Bay of Bengal; ......", and that "There can be no doubt, at all events, that by the fifth century AD. Indian culture was widely known in South-East Asia, ..."[3] But on the whole the current researchers' attempt to analyse the emergence of such extensive commercial activity centred in India possibly touches the core of what we propose to illustrate in this article : the growing incidence of internal commercial enterprise, the networks of which spread tentacles through a very wide geographical horizon, which facilitated the development of such extensive external commerce as noted above. Himangshu Prabha Ray, Ranabir Chakraborty and others discuss the entire paradigm, which bred this substantial commercial network.[4]

I have tried to relate the volume of codes included in the ancient Indian *smritis* with this phenomenon, for it appeared to me to be the most crucial evidence for commerce. Legal discussions on any issue is a result of familiar existence of those issues in day to day life, and the disputes arising out of this familiar existence.[4]

I have noted a gradual increase in the focus on commercial and especially guild operations in the *smritis* throughout the time, between the 2nd century and the 7th century AD. The gradual increase in the volume of discussions on commercial contracts etc. in the *smriti* literature, from the 2nd century AD onwards, indicate the necessity felt for regulations to keep pace with the growing business intricacies actually faced in practical, day-to-day operations. The dynamics of the early Indian business could be brought to light by a careful study of these changes and enlargements in regulations observed in the *smriti*. A historical analysis of these regulations in the *smriti* literature would throw much light on the nature of the early Indian customary and traditional law in relation to the practices of commercial nature. The *smritis* formed the core of Indian customary and traditional law. These customs assumed the stature of codes when brought to practical operations. The abiding importance to these codes in the subsequent legal history is evident. William Jones' attempts to publish a compendium or Digest of Hindu Laws was a part of the colonial policy of ruling an Indian community better by getting to know it more thoroughly. At one point of time, the colonial administrators had felt the necessity of including the Indian customary laws in the colonial system of juridical administration. The ancient *smritis* with their added on commentaries had become inseparable part of every-day life in pre-colonial and colonial Indian society. What we now need is to seek in history the roots of what we may now term as quasi-legal principles concerning business rules. This will not only illustrate the development of commercial enterprises but also illuminate the development of juridical management of these enterprises.

The main sources of this research paper are :

Smritis and normative literature :

1. *Manu Samhita.*[5]
2. *Arthasastra Commentary of Bhattaswami.*[6]

3. *Vishnu Dharmasastra.*[7]

4. *Yajnavalkya Smriti* with the commentary of *Mitaksara* by *Vijnaneswara.*[8]

5. *Narada Smriti.*[9]

6. *Naradiya Manusamhita.*[10]

7. *Brahaspati Smriti.*[11]

8. *Katyayanasmriti Katyayanismritisaroddhara.*[12]

Approximate time structure for the above literary sources :

Arthasastra – 200 BC – 200 AD

Manusmriti – 200 BC – 200 AD

Vishnusmriti – before Yajnavalkya, i.e., about 100 AD – 300 AD, according to P.V. Kane.

Yajnavalkyasmriti – 200 AD – 300 AD.

Narada – 200 AD or, according to S.K. Desai – 4th or 5th century AD, according to Julius Jolly – 6th century AD.

Katyayanasmriti – 300 AD – 600 AD.

Brahaspatismriti – 4th century AD – 6th century AD.

Other Literary Sources :

1. Jataka number 546 in vol. VI mentions a list of eighteen *srenis* including the corporation of masons, painters, blacksmiths, carpenters and men skilled in various arts and crafts.[13]

2. References in *Milindapanho*, a Buddhist text, indicates the existence of occupations of goldsmiths, miners, weavers, dyers, perfumers, etc.[14]

3. *Mahavastu*, a Pali Buddhist Cannonical text, refers clearly to following long list of *srenis* :[15]

- Sauvarnika sreni
- Pravarika sreni
- Mani-prastaraka sreni
- Gandhika sreni
- Tailika sreni
- Ghrtakundika sreni

- Golika sreni
- Dadhika sreni
- Modaka karaka
- Saktu karaka
- Gandha tailika
- Kulairika sreni
- Kolikanikaya sreni
- Auda yantrika sreni
- Attavanija sreni
- Karpasika sreni

And others.

Evidently, these were karusilpi ganas, referred in the Arthasastra of Kautilya.

Epigraphic Evidence:

The inscriptions of *Sakas*, Satavalanas,:(2nd Century BC - 2nd Century AD)

1. Nasik Buddhist of cave of inscription of Usavadatta.[16]

2. Mathura inscription of the 23rd year of Kushana king Huviska mentions the fact of a sum of 550 *purana* coins being deposited with a guild of meal grinders out of the interest of which the guild was entrusted to look after the upkeep of a 100 *brahmans.* [17]

3. Buddhist cave inscription at Nasik of the reign of Madhariputra Isvarasena.[18]

4. Junnar Buddhist Cave Inscription. [19]

5. A second Junnar Cave inscription. Mentioning corn dealers' guild.[20]

6. Nasik inscription also mentions guilds of hydraulic engineers and potters.[21]

7. Bhilsa Topes – Specially interesting : talks about guild representatives from Vedisa, Katakanu, Mahismati, Arapana (Mathura, Sanchi records).[22]

8. Besnagar donors were guild merchants from Taxila etc.[23]

9. Kanheri Buddhist cave inscription also refers to

such merchants from different regions.[24]

10. Nasik inscription also mentions guilds of hydraulic engineers and potters.[25]

Later Inscriptions:

11. Mandason stone inscription of Kumara Gupta and Bandhuvarman of e. 437-38 and 473-74 AD, mention guilds of weavers.[26]

12. Indore plates of Skanda Gupta refer to guilds of oil millers.[27]

13. One Basarh seal mentions *sresthi sarthavaha kulika nigama.*[28]

14. Another Basarh seal bears the word *sresthinigamasya* referring to the seal of guild of bankers.[29]

15. Nirmand Copper Plate Inscription of the *Mahasamanta* and *Maharaja* Samudrasena, AD 612-613 refers to one Udaytokara as *Gana Srestha Chief* of a guild.[30]

16. Western Chalukya inscriptions... Inscriptions of the region of King Tralokyamalla Somesvara I, of 1050 AD mentions a corporate constitution.[31]

17. Dubukund stone inscription of Vikramsimha of Macchapaghata of *Vikram* era 1145 or 1088 AD.[32]

From mixed references, we get the picture of a concept of institutional approach to occupations. Commerce was evidently not the only occupation within guild parameters. So, when we discuss guilds in general, we cannot talk solely of commercial enterprise. But it is apparent that the craft guilds doubled up as commercial houses so far as the selling of their goods is concerned and that they also had the aspects of investment and profit-sharing as in any commercial venture. There were also separate guilds of merchants in different commodities. However, when we are looking at the sources here, we are trying to assess the commercial role of the early Indian *srenis* and the regulations connected to particularly this aspect of their operations. Of this, we shall see that there is no dearth of evidence. The *smritikaras* of Gupta and post-Gupta periods refer to sambhuya samutthana or partnership;[33] and liabilities of partnership in business or profit-making enterprise.[34] They also discuss about regulations protecting both the rightful seller and innocent buyer under the section asvamivikraya.[35] Profit share and other privileges and duties of members of a corporation of merchants and artisans have been treated in details and regulations have been laid down.[36]

A few suppositions to begin with :

It must be clearly stated at the outset that by referring to the smritis and Arthasastra of Kautilya, this paper brings to light the quasilegal structures found in the early smriti literature regarding what was termed as sreni or nigama, a kind of corporation of merchants or artisans or other professionls. The nature of the literature referred here is also discussed in the context of their legal contents and the significance of this legal content in the light of modernday definition of law. The main intent of this reference is to find out exactly how commerce was understood and looked up in the society the smritis portray, and find whether the society was intent on regularizing commercial activity through codifications. A survey of the literature indicate certain facts :

- The high probability of artisan guilds and commercial guilds acting jointly. Laws often overlap for these two separate aspects of productive economy. Business, therefore, was as understood within the scope of these guilds.
- Definitions of partnership often extended beyond commercial ventures.
- Above all, guild laws featured strongly among the matters discussed in these 'juridical' texts. Lack of details of business law in the early smritis may be due to the fact that they were common knowledge and the requirement for codifying them in dharmasastra framework was not yet felt. Most of the internal matters of debate, dispute & title involving legal act, were taken care of by particular guild administrators, who may have followed some manuals, which are not available to us in separate manuscript form. But with time it is apparent that joint venture of commercial nature had assumed a significant proportion and that the political and social authorities were required to intervene in these matters. This necessitated the regularizing of

codes for common reference.

- The focus on transportation of goods and hired servants etc. indicate format of trade enterprises of the times.
- The epigraphic and literary records should be considered in conjunction to get the real picture of commerce.
- According to Mulla book the smritis composed between the 2nd century BC and 7th century AD., deal mainly with law properly so-called as would appear from their contents. They treat law by itself without any reference to the rules of penance, diet or other religious and moral strictures.[37]

Here we have to enter into a discussion of certain definitions and connotations in order to be able to do full justice to the topic of discussion.

A look at what is law :

There is an extremely interesting reference to the wide connotation of a law with reference to a case law in the All India Report of 1965. The definition came as a case law that, "custom and usage having in the territory of India the force of the law must be held to be contemplated by the expression "all laws in force".[38] More importantly, the Constitution of India, article 13, defines "Law includes custom or usage having the force of law."[39] It would be of interest to those who want to traverse the scope of legal history of early India, that the Constitution of India, article 13, brought this definition into exercise with reference to a particular case. This was published in the All India Report of 1965 referring to the case of Govindlalji versus the State of Rajasthan, AIR 1963. SC 1638, 1650. The statement that was issued ran on the following lines - "An absolute monarch was the fountain head of all legislative, executive and judicial powers and it is of the very essence of sovereignty which vested in him that he could supervise and control the administration of public charity ....[40] (Ibid, p. 378) This statement squarely put the issue of legal and judicial authority within an ancient frame of reference in this particular instance, as late as the 20th century. It reminds us of Aristotle's praxis that "Customary laws have intrinsically more force, and pertain to more important matters than written laws; and that a man may well be a safer ruler than the written laws, but not safer than the customary law."[41]

Taking these two wide definitions of law and the issuing authority of law, we may not be wrong in assuming at least that the *Smriti* Literature and *Arthasastra* of *Kautilya,* which form the main evidence for this paper, contain proto-legal codes. These texts specifically refer to 'dharma' or law issued from customs or *'dharmasasthya'* taken together with evidence - *'vyavaharika'* in courts. These codes had functioned as regulations of justice in contemporary society. Most interestingly, the Arthasastra, a text composed between the 2nd century BC and the 2nd century AD, in the background of the emergence of territorial rastras in early India, also, quite logically, talks about royal ordinances or *'rajasasana'*[42]. The text declares the king to be the *'Dharmapravarataka'* or the fountainhead of justice. Sacred law or *dharmasthya,* evidence or *vyavahara,* history or *charitra* and royal edicts or *'rajasasana'* are described as the four legs of law in this text.[43] Following this example, the later composed *smriti* literature devote separate *prakarana* for *vyavahara,* or compendium on civil regulations.

In defence of early Indian *smritis* we may point out that their contents, especially the sections concerning *vyavahara,* or civil procedure, were the accepted legal codes for the Hindus in colonial India till as late as the last decades of the nineteenth century.

If we look at the evolution of the Indian Contract Law some interesting historical facts come to light. The Charter of the 18th century which established the Courts of Justice for the three Presidency towns of Calcutta, Madras and Bombay, introduced into their jurisdictions the English common and statute law in force at the time so far as it was applicable to Indian circumstances. It is, however, a matter of controversy whether English law was introduced by the Charters of 1726 so as to extend to India the statutes passed upto that date only, or subsequently also by the Charters of 1753 and 1774 so as to embrace statutes upto 1774. The indiscriminate application of English law to Hindus and

Muslims within the jurisdiction of the Supreme Courts led to many controversies. The statute of 1781 empowered the Court of Calcutta, which was then the Supreme Court, to obviate this. Following this the statutes of 1797 empowered the Courts of Madras and Bombay, being the recorder's court, to change the situation. The Acts empowered the Courts concerned "to determine all actions and suits against the inhabitants of the said towns, provided that their succession and inheritance to lands, rents, and goods, and all matters of contract and dealing between party and party, should be determined in the case of Mahomedans by the laws and usages of Mahomedans, and in the case of Gentoos by the laws and usages of Gentoos, and where only one of the parties should be a Mahomedan or Gentoo by the laws and usages of the defendant." The effect of these statutes was to supersede English Law so far as regards Hindus and Muslims in the case of contracts and other matters enumerated in the statutes and to declare the right of Hindus and Muslims to their own laws and usage. This continued till the enactment of the Indian Contract Act IX of 1872. It is clear therefore, that till this time the contract law was substantially formatted on the extant regulations of the indigenous codes, which drew largely upon the smritis referred to here, so far as the 'Gentoos' are concerned.

About the Legal Nature of the Smriti Texts :

S.A. Desai describes Three Stages of Indian Legal Literature, viz.,[44]

I. The Vedic epoch and the Pre-Sutra Period.

II. The era of Dharmasastras :

(a) The Sutra period.

(b) The Smriti period.

III. The post-Smriti period.

Desai categorically states that "The Smritis or Dharmasastras are the earliest extant treatises from which our knowledge of the line of development which Hindu law had pursued during the second epoch of its history is derived"......"Composite in their character, the principal smritis blend religious, moral, social and legal duties". ....

"The critical attitude to Smritis as legal codes comes from the angle of Eurocentrism."[45] Desai, an advocate, deals with this perception in the following manner: "The smritikaras were not always punctilious about stressing a clear distribution between the positive or lawyer's law and moral law, but this is not to suggest that they were unmindful of this distinction. When necessary they took care to define this distinction as for instance in the case of the pious and legal obligation of a son to pay the debt of the father when the debt was not for an immoral or illegal purpose". He comes to the point of evaluation of smritis as compilations of proto-legal codes in the following manner: "The charge levelled by some Western scholars against the authors of the Smritis for a want of precision and discrimination between moral and legal maxims is unreasonable and unfounded ..." "A clear perspective of Hindu Law is not possible unless it is properly appreciated that the blending of religion and ethics with law by these jurist theologians was in a large measure the natural results of a philosophy of life......." The acceptance by a corporate society of the connotation of duty *(Dharma)* which associated religions and ethical concepts with secular matters was bound to be projected into its codes of positive law." Desai puts forward some details in order to highlight the wide concept of the ancient Indian jurists. He describes, "It may also be observed that *Yajnavalkya* and some other *smritikaras* divided their treatment of subjects into 3 sections, *Acara* (or custom), *Vyavahara* (*civil* law), and *prayashchitta* (atonement of moral sins). The first and the last relate to rules of religious observances & expiations. The later smritis in fact deal more and more on *vyavahara* and discuss it in separate *prakaranas* or sections." Coming to the modernday connotation and format we appreciate that it is from the angle of Austinian principles that ancient smritis have been criticized. Bentham had stated that the "traditional law of ancient India would be termed as "morality" because that law was not a direct or circuitous command of a monarch or sovereign number to persons in a state of subjection to its author." Desai states that the "smritis, some of which deal exhaustively with various topics of laws and are generally referred to as Institutes or Codes were not codes in the strict sense in which a code is not understood, that is a single comprehensive legislative document on a particular topic or branch of law. The extant smritis were compiled at different time and in different parts of the country but they all purported to record on traditional law. The smriti was not autonomic law, which is the result of true form of legislation or promulgated by the state in its own person. It was not imposed by any superior authority *in invitos*. There was no dogmatic insistence upon any fundamental notions of command of a sovereign and habit of obedience to a determinate person. What was accepted was the rule-dependent notion of what ought to be done as agreeable to good conscience and in conformity with the cherised article of belief that the fundamental rules of law had been derived from a divine author."[46] A legal system is a system of rules within rules; and to say that a legal system exists entails not that there is a general habit of obedience to determinate persons but that there is a general acceptance of a constituent rule, simple or complex, defining the manner in which the ordinary rules of the system are to be identified. One should think not of the sovereign and the independent person habitually obeyed but of a rule providing a sovereign and independent persons habitually obeyed but of a rule providing the sovereign as ultimate test in accordance with which the laws to be obeyed are identified. The acceptance of such fundamental constituent rules cannot be equated with habits of obedience of subjects to determinate persons, though it is of course evidenced by the obedience to the law.[47] The general effective motive, according to these *smritikaras,* was observance of *Dharma* and the sanctions recognized by the people themselves. Enforcement of law *(Danda)* in the nature of things proceeded from the sovereign but one view of the genesis of legal institutes was that the king and the law were created by people. This is quite clear when we refer to the descriptions supplied by the *Pali* Buddhist *Jataka* tales, where the Judge, whether at the lowest rungs or the highest moral authority in the rastra, the king, is often criticized for wrong decisions. Moreover, a look at the laws regarding corporations, sales & purchase, wages contracts, services profits & loss, sharing of profits etc. contained in the later *Smritis* of *Narada, Katyayana* and *Brahaspati* indicate in a positive way that regular acceptance of a 'divinely ordained regulatory code' was not religiously followed by the people in practice. The existence of disputes is evident from the number of legal titles enjoined to be followed in the works of the *smritikaras*. Disputes on above and many other questions were rampant, requiring a detailed treatment in legal treatises to construct a disciplinaryprohibitive format.

A Look at Business :

Definition of Business in the August issue of AIR, All India Reports 1994, Nov. 26, referring to a case law from Madhya Pradesh,[48] is stated in the following manner that "business" is a word of indefinite import and has a very extensive and wide meaning. In general sense "business" means practically anything, which is an occupation, distinguished from pleasure. It encompasses within its folds any venture in the nature of trade, commerce, manufacture or any professions are business". This is probably the widest legal connotation of business. In a more focused definition the term business is used in the sense of an occupation, or profession, which occupies the time, attention and labour of a person, normally with the object of making of profit. To regard an activity as business there must be a course of dealings, either actually continued or contemplated to be continued with a profit motive and not for sport or pleasure.[49] In a narrower, specific sense we may see "business in a particular commodity must depend upon the volume, frequency, continuity and regularity of transactions of purchase and sale in a class of goods and the transactions must ordinarily be entered into with a profit motive."[50] (Ibid, p. 111).

In this last sense, although we cannot graph the exact volume of transactions on particular commodities carried out by specific guilds in early India, there is a definite indicator to continuity of transactions over long periods. The commodities, the artisan and mercantile communities, their wealth-generating activities with a profit motive, profit in terms of fixed and liquid capital, practices of investments and security bonds, are all described in both literary and archaeological evidences. These references make the picture clear. The reality of the "business" of commercial guilds or sreni and merchants or sresthi operating within sreni is conspicuous. We observe a continuous profit-making occupation in the context of early and early medieval India. However, in no way can we provide exact evidences to compare these transactions with the order of business in the modern world. What is required here is a bent of perception to read the meanings and indications of evidences, in order to understand how a past society lived and worked or framed its rules of existence.

Apart from the references we have already drawn to illustrate the nature of commercial enterprise in early India as revealed in the literary and epigraphic sources, let us mention a few more to highlight the fact that profit - making commercial transactions were a part of professional life in that context.

References to commercial enterprise:

A very early reference in the *Aitareya Brahmana* contains an allusion to profit-oriented ventures. The Vaisya class is mentioned here as " the earthly *Vaisya Ganasah",* the mortal group of vaisyas, who had acquired wealth through cooperative effort.[51] (Aitareya Brahmana III, 30, 114 (12)). A large scale business activity through the operation of guilds is not evident in this context and most probably the reference is to the past and the Harappan enterprises, which were by all accounts, of magnum stature. However, the *Pali Jataka* tales belong to a time scope that approximately takes up three or four centuries of history in northern India and matches the time that witnessed the flow of external trade in India both westwards and eastwards. We may briefly refer to some points here. The *Saindhava Jataka*[52] (Jataka story, vol. III, no. 339, p. 83) talks of *assavanijo* or horse dealers, a group of merchants who specifically traded in an item that connected them to Sind. The *Phala Jataka*[53] (Jataka, vol. I, no. 54, p. 135) talks of caravan traders or *sattavahaka.* And, most interestingly, the *Baveru Jataka* refers to *samudda vanija*[54] (Jataka, vol. III, no. 339, p. 83) oceanic merchants. *Gautama Dharmasutra* mentions guilds of cultivators, traders, herdsmen, moneylenders and artisans[55] (*Gautama Dharmasutra,* XI, (21)). *Gautama* tells us that they had authority to lay down rules for their respective classes[56] (ibid, XI, (21)). The text alludes to guilds in connection with persons who lived by trade or by handicrafts or the use of bow and arrow or by playing musical instruments. Clearly these are guilds or joint group organizations of professionals of the same class. But among these guilds there were specific organizations, which undertook profit-making exchange production and commercial ventures. Guilds of merchants were especially called *Vaidehaka* in the *Arthasastra.* In fact artisans guilds were also compounding as commercial guilds in some respects as is evident from the textual and especially the epigraphic records. *Muga pakkha* and *Maha Ummagga Jataka* stories[57] (Jataka, vol. VI, no. 538, p. 14, 22) refer to eighteen guilds, of which a few are such profit making business ventures.

So far as the definitions of business is concerned we find that it is as widely understood as the above modernday connotation, or perhaps more loosely. Let us see what the *smritis* say regarding this. As such we find no direct discussion of the meaning or application of the term *vanijya* in the sense of business in these texts. But a brief outlay from various portions of the *smritis* could throw light on what the jurists read as business and how they approached the problems ensuing from such activities in the contemporary society. The problematic angle could sufficiently illuminate the conception of 'business'. First we refer to a definition:

Yajnavalkya enjoins "A number of traders, carrying on trade or making profit, shall share profit and loss according to their respective share or according to the compact made between themselves. If any member or a company does not act, or acts as forbidden by the general body, or without their permission, or negligently, and thereby causes a loss, he shall have to indemnify the others for the same."[58] (Yaj, II, 262, 263.) Here there is the clear implication of business.

Now there are other portions, dealing with the various activities concerning 'business', which may throw light on the nature of commerce the later *smritis* are referring to. There are issues of the seller's identity:

Brahaspati, for example tackles this problem in the

following manner. He states, "when a sale has been effected in the presence of merchants and also the king's officials are aware of it, but the vendor's habitation is not known or when the purchaser is dead, the true owner can recover his property provided that he pays half the price of the article to the bona fide purchaser."[59] (Br., p. 127, VV. 10 - 11). However, the regulation is wide open and may actually refer to a false sale.

But rather *Narada* enjoins certain injunctions on the question of the purchaser, his rights and liabilities, which may refer to 'business' proper. He lays down that, " A person who purchases any commodity from a person who is not its owner, is absolved of the guilt if he proves that he purchased the article in good faith without knowing that the seller was not authorized to sell it; but he has to return the article to the true owner. Purchasing an article at a fair price and declaring the purchase are indications of the other's good intentions.[60] (Nar, p. 155. V. 4)

Two most important additions in this respect are made to the titles of law in the *Naradasmriti,* composed after the *Yajnavalkya smriti:* One is a title concerning repentance of the purchaser after buying a commodity termed: *Krttanusaya.* The other is formulated concerning the non-delivery of a thing sold, termed: *Vikriyasampradana.* We shall discuss other aspects in *smritis* later in the main body of the evidence, which will throw light on how 'business' was conceived, operated and rules formatted to guide such activities according to codes.[61] (Nar. V. 1; V. 2). *Narada* also takes care of issues like buyer's rights, liabilities, seller's rights and responsibilities, pre-emption, adequate and inadequate price, conditional sale etc.[62] (Nar, VV. 5 ff)

Evidently, the *smritis* were discussing exchange of goods and property along with commodity exchange. Specifications of business were not understood in modern terms. But what is of interest to the historian of early India is the emergence of a clear and problem-specific guideline for commercial transaction. The continuance of commercial exchange is inherently implied in the formation of titles of 'law' or 'vyavahar' in case of sale and purchase modes and the legal moral status of these modes.

Next let us deal with the modernday connotation of company and 'Company Law'. We take this term because the definition of business begins with a reference to company: Business is defined as the commercial enterprise or establishment of commercial practice.

Formation of Company or Corporate: [63]

The board of company law administration, referred to as Company Law Board, was established by the Companies Act, 1963. The statement of objects and reasons stated that "it is considered desirable, for the better and convenient administration of the Companies Act, to set up a board which will be entrusted most of the powers and functions of the Central Government under the Companies Act or other laws. The board will function subject to the control of the Central Government in all matters".

Further section 139 of The Amendment Act of 1988 [64] has established an independent Company Law Board, which would exercise the judicial and quasijudicial functions hitherto exercised by the courts or the Central Government, besides the power already statutorily vested in the Board by the Amendment Act of 1974. The Central Government is empowered to appoint chairman and members of the board and to frame rules to prescribe qualifications and experience of the members. The Board may regulate its own procedure and is to be guided by the principles of natural justice and has to act in its discretion."

How does the ancient *smritikaras* define the *sreni* or the *nigama?*

Yajnavalkya enjoins, "A number of traders, carrying on trade or making profit, shall share or according to the compact made between themselves. If any member of a company does not act, forbidden by the general body, or without their permission or negligently, and thereby causing for loss, he shall have to indemnify the others for the same". [65] (Yaj. II, 262, 263).

He had also stated the qualification of the leader of such guilds: "Persons, conversant with the Vedas, pure minded and shorn of avarice, had to be placed at the head of public body like a guild. All had to follow the words of those who spoke in the interest of a public body. This was also the law for a guild *(sreni)* or the companies of traders and artisans *(nigama)* of various castes coming from different countries for trading purpose[66] (Yaj, II, 262, 263. This is explicit. *Yajnavalkya is* talking about business transactions across caste and regional boundaries. About regulations the common custom has also been pointed out that the *pramukhya* or the Chief of the guild should exercise authority. But there is an extended authority enjoyed by the king too by these times (3rd - 4th Centuries AD) : *Yajnavalkya* lays down that "a ruler should prevent dissensions among them and should make them follow their previous callings, if they had left them." "Learned persons were expected to be selected as the members of a guild and their advices were to be followed. They had to drive away any deceitful member, after having deprived him of his share and had to appoint in the place of an incapable member one who could conduct the business of the guild properly. This law was also applicable to bands of priests, cultivators and artisans, implying their corporations also." [67] (Ibid, Ch. II, (268), p. I08). Obviously then, the third century AD *smritikaras* took the entire conduct of professionals grouped together within the purview of *"sreni"*. Here, therefore, the joint operation of the professionals is in question so far as the legal relations of the members are concerned. Corporations of businessmen are not treated separately while describing the regulation for formation of *sreni.*

A brief review of the list of personnel mentioned in connection with *sreni* operations could throw light on whether a pattern of guild format emerged at the same time that saw the inclusion of codes on corporations and their 'business'. The *Nigrodha Jataka* gives an interesting dimension to the question of guild constitution when it mentions an officer being charged by a king of a *rastra* to the post of the treasurer or *bhandagarika* with which went the duty of judgeship of all the merchant guilds. The *Jataka* also informs us that this was a completely novel instance as there was no previous office of that nature.[68] Probably we could read the significance of this reference in terms of a growing incursion of royal authority in the sphere of guild activity. Yet, the law of the guild was an item by its own as we shall see. At one point probably there was an overlap of authority, which shifted according to the historical context. *Manusmriti* had laid emphasis on guild law for example, while Kautilya Arthasastra was more in favour of royal authority superseding guild authority.

There was a hierarchical list of guild officials, which illustrate the scope of guild activity. The chief of a guild was termed *Pramukhya* or *pamukha* in *Pali*. Squabbles between *pamukhas* of two guilds at *Savitthi* and *Banaras* have been mentioned. *Jyesthaka* or *jetthaka* in *Pali is* another term for the chief of operations. A host of titles like : *Maha setthi, Anu setthis, uttara setthi, janapada setthi* and *Rajagaha Setthi* appear in a Jataka tales like *Kuta Vanija Jataka, Sudhabhojana Jataka* and *Culla Setthi Jataka*, etc.[69] Evidently most of these Jataka tales belong to the post-Maurya times. Reference to Rajagaha Setthis could indicate inferring of special positions to some leading merchants by the Royalty. As to the hierarchy within the ranks of setthis, we have corroboration from the play of *Sudraka, Mrcchakatika,* which reveals that such guilds operated jointly under the *nagarasresthi* and that there were specific localities within cities where the merchants' quarters were situated. *Dandin,* a little later, mentions *vaingjanasamaja,* or assembly of merchants.[70] Contrary to the theory advanced by R. S. Sharma and others of a declining trade, the references to mercantile and artisan guilds compound in the Gupta and post-Gupta times, especially in the epigraphs. While the Gupta period *smritis* generally provide a more comprehensive picture of guild activities than the earlier literature. Epigraphs recording donations and grants mention *Sresthin* and *vaniya* [71], *sathavaha* and *vyavaharin.*[72] Evidently, there were various categories of merchants. The Nirmand copper plate mentioned above speaks of the *ganasrestha,* or the chief of a *gana* or corporation.[73] The *Sangam sahitya* text, *Silappadikaram* gives a graphic description of a *sresthi,* a leader of a hundred goldsmiths, in the city of Madura.[74] Evidently the background is comprised by the new upsurge of Indo-Roman trade spreading into the peninsular. However, the explicit description of a constitution of a corporation comes from a Western Chalukya inscription of the llth century AD. An example, which perhaps illustrates the final spurt of commercial enterprise on large scale in early medieval India during the times that witnessed the rising glory of the Cola rulers. In fact a number of South Indian inscriptions dated between the 8th and the 10th centuries mention commercial corporations and their activities. The five hundred lords of the famous city of *Ayyavole*[75] for example set the standard that the mercantile enterprises had reached in the peninsular India in early medieval times.

Although my discussion focuses on the smritis written between the 2nd and the 7th centuries AD, yet, the description of an 11th century corporate constitution could set the records straight whether trends of regulated, joint, commercial enterprise had a long life in early India. The inscription of the reign of Western *Chalukya* king *Trailokyamalla (Somesvara I)* dated 1050 AD mentions the fact that in a group of royal authorities were present in the official procedure of a renewal of the revenue status of a corporation, which had gone awry due to wars with the Colas.

The features of the discussed format of revenue constitution were as follows:

1. The shops and houses were to have their four sides of access situated in the grounds of the lands of *Karagambadu.*

2. They were allowed to stand, exempt from all imposts *(sarva - badha - pariharam gettu).*

3. From the year *Nanadana* onwards, they were to pay only the *sarva - aya,* that is the dues of hereditary servants annually.

4. The fixed landrent payable by them under the statutory constitution of the Department of Charities was fixed at 18 gold *gadyanas.* (currency denominator).

5. This constitution of the Eight *Sethis* was not applicable to the country, nor that of the country to the Eight *Setthis.*[76]

The above epigraphic note does in no way compare to modern day company constitution. But to put the matter straight, the question here is not a direct comparison with modern practices and understanding, but to trace back the path through which indigenous enterprise had travelled to the present status. Could we distinguish signs of an indigenously developing business profession, cohesive, joint, financially traced out, formatted into regulatory mode ?

A brief survey of some of the lawheads will reveal just how much was evidently there. It is apparent at least that the smritis were, in some instances, discussing purely business activities in details. The headings run on issues like:

- Sale and Purchase.
- Seller's liability.
- Stock in Trade.
- Allocation of Shares.
- Insurance on Seafaring Commerce, etc.

These titles indicate involvement in the regulatory areas of business deals, joint organizations of merchants and the issues arising out of their operations.

We shall now turn to the detailed discussions of some of the topics of regulation, which will leave no doubt as to the thrust of the specific codes on profit-making or business-oriented professions.

The connotative frame-work is primarily traced out above in great details precisely because the task appears to be too lofty. It required a clear delineation of orderly arrangement within which the scope of the subject is laid down. The treatment of the questions regarding: the stature of the *smritis* read as legal codes, the commercial ventures of early days seen as business, the selected *srenis* of *setthis* regarded as corporate commercial bodies, were vital to the topic.

Let us now look for specific issues discussed from the angle of business regulations in the main *smritis* of the times between the 2nd century and the 6th-7th centuries AD. A survey reveals the growing volume of not only specific definitions and rules concerning corporations of merchants or *srenis,* but also regulations concerning labour and wage disputes, sale and purchase etc. These formed parts of the entire paraphernalia for commercial ventures and business operations in our context. References to regulations in the *Arthasastra* and *Smritis* also illustrate the gradual changes taking place both in the domains of business as well as political-legal authority.

In *Manusmriti* we have very rudimentary rules regarding sale and buying or purchase, ownership of bought and sold item, rescission of sale and purchase and disputes between master and servant over work and wages, etc.[77]

In 2nd Century AD Manu had not referred to guilds in particular, except to state that a king who knew the sacred law, had to inquire into the law of castes *(jati),* of districts, guilds and families and thus had to settle the law of each.[78] The question of fulfilling respective duties was rendered a religio-ethical compunction in the *smritis* more emphatically than in earlier normative literature. The *smriti* thus stressed the moral dictum, 'for men who follow their particular occupations, and abide by their particular duty, became dear to people, though they may live at a distance'.[79] The question why the *Manusmriti* does not deal exhaustively with business law, can perhaps be explained by the fact that commercial operations had not been conceived as a part of the moral jurist's precinct. It is also implied that the *srenis* had their own regulations, which the king of the realm had to abide by, when dealing with a member of the *sreni.* So it was not yet necessary to include these in the *smritis.* However, the economic environment of the times was characterized by surging commercial activities in and out of the Indian subcontinent. The *Kautilya Arthasastra* had referred to the guilds of that time in broad terms. It seems that in a broader sense, the *'sreni' was* a connotative term for groups of people in the same occupation. It was applied both to non-monarchical sanghas, warrior communities or Kshatriya srenis, as well as to commercial, occupational and craft corporations. *Kautilya* had referred to a few regulations guiding the role of members of guilds[80], which indicate that the composers of *Arthasastra* kept abreast of contemporary guild laws. The guild laws also appear to be effective. Quite apparently, therefore, the necessity for preparing law

Arthasastra deals in details in labour laws, probably in order to cope with the problems arising in the state-regulated workshops, in the Maurya *rastra.* Taking the *Arthasastra* (2nd BC to 2nd AD) into consideration, one could say that regular activities of guilds were conducted with reference to individual guild laws. However, the precedence of the *Arthasastra* labour regulations set an example, no doubt, for the *smritis,* when they started to arrive on the scene from the 2nd century AD onwards, devoted some sutras to the labour question, which were included in the *vyavahara* sections.

But so far as the specific scope of corporations and their operations are concerned, it was only with *Yajnavalkya,* after Manu, between the later part of the 2nd and the 3rd centuries AD, that more detailed regulations on business activity in corporate establishments started to evolve. Most probably, these were brought into the main forum of law of kingdoms. With *Narada, Brhaspati* and *Katyayana.*

The rudimentaries of guild operations regulations are to be found in the *Arthasastra* itself. The text states specially that guilds of workmen, workers employed by companies as well as those, who carried on any co-operative work, sambhuya *samutthatarah,* had to divide their earnings either equally or as agreed upon among themselves. The same principle was applicable in the case of priests and artisans. As we learn in connection with the latter, the agreements were not only in respect of the division of wages but they had to state clearly the time, place and the form of work, *'desakalakaryapadesam'* . In fact the *Arthasastra* states that those 'artisans who postponed their engagements on the excuse that no such agreement had been entered into had, excepting in times of troubles and calamities, to pay a fine twice the amount of their wages'.[81] In all likelihood the practice or system of having such agreements must have prevailed in the case of all guilds or else they could hardly have functioned as corporate entities in executing their work and in sharing their earnings or in possessing their properties.

Another important thing to be noted in the *Arthasastra*

possessing their properties.

Another important thing to be noted in the *Arthasastra* is with regard to the detailed regulations for labour and contracts that the text provides.[82] The disputes concerning labour contracts made it necessary to have *bonafide* witnesses. For witness account was an important aspect of judicial operations in early India. The *Arthasastra* clearly provides for the system of witness: the cardinal principle being that all disputes would depend for main settlement on the evidence to be furnished by neighbours.[83] This system came to be handy in all matters of dispute and was possibly an innovation of the times. In fact much of the legal and juridical contents in the *Arthasastra* reflect the growing body of political and legal control systems within an emerging rastra-polity framework. In case of corporate operation the main bone of contention must have been the problem of wages. In such matters also disputes were to be settled on the strength of evidence furnished by witness. In the absence of such witness, the master or employer, who had engaged the servant was to be examined. Failure to pay wages was punishable with a fine ten times the amount of wages, termed *'dasabandha'*. Misappropriation of wages was punishable with a fine five times the sum of the wages claimed, *'pancabandhova'*.[84] Creation of such terms imply long usage being formalized by regulative codes. Another interesting reference is made to experts or *kusalah*, who fixed the wages of the workers in case of disputes.

These stray references in the *Arthasastra* illuminate the picture of emergent guilds in the background of a growing centralization of political authority. Rudiments of regulations were coming to the fore as the index of such a development, which were required to control the sources of revenue by certain sets of principles. Reference to *kusalah* or experts in settling disputes over labour contracts, however, imply the prior existence of regulation, which had probably not been centralized in codes. Manu's reference to guild laws as a separate body of code, acknowledged by tradition, rulers, dharma injunctions, indicate a separate code existing, probably regulated by a *sreni pramukha* or *jyestha* mentioned the *Jatakas.*[85] This is well observed from the *Nigrodha Jataka* (E.B. Cowell translations), which emphatically and explicitly states that the office of the *Bhandagarika,* which had not existed earlier, was specially created with dual responsibility. The Cambridge History of India[86], volume I, states that this probably arose in order to settle disputes among guilds. The term *Srenidharma,* anyway, had a regulatory character and took its place among social regulations. For this was a term commonly found in many literary compositions from 2nd BC onwards. According to Manu, even the king had to keep track of *srenidharma. Visnusutra,* dated after the *Manusmriti,* prescribed that one who violated the established rule of the corporation, was to be banished.[87] Such strong prescriptions would prove beyond dispute the common acceptance and knowledge of the authority of *srenidharma.*

However, in the absence of any regular code of guild laws in this period, we may express doubt as to variability of these laws in specific cases, from country to country, guild to guild, settlement to settlement. This problem is done away since the days of *Yajnavalkya* in the 3rd-4th centuries AD, when the *smritis* began to embody detailed regulations applicable in the fields of commercial operations and craft-production.

We must first begin with the legal procedure described in *smritis* for founding *srenis.*

Formation of sreni/corporation :

The first proper reference to the principle of forming a corporate body of professionals or *sreni,* as it was termed in early India, is available in the *Yajnavalkya Smriti. Yajnavalkyasmriti* set down the rule "A number of traders, carrying on trade or making profit, shall share or according to the compact made between themselves. If any member of a company does not act, forbidden by the general body, or without their permission or negligently, and thereby causing or loss, he shall have to indemnify the others for the same".[88]

The text had also stated the qualification of the leader of such guilds: "Persons, conversant with the law (sic), pure-minded and shorn of avarice, had to be placed at the head of public body like a guild. All had to follow the words of countries for trading purpose.[89] It is talking about business transactions across caste and regional boundaries, which thus had to follow the common custom pointed out, that the *pramukhya of* the guild had precedence over other members. But there is an extended authority enjoyed by the king of the domain too. After Arthasastra, this is the second time (3rd century - 4th century AD) that a *smriti* lays down that a ruler should prevent dissensions among the members of sreni. Apparently it was the task of a king that he should supervise that learned, qualified persons were selected as the members of a guild and that their advises were followed. The members were empowered to drive away deceitful members, after having deprived them of their shares and appoint in their place a member who could conduct the business of the guild properly.[90]

If we go by *Naradasmriti,* which is said to be either preceding or contemporary with *Yajnavalkya,* there is a clear definition of corporation: " where traders or others carry on business jointly, it is called partnership, which is a title of law.[91] The definition went further, (Nar, III.22) "Where several partners are jointly carrying on business for the purpose of gain, the contribution of funds towards the common stock of the association form the basis (of their undertakings), therefore let each contribute his proper share." It seems, therefore, that the *Naradasmriti* was more focused on the formal definition of *sreni* than *Yajnavalkyasmriti.*

The leap made from *Manu* to *Yajnavalkya* and *Narada* is clear. The latter deals in the details of the constitution, membership and legal position of corporations. While *Manusmriti* had left the *srenidharma* to the individual guilds, requiring the king only to be conversant with them and abide by them, the latter assigns the political authority jurisdiction over the guilds.

Yet, it took a century or two more for the regularization of a formal, legal procedure of which should precede the formation of the sreni. This is first provided in *Brhaspati Smriti,* between the 4th and the 6th centuries AD.

The *Smriti* states down the following rule. The "guilds had to set about their tasks after mutual confidence had

Smriti, between the 4th and the 6th centuries AD.

The *Smriti* states down the following rule. The "guilds had to set about their tasks after mutual confidence had been established by means of the sacred libation *(Kosa),* followed by a stipulation in writing *(lekhakriya)* or through arbitrators *(madhyastha).*

Kosena lekhakriya madhyasthairiva parasparam
Visvasam prathamam krtva kuryuh karyanyantaram.

Kosa is also known as *pramana*/evidence, or *sapatha*/ pledge/.[92] *Lekhakriya* or stating things down in writing, was necessary for recording in writing the real purpose of the organization. If, as we have already discussed, the *Arthasastra* rule presided to determine the place, time and purpose, their determination was all the more essential. The *madhyasthya* is an arbiter, guarantor of good faith.

Brhaspatismriti went further in furnishing same details about the officers of such corporations [93] : "Two, three or five persons shall be appointed as advisers of the association: their advice shall be taken by the villagers, companies (of artisans), corporation (of co-habitants) and other fellowships." It is clear that the *Brahspatismriti* took into consideration all corporations while speaking about membership including trading and artisan corporations. The authoritative status of the *sreni pramukhya* implied in this regulation provides insight into the local power structure emerging in the Gupta, post-Gupta times. In fact the gradual development of local self-government, culminating into the proto-types of the *cola sabha* administrative bodies, may be discerned to have roots in such features as this. We have already referred to the guild constitution mentioned in the *Calukya* inscription of the eight setthis. Although the concurrence of the king and the royal officials of the *rastra* was manadatory in this matter, the formal status of the guild is well expressed. They stand immune to the regulations of the rastra dharma codes. This is more evident in the fact mentioned in the *Damodarpur* Copper Plate[94] of Gupta ruler, Kumaragupta, which includes the *Jyestha* or the *sreni* chief, the *prathama kulika* (chief of artisans) and the *prathama kayastha* (chief of scribes) in the list of officials supervising the administration of a town council.

It is true that many of the above regulations often sound rather descriptive and are more in nature of normative injunctions. However, the early Indian society abided by these injunctions and though these texts are not in the nature of regular legal codes from an accepted sovereign or authority, yet the tradition or *"dharma"* voiced by jurists was as much as a code in the context of early India.

Let us look at the later *smritis* and find how they are defining corporations and their activities. *Narada smriti* defines partnership as "the conduct of business by traders or others jointly." "This is the third title of law."[95] Katyayana-extended the application of the term to the business of artisans and of `inseparated' brothers.[96] Kat, v v 633 ff. The amount contributed by each partner towards the understanding formed the basis of partnership and each partner was entitled to receive profit according to his share in the partnership. Brhaspati[97] like Katayana[98] applied the provisions of the law of partnership to the artisans. "Artisans of different grades shared the profit in the proportion of one, two, three or four shares according to their grades."

Privileges and Responsibilities of Members :

The law was not all about profit but about the total sphere of their involvement business. The members of the guild enjoyed the privilege to form regulative codes not only for operative and functional aspects, but also for the moral guidance of the members concerned. According to *Brhaspati* the Corporation met as a body, in a "house of assembly" for transacting business and they seem to have drawn up rules, which required the king's approval.[99]

Narada and Katyana have elaborated about the liabilities of the partners in business. Every partner was stated to be sharing the profit as well as the loss in proportion to his contribution and had to bear the expenses for keeping the valuables. Similarly, the partner who caused loss to the property, either because of his negligence or without authorization from other partners, is liable for the loss so caused.[100] But if anyone of the partners preserved the property from danger he was entitled to a tenth part of the property rescued as a reward.[101] Involvement in joint action went beyond the regular operations. On the death of a partner his share went to his heirs and in the absence of heirs it reverted to the surviving partner.[102] This provision is in conformity with the provisions of section 251 of the Indian Contract Act IX passed in 1872.[103]

A very significant change in attitude towards business and production personnel is noted among jurists of different periods. Kautilya, between 2nd century BC and 2nd century AD and Manu in 2nd century AD, disqualified artisans as witnesses in judicial procedure. But Narada, between 2nd century AD and 3rd century AD, modified this view. According to him, "among companies of artisans, guild merchants and other artisans, they or merchants could be witnesses and members of an association among other members of the same association."[104] [Nar. I, II (156)]. This is a definite indication of the growing legal status of the guild members and the importance of the guild courts, recognized in positive injunctions of the smritis. However, paradoxically, the injunction also means that the *smritis* had assumed the supervisory status powerful enough to command how the guild courts were to operate.

The privileges were formalized into *dharmasastra* codes. They include the authority to expel a member, appoint a substitute, remove a chief or officials of a corporate body[104]. Yajnavalkya added that a member who was found guilty of corruption from any angle, could be expelled or removed from the guild and such a punishment was only› inflicted after depriving him of his share.[105] A major indication that the king was the ultimate count of justice and considered an arbiter in corporate matters is clear from Brahaspati's following injunction; when a dispute arose between a guild and its chief the king was to decide it and bring them "back to duty".[106] *Narada* also recognizes the sovereign authority of the kings above the sanctions of guilds : "a ruler could prevent various corporations from combining together, arming of associations without adequate reasons, fights between them embarking an action in opposition to his own interests or aims and also when they were despicable.[107] These injunctions in *Brhaspati* and *Narada* are probably reflective of the growing recognition of the political authority superseding corporate bodies. The days had changed since the times of Manu, when the king was enjoined to observe *srenidharma.* Probably these minute analyses will help as to observe the evolution of political and legal institutions and authority in the context of early India."

Glimpses of a few regulative codes would substantially illustrate the focus on business law in the different post-Manu *smriti* compendiums.

Allocation of Shares :

This was a major concern in joint business operation.

Naradasmriti being the earliest among these, we begin with that text.

Narada: "Where several partners are jointly carrying on business for the purpose of gain, the contribution of funds towards the common stock of the association forms the basis of their undertaking. Therefore let each contribute his proper share".[108]

"The loss, expenses and profit of each partner are either equal to those of the other partners, or exceed them, or remain below them, according as his share is equal to theirs, or greater, or less".[109]

Brahaspati was more explicit. He enjoined : "As an equal, smaller or larger share (of the joint stock) has been contributed by a partner, in the same proportion shall he defray charges, perform labour, and obtain profit."[110] "of those who lend (jointly) gold, grain, liquids and condiments, or the like, the gain shall be equal to their respective shares (of the joint expenditure), whether equal, more or less."[111]

Now this last clearly identifies the joint stock of goods and the equal or respective share thereof - in partnership or corporate enterprises. Each guild had no doubt its own stock in trade, which was in fact the foundation of its commercial existence. Rules were laid down in later *smritis* like *Narada* regarding the rule of stock: " the junction of stock is the basis of the transactions of men carrying on business jointly with a view to gain; therefore each should contribute his share to be common exertion".[112]

The constitutional aspects of the guilds were formulated with both the mercantile as well as any other joint organization of professionals. However, that the smritis were deeply concerned in matters pertaining to commercial enterprise is evident from certain other titles discussed in the later law-books especially. One of the prime issues was of the payment of the commercial revenues. The *smritis* in majority, starting with the Yajnavalkya smriti, were composed and followed in a time-frame when the political paradigm of the society had mainly been circumscribed within small to middling kingdoms, juxtaposed with each other in diplomatic bonding and/or enmity, as each situation was set. An uniformity between the *smritis* on revenue matters should be taken as a sign of that uniformity being customized at least throughout the sanskritized communities over a substantial geographical area. Therefore, this portion of the smriti does not only illuminate the revenue status of the commercial ventures but also the customization of the revenue pattern itself. The following description does not only reveal this clearly but also illuminates cases of transgression and that in such cases effective restrictions could not be imposed. The *smritis* tried the mode of statutory warning.

Commercial dues and royal duties:

The king was traditionally the recipient of 1/6th of the sale proceeds as *sulka*. Evasion of sulka was punishable. Yajnavalkya provided a formal law on this question This title enjoined, "one who made a false statement regarding the quantity of articles in order to evade payment of proper duty or went away from a place where such duty was collected, was to be fined eight times the value of the article."[113] *Naradasmriti* is more specific in laying down the terms for *sulka* and toll duties. "A trader on reaching a toll-house should pay the legal duty. A prudent man should not avoid it. If he evades a toll-house or if he buys or sells at another than the legal hour, or if he does not state the value of his goods correctly, he shall be fined eight times the amount which he tried to evade."[114] Another interesting information is available concerning commercial operations, which is termed `vyavahariki'. This is described in the *Arthasastra*, *Mànusmriti* and *Yàjnavalkyasmriti* as commercial interest. This was a flat rate tax levied on commercial enterprises *'samudrarnam'*. The interest on the loan amount is clearly stated to be 20% per month. Reference to it in the above texts,[116] across a time-frame running from the 2nd century BC to 3rd century AD illuminate the surge in commercial operations throughout these centuries, a fact that is borne out by epigraphic and numismatic evidences too.

Sale and Purchase Regulations:

Business ethics had been considered another important area of juridical involvement. *Narada smriti* and the *Katyayana smriti* provided regulations on a seller's liability as well as the matter of price regulation. The sale of a commodity presupposes payment of price as its value before the delivery of goods to the buyer. Prices were regulated under some kind of administrative authority. Although the authority is not specifie, the norm ran that : A price which is either more or less than the fixed price is inadequate and whatever is sold at improper price can be annulled at any time."[117] How far such norms of regulated exchange could be implemented, and the mode of such implementation, especially on large–scale commerce, is a matter of doubt. Nevertheless, there is also a body of law that concerns the liabilities of seller. The injunctions on a seller to deliver to the buyer the property sold immediately after completion of the sale was a checking measure against tempering. If the seller failed to deliver the goods he was to surrender to the buyer any profit derived by him.[118] The seller was responsible for the loss or damage of goods which was not yet delivered to the buyer.[119] Again *Yajnavalkya* tried to assure correct demeanor from the delivery and buyer end, by laying down the regulation that if the buyer had paid earnest money and the vendor failed to give effect to the sale for some reason then the vendor had to pay double the amount paid to him. But if the buyer failed to take the delivery of the article he lost both the article and the money paid by him. *Visnusmriti*, a slightly later composition in the post–Gupta period went a step further in regulating commercial enterprise. This *smriti* imposed the highest punishment on the members of a company who tampered with the sale of goods, and prevented the sale of a commodity, which happened to be abroad. He also laid down the same commercial enterprise. This *smriti* imposed the highest punishment on the members of a company who tampered with the sale of goods, and prevented the sale of a commodity, which happened to be abroad. He also laid down the same punishment for those members of such a company who sold an article belonging to the whole company for more than its worth, on their account.[120]

The issue of service and wage contracts was an area that the smritikaras included under regulations following the example of the Arthasastra of Kautilya. Evidently, these regulations arose out of the necessity to regularize contractual labour for smoother operations of production and commerce. Here a brief reference to the regulations is included, keeping in mind the prime concern of the article, that is the aspects that were related to commercial ventures.

Non-Payment of Wages (*Vetanasyanapakaram*)

Brahaspati speaker of 3 titles of law, which could be described as service laws and which deal with the hired servants and the relation between master and servant. These laws include (i) non-performance of service, (*abhyupetasusrusa*), (ii) non-payment of wages (*vetanasyanakarma*), and (iii) disputes between master and servant (*svamipalavivada*).[121]

Narada includes the following persons within the category of wage-labour, all of whom are clearly associated with commercial enterprise.

1. A transport agent who agrees to carry to its destination the merchandise. If he abandons the work, he is liable to pay 1/6th of the wage fixed. Similarly, if the employer does not pay the stipulated wages, he should be made to pay the wages together with a fine.[122]

2. A merchant who undertakes to carry beasts for draught or burden having hired them and then refers to do so is made to pay the stipulated wages, should be made to pay the wages together with interest.[123]

Also : When the merchandise has been damaged by the carrier's fault, he shall have to make good every loss, not including such losses as may have been caused by fate or by the king.[124]

Katyayan's rule in respect of the non-payment of wages are very brief. According to him a trader, a cowherd, or a man practising husbandry, fall under the category of hired persons and they are entitled to receive one-tenth of the profit when the wages are not fixed. In the case of theft of the goods transferred to hawkers employed by artisan guilds for selling, the (hawker, who is described as a hired servant) hired servant is entitled to get wages in proportion to the distance already traversed by him.[125]

There is a special provision in *Katyayanasmriti*, described by the term *Silpinyasa.*[126] This is a special deposit of raw material deposited with an artisan, as in the colonial days the tradition of *dadan* or *dadni* involved depositing supplies and commissioning craftsmen for stipulated jobs.[127] It is quite obvious that the system led to occasional disputes just as service contract did. The *Katyayanasmriti* with its late commentary belongs to a more developed stage of both commercial and regulative organizations. Hence it includes some observations on minute transactions in commerce. The text laid down that "if an artisan does not return the thing deposited with him within the stipulated penod, he should be made to pay its price even in the cases, where the loss is due to an act of God or king. The artisan, however, is not responsible for the loss of an article which was very defective at the time of bailment. unless the loss is due to his own fault."

The regulations and precepts that follow on matters like: Judicial power of guilds, witness of guilds, commercial powers, sale and purchase, stock-in-trade, allocation of shares etc. are given in a legal format and quite likely operated in judicial cases. We also have to consider the fact that in early India the judiciary embraced the legal sanctions in a unified body. Law was important insofar as judicial actions were concerned. Law and judiciary were not treated separately. It is in connection with the judicial disputes over sreni operation that the above codes were formulated. They are either normative or practical in nature.

The discussion regarding the *srenis* and *sreni-dharma*

point to an understanding of the operations of trading as well as manufacturing corporations. It is also evident from other sources that trade and marketing corporations were sometimes jointly operating so that a corporation comprised both manufacturing and trading sections. The main legal structure available on commercial *srenis* exist in quasi-codes in the smritis. These deal with their constitutions, sale and purchase modes, profits and shares, liabilities of members or partners. We have to recognize the limited scope of the legal texts as well as the narrow scope in which these texts discussed 'business'. Business here is restricted to the sense of mercantile and production activities and the associated disputable areas. Here we find no elaborating on financial legalities, legalities of partnership, liabilities of partners on a broader framework, mortgage, shares or legal involvement of members in guaranteeing business or legalities of business investment.

Neither did the trading activities involve all the aspects of a modern business enterprise. The *smritis* reflect the simple nature of 'business' as it was understood to operate within the given economic, political and legal parameters of the times. We have to look at the matter of this early `business' from the contextual angle and note the special nature of *smriti* texts. They reveal the nature of the legal structure that was prevalent in early and early medieval Indian society. Only a historical and contextual angle of perception would render a connected and true picture of early Indian business and regulations concerned with it. We have already discussed the point of *smritis* as code. We have analysed what these texts provide regarding corporate operations. The regulations surveyed above appear to approach the format of business within that given framework.

Notes and References

1. H.G. Rawlinson, 'Early Contacts Between India and Europe' in A. L. Basham, ed., A Cultural History of India, New Delhi, 2002, reprint p. 433.
2. Ibid, p. 434.
3. Alastair Lamb, 'Indian Influence in Ancient South-

East Asia', in A. L. Basham, ed., op. cit., pp. 444, 445.

4. Himangshu Prabha Ray, The Winds of Change Buddhism and the Maritime Links of Early South Asia, New Delhi, 2000, reprint, p. 189; David Whitehouse, 'Epilogue: Roman Trade in Perspective, in Vimala Begley and Richard Daniel De Puma, eds., Rome and India: The Ancient Sea Trade, Delhi, 1992, p. 216ff; Ranabir Chakrabarty, 'Introduction', in Ranabir Chakrabarty, ed. Trade in Early India.
5. *Manu Samhita* with the commentary of *Kulluka,* Cal. 1930, Translated, G. Bhuler, SBE Text also edited by J.R. Gharpure, Bombay, 1920.
6. *Arthasastra* Commentary of *Bhattaswami* by T. Ganapat Sastri, Mysore, 1924.
7. *Vishnu Dharmasastra,* ed. By M. N. Dutta, Calcutta 19th Century; J. Jolly, SBE, Vol. II.
8. *Yajnavalkya Smriti* with the commentary of *Mitaksara* by *Vijnaneswara,* ed. by Vasudeva Laksman Sastri, Pansikar, Bombay, 1926. 3rd edition. Translated by M. N. Dutta, Cal 1908, 93 vols.
9. *Narada smriti,* edited by Julius Jolly, Calcutta 186 *Naradiya Manusamhita,* ed. by Sambasiva Sastri, Trivendram, 1924.
10. *Brahaspatismriti* ed. By K.V. Rangaswamy Aiyangar, Gaekwad Oriental Series Vol. LxxxV, Baroda, 1941.
11. *Katyayanasmriti* or *Katyayansmritisaroddhara,* Text, Translation, Notes & Introduction and edition, P.V. Kane, Bombay, 1933, Vyavahara Law and Procedure.
12. Jataka story no. 546, Vol. VI, E. B. Cowell, ed. and trans., Delhi, 1990 reprint.
13. T. W. Rhys Davids (tr.), The Questions of King Milinda, pt. II, pp. 209 - 11, Sacred Books of the East series, Vol. XXXVI, 1890, p. 195.
14. Mahavastu, III, p. 442; 8 ff.
15. Epigraphica Indica, Vol.VIII, no. 12, p. 82. EI Vol. X, no. 1133, p. 128.
16. EI, Vol. II, no. 10, p. 61.
17. Ibid, VIII, p. 88. EI, Vol. X. no. 1137, p. 127.

18. Archaeological, Survey Annual Report, Western India, Vol. IV, no. 24, p. 96; EI, Vol. X., no. 1162, p. 132.
19. EI Vol. X, no. 10, p. 04; EI, Vol. X., no. 1180, p. 136. ASI, (Annual Report), 1908, p. 133.
21. EI. Vol. 1, No. 361, p. 43; Ibid, Vol. II, no. 111, p. 109; Ibid., Vol. X, nos 296- 98, p. 45.
22. IA, Vol. XXXI, no. 16, p. 228 and no. 118, p. 236.
23. EI, Vol. X, no. 98, p. 102; ASWI, IV, 19. p. 82; EI, Vol. X., no. 25, p. 124; EI, Vol. X, nos. 1140 & 1148, p. 130.
24. EI, Vol. X, List no. 137, p. 127.
25. Fleet, Corpus Inscriptionum Indicum, III, no. 16, p. 84.
26. Fleet, Corpus Inscriptionum Indicum, III, no. 16, p. 71.
27. A.S.I R, 1903 -4, p. 107.
28. A.S.I R, 1903 - 4, p. 107.
29. Fleet, CII, III, p. 287.
30. EI Vol. XV, no. 6, pp. 77-78, 79-80.
31. Indian Antiquary, IXX, no. 170, p. 361, also IA, XV, p. 35; EI II, no. XVIII, pp. 232-236.
32. Narada, V. I; Brhaspati, V V, 34 f; Katyayana, V V, 633 ff.
33. Narada, V. 5; Katyayana, V. 636.
34. Narada, V. 1 & 2; Katyayana, V. 612.
35. Brhaspati, XVII (11); XVII (18).
36. Narada, X. 3; III. 2; III.3; Yajnavalkya, 268.
37. Mulla Principles of Hindu Law, Vol. I, Satyajeet A. Desai, New Delhi, 1998 reprint, p. 2, 8.
38. All India Report of 1965 (SC 314, 316) reiterated in Surendra Malik, "Supreme Court on Words and Phrases", Lucknow, 1995, reprint, p. 378.
39. Ibid., p. 378.
40. AIR 1963. SC 1638, 1650. This case law is cited in Surendra Malik, "Supreme Court on Words and Phrases". Lucknow, 1995, reprint, p. 378.
41. Aristotle, Politics, Ill., 16 - 9.
42. Arthasastra, (Bk lII) Ch. I.

43. Ibid., Bk III, Ch I , 150.
44. S.A. Desai, op. cit., New Delhi, 1998, p. 4.
45. Ibid., p. 8.
46. Ibid., pp. 8-10.
47. Hart, Introduction to Austinian province of Jurisprudence Determined, pp. xi-xii.
48. August Issue of AIR, All India Reports 1994, Nov. 26, referring to a case law from Madhya Pradesh, p. 106.
49. Surendra Malik, Supreme Court on Words and Phrases, Lucknow, 1995, reprint, pp. 110-111.
50. Ibid p. 111.
51. Aitareya Brahmana III. 30, 114 (12).
52. Jataka story, Vol. III, no. 339, p. 83.
53. Jataka, Vol. I, no. 54, p. 135.
54. Jataka, Vol. III, no. 339, p, 83.
55. Gautama Dharmasutra, XI, (21).
56. Ibid.
57. Jataka, Vol. VI, no. 538, pp. 14, 22.
58. Yaj., II, 262, 263.
59. Br., p. 127, VV. 10 - 11.
60. Nar, p. 155. V. 4.
61. Nar, V. 1; V. 2.
62. Nar, VV. 5 ff.
63. A. Ramaiya. Guide to the Companies Act, Nagpur, 1995, reprint, p. 134 ff.
64. Constitution of Board of Company Law Administration. Cited in Ibid, p. 139.
65. Yaj. II, 262, 263.
66. Yaj, II, 262, 263.
67. Ibid., Ch II (268), p. 108).
68. Jataka, Vol. IV, no. 445, p. 27.
69. Jataka, Vol. 11, no. 218, p. 127; Vol. V. no. 535, pp. 202 - 218; Vol. I, no. 4, pp. 14-20,
70. Sudraka, 2. 3; Dandin, dasakumara, text, p.l 17).
71. EI, I, p. 382; ibid., X, no.24, p.5.

77. Manu, VIII, 199 - 223.
78. Manu, VIII. 41, 42 , p. 26.
79. Ibid, VIII. 42.
80. Arth Bk III, Ch XIV, p. 210; Bk IV, Ch I, p. 227.
81. Ibid, Bk IV, Ch I, p. 227, Text p. 201.
82. Ibid, Bk III, Ch IX.
83. Ibid, Bk, III, Ch XIII, pp. 191, 208.
84. Bk III, Ch XIII, p. 208.
85. Nigrodha Jataka in E.B. Cowell, translations, op. cit. Vol. I, pp. 206-7.
86. The Cambridge History of India, Vol. I, pp. 206-7.
87. Visnu V (18) SBE, Julius Jolly, Vol. VII, p. 38.
88. Yaj. II, 262, 263.
89. Yaj, Ch III (94-95).
90. Ibid, Ch II (268).
91. Naradasmriti, Third title of Law, 1 / III. I.
92. Nar, III.22.
93. Br. XVII (7), p. 374 SBE, vol. XXXIII.
94. Epigrapica Indica, Radhagovind Basak, ed., XV, pp. 113 ff.
95. Narada, V. I, p. 133.
96. Katyana, V V. 633 ff. p. 78.
97. Br. V V. 34 ff, p. 135.
98. Kat, v v 633 ff.
99. Br, XVII, (11).
100. Kat, V V, 633 ff. Nar X 3; Br KVII. 18.
101. Narada, V. 5, p. 133; Kat. V. 63, p. 78.
102. Br. V. I; Br. X. 22.
103. Madhukar M. Patkar, p. 132
104. Nar. I, II (I56).
105. Arthasastra, Bk III, Ch XIII, p. 208.
106. Br. XVII.20.
107. Nar, X (4.5,7) SBE, XXXIII, pp. 154-55.
108. Nar, III, 2.
109. Nar, III, 3.
110. Br, XIV, 3.

106. Br. XVII.20.
107. Nar, X (4.5,7) SBE, XXXIII, pp. 154-55.
108. Nar, III, 2.
109. Nar, III, 3.
110. Br, XIV, 3.
111. Br, XIV, 4,
112. Narada-, III (2), p. 57.
113. Yaj, (265), p. 108.
114. Nar. III. 12 -13.
115. Arthasastra, Bk. III, Ch. XI, p. 197.
116. Arthasastra, Bk.'IIII, ch. XI; Yajnavalkva II (39), pp. 68 - 69.
117. Kat. V V. 705 - 7, p. 86.
118. Nar, pp. 157 - 8, V, 4.
119. Nar. p. 188. V. 6.
120. Visnu V, (125-26), p.35, SBE, Vol., VII.
121. Br. XVI, 9.
122. Brahaspati, (vi, 6) title of law no. 6.
123. Nar. (VI, 7).
124. Nar. [VI, 9]
125. Kat, p. 82, V. 663.
126. Kat, p. 82, V. 663.
127. J.R. Gharpure (ed.) Katyanasmriticandrika, Pt. II. p. 182.

3

Business in Early Bengal (Pre-Gupta Phase): A Numismatic Approach

Suchandra Ghosh

Paucity of relevant data does not allow us to conclusively comment upon the 'business' history of Pre-Gupta Bengal, if we take the term 'business' signifying the functioning of a complex system. On the other hand, if one adheres to the simple dictionary meaning of the term 'business' implying a 'commercial or mercantile activity engaged in as a means of livelihood', then Pre-Gupta Bengal did have a history of mercantile or commercial activity.

A perusal of early Indian sources is an indicator of the fact that early India could definitely boast of different categories and levels of merchants like *vanik* (petty merchant), sreshthi (very rich merchant), *sarthavaha* (caravan trader), *nauvittaka* (ship owning merchant), *raja sreshthi* (royal merchant) etc. and different types of exchange centres like *hatta, putabhedana, mandapika, pentha* and *nagaram.*[1] Presence of such wide categories of markets and merchants is a definite pointer to business activities which demanded a medium of exchange like coins, among others. The appearance of coined money in remote times certainly suggests a complex socio-economic situation, which must have witnessed a considerable growth of commerce, a strong political structure and a sharply differentiated social structure distinct from a simpler way of life.

Thus coins are invaluable source for a proper understanding of the economic history, especially the history of trade of a given period. Unfortunately this very important source of economic history is not always taken into consideration while examining the economic history of early India in general.

Earlier historians, writing on Bengal's history, could not highlight much on the pre-Gupta phase of the history of

Bengal for want of reliable archaeological and textual materials. But with the spurt of archaeological discoveries in Bengal like potteries, seals, sealings, sculptures, coins etc. in the last three decades, the situation is much better now. Historians are now able to reconstruct the history of pre-Gupta Bengal with more conviction. The present paper seeks to examine the business potential of pre-Gupta Bengal (including present day West Bengal and Bangladesh) on the basis of the available numismatic data[2] and related archaeological findings.

Though many areas in north India experienced regular metallic currency from c. 5th century onwards, the definite evidence of the introduction of metal money in Bengal cannot be pushed beyond c. 3rd century BC when Pundravardhana or North Bengal probably came under the Maurya rule. That Bengal began to experience the circulation of metallic pieces from this period onwards is clearly evident from the availability of silver punch marked coins from excavated sites like Mahasthangarh (Bogra dist. Bangladesh), Bangarh (South Dinajpur dist. West Bengal), Chandraketugarh (North 24 Parganas, WB), Mangalkot (Bardhaman dist. WB) and also from various places in Medinipur, Bankura, Murshidabad districts in West Bengal.[3] The recent discovery of fairly high number of punch marked coins from Wari-Bateshwar near Dhaka (Bangladesh) is highly significant.[4]

It is interesting to note that punch marked coins occurred simultaneously with the Northern Black Polished Ware, itself a deluxe pottery and possibly an item of trade. Mention should be made here of the Mahasthangarh fragmentary inscription, palaeographically assignable to 3rd century BC.[5] It records the filling of a royal treasury (*kosa*) at Pundranagara (the earliest known urban centre of Bengal, now Mahasthan in Bangladesh) with *Ganda* and *Kakani*. The two terms according to many scholars stand for two types of coins in circulation. Alternative interpretation was cowry shells counted in the unit of four (ganda). Arthasastra uses the term *kakani* to mean a minute coin (II, 12) and also to indicate a Kapardaka or cowry (III, 20). We are obliged to accept the latter meaning since no such minute copper punch marked pieces have been unearthed here. Therefore along with coins we have parallel presence of cowries as a medium of exchange. There is little doubt that punch marked coinage reached Bengal from the Ganga valley as an impact of the expansion of Mauryan control over North Bengal. These coins were struck on the Karshapana standard (32 rati or 57.6 grains). Apart from the silver punch marked coins Bengal knew the use of copper and *billon* (silver + copper\tin) punch marked coins, which were struck on the silver Karshapana standard. Silver was the most common medium for striking punch marked coins in Bengal and stratigraphic evidence do not suggest the continuation of this coinage beyond 1st century BC in Bengal. The use of copper and *billon* punch marked coins is a pointer to the fact that minted currency in baser metals were meant for petty transactions. This finds corroboration in the words of Renfrew,........ 'the existence of any low denomination coinage used within the jurisdiction of the issuing authority, is an indication of market exchange.'[6] Thus when a base metal coinage circulates in the area intended for its distribution and use, there is a likelihood of market orientation. Copper was also used for striking cast coins which have been found from a number of archaeological sites like Harinarayanpur, Deulpota, Chandraketugarh, Atghara (North and South 24 Parganas), Tamluk, Dihar and Pokharna (Bankura), Mangalkot, Bangarh, Mahasthangarh.[7] Stratified evidence of the cast copper coins from these archaeological sites in West Bengal and Bangladesh suggests the introduction and circulation of cast copper coins during 1st and 2nd century BC, though in certain areas these might have continued to be in use up to c. 2nd and 3rd century AD and even in the Gupta age. Among the various devices used in these coins, we have the device of a boat or a ship. This may allude to the riverain activities in the areas of the provenances of the coins concerned. Attention may here be drawn to the fact that the Satavahanas introduced coins bearing the image of ship to be circulated in the Andhra and Coromandel coastal region in the 2nd century AD.[8] The introduction of the ship type of coins for the eastern Indian coast by a strong political power like the Satavahanas perhaps underlines the importance given to trade, be it coastal or maritime by this dynasty. That the entire east coast formed a part of a network extending from the Vaigai delta in the south to the Ganga delta in the north and into northern Srilanka and areas of South-East Asia is well illustrated by the availability and distribution of Rouletted Ware. A re-examination of the Arikamedu material by Vimala Begley suggest that it was an indigenous pottery tradition and not a Roman import. Only the technique could be borrowed from west and can be dated from 200 BC to 300 AD.[9] The wide distribution of rouletted ware from Chandraketugarh to Arikamedu and epigraphic evidences of contacts between deltas of the Ganges, of the Krishna and of the Godavari have been rightly interpreted as indicators of a coastal commercial network along the east coast.[10]

The device of ship represented on a coin from deltaic Bengal is not the only indication of riverain coastal activities in this region. This has been supplemented by representation of ships on seals found from Chandraketugarh and datable to 3rd century AD. Seals being often stamped and inscribed are generally dependable trade and administrative documents. A round terracotta seal impression, now in the collection of the State Archaeological Museum, Calcutta, displays within a circular boarder a masted ship, a svastika symbol, a figure of a horse on its board and a marginal legend. The implications of a horse on board a ship has been extensively discussed by Prof. Ranabir Chakrabarti.[11] In the legend written in Brahmi-Kharoshti mixed script as deciphered by Prof. B.N. Mukherjee we find reference to a class of ship named trapyaka. A similar seal from Chandraketugarh itself and belonging to the same period displays within a circular border a masted ship and stylized stalk of grain in the right hand field.[12] The precise purpose of showing the stalk of grain or the horse was unmistakably to highlight the product the ship carried on the trade documents in question. There is a definite correspondence between trapyaka class of ship referred to in the seal and the class of ship named trappaga, described in the Periplus of the Erythraean Sea (c. late 1st AD) in the context of the account of Barygaza, one of the celebrated ports of early historical times.[13] Trappagas were a type of craft also meant for coastal voyages. The *Angavijja*, a Jaina text of the 4th century AD mentions a craft called tappaka.[14] It has been earlier shown that Bengal was a participant in a coastal trade network and naturally the trapyaka type of middle category vessels were in operation in the eastern seaboard and deltaic areas of Bengal for transportation of commodities including as precious an item as the horse.

It is important to note that Bengal perhaps could boast of water crafts having a distinct type. A definite category of vessels called 'vangam' is mentioned in the early Tamil literature. Verse 368 of *Puranaunuru* (1st or 2nd century AD) refers to a Vanga ship that lost its direction in strong winds.[15] There is iconographic distinctness in the type of water craft displayed on the coins and seals from lower Bengal from the ship type of coins issued by the Satavahana rulers for use in the Andhra and Coromandel coast.

Subsequent to the cast copper coins the numismatic scenario in Bengal is illuminated by the presence of a large number of Kushana coins. Since the region of Bengal did not form a part of the Kushana empire, these seem to have reached Bengal by way of trade. In this context it would be proper to refer to the recently discovered inscription of Kanishka I from Rabatak in the Baghlan area of Kataghan in Afghanistan.[16] It appears from the inscription that in the east Kanishka's empire extended up to Ziri Tambo i.e. Sri Champa. It was located in the area of Champanagar and Champapura in the Bhagalpur district of Bihar. Thus it was very natural that Kushana coins penetrated into Bengal from a neighbouring region. It is however significant to note that Kushana copper coins in Bengal far outnumber their gold counterparts. Gold coins might have been brought here as mementoes. Copper coins have been found from the north and south 24 Paraganas, Bardhaman, Medinipur and Hoogly districts. This indicates the regular circulation of Kushana copper pieces in the Radha region to the west of the Bhagirathi from c. AD 1st to about 3rd centuries. There is little doubt that the Kushana copper coins, albeit being imported into Bengal, formed a regular currency in this area. Its outcome can be seen in the emergence of a large number of imitations of the Kushana copper coin types. These copper pieces imitated Kushana devices but followed the

Karshapana weight standard, instead of the Attic tetradrachm metrology. Considering the combinations of these two features, these imitations have been designated as Kushana Radha coins.[17]

From the emergence of a large number of imitations of the Kushana copper coin types, it can be deduced that there was an organized authority (of a state or a merchant guild) who developed a system of coinage based on the well known Kushana types. That coins were evocative of wealth and prosperity is suggested by a terracotta plaque of this age, discovered at Tamluk which displays a filled up vase (purnaghata), a traditionally auspicious symbol of prosperity as having coins overflowing it and also covering the ghata.

The presence of an organized authority in the same period is also reflected from the various archaeological discoveries from the lower parts of present day West Bengal. These regions have yielded potsherds and terracotta seals bearing Kharoshti and Kharoshti-Bramhi legends. The contents of these inscriptions are varied, while some carry personal names, others refer to agriculturists, traders and religious formulae.[18] Since Kharoshti was a script used only in the north-western part of the subcontinent, one may naturally question its presence in Bengal. However with the decipherment of these inscriptions by Prof. B. N. Mukherjee, we are now in a position to assume that Kharoshti and Kharosthi-Bramhi was in use in the lower parts of West Bengal from about the second half of 1st century AD to about early 5th century AD. It was developed there by a powerful community hailing from the Kharosthi using zone in the north-western section of the Indian subcontinent. These immigrants settled in coastal Bengal, mainly as agriculturists and traders and became quite powerful economically and politically. The agricultural prosperity of a person can be very well attested from a seal inscription where he is referred to as a *Kodihalika* i.e. a person having a crore of ploughmen.[19] Obviously he must have been a large scale agriculturist, employing several cultivators to till his vast arable land.

Largest concentration in lower West Bengal of the finds of early Bengal's archaeological artefacts indicates economic prosperity among at least a certain class of people. Copper coins of the period concerned betray the use of coin money of low value for ordinary transactions. Their participation in trade facilitated the emergence of a metrology of local copper coins based on a combination of Kushana and indigenous monetary systems. Agricultural base and exploitation of copper mines of nearby Singbhum region also gave fillip to commerce.

It would not be out of place to mention here that the Rakha hill area of the Singbhum district has yielded Puri-Kushana coins of c. 3rd to 4th century AD. The Puri-Kushana coins were in circulation in Orissa and northern Andhra. The close correspondence between the Puri-Kushana and Kushana Radha/ Vanga copper coins (though the two being not identical) strongly suggests that all these could have formed parts of a complex system of currency used in upper Andhra, Orissa, West Bengal (including the coastal zone) and the adjoining regions of South Bihar during the period from the 1st century BC-AD to about AD 4th century.[20] This could facilitate inter zonal exchanges through medium of coinage.

Bengal's contact with the greater part of the Ganga valley can be understood if we keep in mind that for the land-locked north India, the Bengal delta provided the only outlet to the sea. The Jatakas are replete with anecdotes of voyages by merchants from Varanasi of Champa (near Bhagalpur) to Suvarnabhumi or Suvarnadvipa. Such merchants seem to have first undertaken a riverine journey along the Ganga to the Bengal coast wherefrom a sea voyage was next made to South-East Asia. Recently discovered Kharoshti inscriptions near Chunar[21] in the heart of the Ganga valley and the remarkable rock shelters in inscriptions in Kharoshti and Bramhi discovered in Nawada (Jharkhand) and Giridih (Bihar)[22] clearly suggest overland linkages of north-western India with the middle Ganga valley and finally with the Bengal littorals. One of the cave inscriptions datable to 1st century AD refers to Sarthavahas. Thus the cultural history data help us in tracing the route followed by the people in their long and arduous journey from the north-west to Bengal.

A look at the literary and archaeological sources help us in forming an idea of the products and nature of products which were available and transacted. The seals discovered from lower Bengal is an unmistakable pointer to the flourishing agrarian economy in the Bengal coast. The most important crop was of course paddy. An inscription in a vessel reads ' Vapayakosha', thereby indicating that it was a vessel for a sower.[23] Such vessels must have contained a specific amount of seed of a particular grain to be sown on a given amount of land. Reference to a Kodihalika i.e. a person possessing a crore of ploughs has already been made. In addition to this, in an inscription we find reference to another person *Yasa* who is described as rich as a *Yaksha* in grain (sasye yakshasya).[24] Thus lower Bengal could boast of rich agriculturists. In the 1st century AD, the Periplus enumerated malabathrum, Gangetic nard and very fine quality muslins called Gangetic as items of export from the port of Ganga.[25] Attention here may be drawn to the remarkable loan contract document written on a papyrus between two Greco-Roman merchants at the famous port of Muziris. From Muziris precious commodities were shipped on a vessel named Hermopollon to a premier Red Sea port, most probably Berenice or Myos Hormos. It is interesting to note that among the six parcels of precious commodities we find the presence of Gangetic nard. [26] The remarkable demand for this particular product is significant. Nard was definitely procured from a northern hinterland and then transported to Muziris from the port of Ganga. The Arthasastra (II, 11) referred to white and smooth dukula (a kind of fine cloth made from the inner bark of a plant) and the high quality *Karpasikas* as *Vangaka.* Silver could have been an item of import. If cowries formed a part of the medium of exchange, they had to be imported perhaps from Maldives. It appears that the products involved in the commerce of Bengal were grains, textile products, spices and horses.

The above survey is an attempt to bring to light the importance of the study of coinage in understanding the business activities of an area in any given period. In case of Bengal an efficient monetary system helped in the development of business potentialities in the area concerned. Pre-Gupta Bengal experienced an organized medium of transaction which gave fillip to its commerce.

Notes and References

1. For an overview of early Indian trade, please see the Introduction of Ranabir Chakravarti ed. *Trade in Early India*, New Delhi, 2001.
2. B.N. Mukherjee, *Coins and Currency Systems of Early Bengal* (up to c. AD 300), Calcutta, 2000.
3. Ibid, 14–18.
4. Enamul Haque et al, '*A Preliminary Report on Wary-Bateshwar Trial Excavation by ICSBA*', in Enamul Haque edited, *Journal of Bengal Art*, Vol. 5, 2000, Dhaka, 297.
5. D.C. Sircar, *Select Inscriptions Bearing on Indian History and Civilization*, Vol. I, New Delhi, 1993 (reprint) p. 79-80.
6. Colin Renfrew, '*Trade as Action at Distance*', in J.A. Sablov and C.C. Lamberg-Karlovsky eds., *Ancient Civilization and Trade*, Albuquerque, 1975 : 3-59.
7. B.N. Mukherjee, op. cit. : 19 – 21.
8. Mala Datta, *A Study of the Satavahana Coinage*, New Delhi, 1990.
9. Vimala Begley, '*Rouletted Ware at Arikamedu : A New approach*', *American Journal of Archaeology*, 92, 1988: 427-40.
10. Himangshu Prabha Ray, '*Trade and Contacts*' in Romila Thapar ed., *Recent Perspectives of Early Indian History*, Delhi, 1995: 142-75.
11. Ranabir Chakravarti, '*Maritime Trade in Horses in Early Historical Bengal: A Seal from Chandraketugarh*', *Pratna-Samiksha*, Vol.1, Calcutta, 1992: 155-159.
12. B.N. Mukherjee, '*Kharoshti and Kharoshti-Brahmi Inscriptions from West Bengal (India), Indian Museum Bulletin*. Vol. XXV, 1990.
13. Lionel Casson, '*The Periplus of the Erythraean Sea*, Princeton, 1989 : 79, sec. 44.
14. Angavijja, edited by Muni Punyavijayaji, Benares, 1957: 49.
15. Swaminatha Iyer, U.V. ed, *Purananuru*, 6th edition, Madras, 1963. This information was kindly given to

me by Prof. B.N. Mukherjee, who in turn received it from Prof. R. Nagaswami. I am thankful to both of them.

16. B.N. Mukherjee, *'The Great Kushana Testament'*, IMB, XXX, 1998: 1-105.
17. B.N. Mukherjee, *Coins and Currency Systems of Early Bengal* (up to c. AD 300), Calcutta, 2000: 26-30.
18. B.N. Mukherjee, *Kharoshti and Kharoshti-Brahmi Inscriptions from West Bengal (India)*, IMB, Vol. XXV, 1990 (first two chapters).
19. Ibid. This seal is now in the Balanda Museum, Hadoa (24 Parganas North).
20. B.N. Mukherjee, *Coins and Currency Systems of Early Bengal*: 36.
21. B.N. Mukherjee, *'Some Recently Noticed Kharoshti Epigraphs in U.P.'*, in Vidula Jayaswal ed., *From Stone Quarry to Sculpting Workshop*, New Delhi, 1998: 238-244.
22. B. N. Mukherjee, *'Discovery of Kharoshti and Kharoshti-Brahmi Inscriptions in Bihar'*, *The Journal of The Asiatic Society*, Vol. XXXIX, No.3-4, Calcutta, 1997: 119-123.
23. B.N. Mukherjee, 'Kharoshti and Kharoshti-Brahmi Inscriptions from West Bengal', No.2.
24. Ibid., No. 35.
25. Lionel Casson, *The Periplus of the Erythraean Sea*, Princeton, 1989: 79, sec. 64.
26. Ranabir Chakravarti ed, *Trade in Early India*, New Delhi, 2001: 68.

4

Seventeenth Century Merchant Capital : The Case Study of Surat

Ruby Maloni

In the context of Surat, and in the light of the historical data available, there are clear indications of the strong presence of merchant capital in western India in the later medieval period. Some traces of Eurocentric notions linger, that at this time Indian commerce was static, and Indian merchants were first playing a rather negligible role in the Indian Ocean trade, and later were, at the most, apathetic or self serving partners of the European trading companies. However, most commercial records of these very companies tend to negate this.

As a primary source material, the Surat Factory Records provide copious information, restricted not only to Surat, but ranging all over the growing trade network of the English East India Company[1]. Undoubtedly, they are fraught with dangers of partiality and bias towards the commercial activities of the English. It is the casual acceptance of these perspectives that has led to generalizations about indigenous governments' disincentives to trade and long suffering mercantile communities. If the Records are examined more closely and critically, in corroboration with other contemporary source materials, the results can be different.

The English and other European trading companies made extensive use of the already existing commercial institutions. Their relationship with Indian merchants offer significant insights into different forms of economic behaviour and the level attained by the local Indian economies. Contemporary business systems and their dynamics can be better understood, and also the activities of the individuals and communities involved.

The commercial image of the period is not one of stagnation and confusion, but of a lively and stimulating milieu, a profile of a flourishing port and a systematic trading network. In seventeenth century India, there was opportunity for all. Surat provides the classic example of the remarkable vitality and resilience of the Indian business system to respond to the large scale transformations of the seventeenth century.

Surat was the unquestioned capital of emporia trading in the western Indian Ocean. In the 'trading world' of the Indian Ocean, Indian merchants and Indian products were dominant.[2] Gujarati traders organized directed voyages with their shipping and capital Western India was from early times a major market for West Asian imports such as silks, carpets, brocade, dried fruit, rose water, wines, dye roots, drugs such as frankincense and myrrh, coffee and horses. Coral was imported from the Mediterranean, and merchants from Aleppo and Cairo purchased a substantial volume of 'Eastern commodities'. From the entire area the surplus of exports over imports was repatriated in the form of bullion and specie. The pilgrim traffic, with its departure point at Surat, was significant, accompanied by a lucrative interchange of products. The Red Sea trade was a traditional sphere of commercial activity for Gujarati merchants. Trade was also firmly entrenched with Achin in Sumatra, with Java and Malaya. At Surat, the trans-shipment of goods from South-East Asia to West Asia took place. The English and other European trading powers involved themselves actively in this intra-Asian trade. In fact, Gujarati traders at Tiku, Priaman and Achin were described by the English as their enemies. Thomas Roe advised commercial traffic from Surat to the Red Sea as far more important than all other projects.[3] Indigenous merchants naturally resented this intrusion and in 1619 Surat traders appealed to the Mughal authorities.

In the Surat region, inter-regional trade was not conducted on a peddling level. The actual structure of Asian markets was much more complex. Any pre-Industrial Revolution economy would be noted for its relatively smaller scale and dimensions, a feature of pre-modern trade. The emphasis placed by Niels Steensgaard on the 'pedlar' is somewhat exaggerated.[4] Small scale traders did operate in the area, but it was in co-existence with merchants whose wealth and power compared favourably with territorial princes.

There was an accumulation of liquid or money capital in the hands of the bourgeoisie. A class with very considerable merchant capital existed, of whom the prime example is Virji Vora. A man of legendary reputation, he was perhaps one of the richest merchants of the world of his time. Some of his exploits verge on the apocryphal. At one time or another he lent large sums of money to the European companies. He dominated the Surat market, and had branch offices at Ahmedabad, Agra, Burhanpur and also in the Konkan, Malabar and the Coromandel coast. He owned a substantial fleet of ships. Virii Vora was not exceptional in the commercial life of Surat. There were other merchant princes like Haji Zahid Beg and Hari Vaisya. The former was so rich that when Shivaji attacked Surat, he demanded from him alone more than three lakhs of rupees.[5] The latter was a prominent broker merchant of Surat. He is often mentioned in both English and Dutch factory records - the Dutch calling him Henry Bessy. By 1631, both the English and the Dutch were deeply in debt to him. Merchants like him, Abdul Ghafur, Haji Abdul Nabi and Agha Rahim owned more than two hundred ships each. Muhammad Chalebi and other members of his family were eminent merchants of Surat. Chalebi had "nearly 2000 Arabs and Rumis" always with him.[6] There were also Chalebis at Aleppo, mentioned by Tavernier and Lannoy, the English Consul at Aleppo. The merchants functioned as an integrated group, as in freighting each other's ships. They also engaged in charitable and civic activities, founding veterinary hospitals, building temples and mosques, reservoirs and *sarais*. Rustam Manek[7], the eminent Parsi merchant, constructed bridges, wells, reservoirs for cattle and an imposing Parsi temple.[8]

With the increase of Indian Ocean trade, rulers and officials began to increase their investment in shipping and overseas commerce in the early seventeenth century. It was common for members of the royal family to engage in trade ventures. Jahangir, Nur Jahan, Shah Jahan and Aurangzeb[9] owned ships trading to the Red Sea. .A large source of capital required for sea-borne trade came from the Mughal aristocracy. Tavernier writes that, 'on arrival for embarkation at Surat, you find plenty of money. for it is the principal trade of the nobles of India to place their money on vessels on speculation for Hormuz, Bassora and Mocha, and even for Bantam, Achin and Philippenes."[10]

Many of the *Shahbandar* and even some Governors or *Mutasaddi of* Surat were prominent merchants before they were elevated to their positions. They continued to be involved in trade on their own private account while in office and may be described as capital entrepreneurs engaged in high finance. The *Shahbandar* as port officer had a hold over the passage of commodities at Surat port, and his office was usually farmed out to the highest bidder. lshaq Beg was appointed in 1621 as *Shahbandar* because he promised to increase the collection of revenue by as much as 200,000 *Mahmudis.*[11] The major work of the office was the assessment and collection of customs dues on the import and export of bullion. Some of the *Mutasaddi of* the city of Surat formerly held the position of *Shahbahdar.* In 1630, the *Mutasaddi* was Mir Musa, who was a wealthy merchant, and owned the famous ship *Salamati.* He traded regularly with the Persian Gulf At one time, he attempted to form a partnership with Virji Vora. He controlled the wheat supply, along with other powerful merchants, and extended a monopoly in lead and indigo also.

Between the government and merchants a vertical link of common mercantile and pecuniary interests existed. While there was an awareness that the newly arrived Europeans, in contrast to the Portuguese, were likely to contribute to commercial expansion and revenue increase, they were also perceived as a threat to the existing trade network of the local merchant community. The Mughal administration could and did take punitive measures against the European trading companies. Several incidents may be cited ; one of them of 1692, when the Surat merchant Abdul Ghafur's ships were seized by pirates. The emperor issued a *hasb-ul-hukm* forbidding the trade of the English, Dutch and French throughout the Mughal dominions unless they provided joint escort service to Mughal shipping.

Merchants had their own areas and means of influence and access to centers of political power, and their internal order of self-management. The world of ports and markets operated with a considerable degree *of* autonomy. Merchants and artisans were generally organized into identifiable communities. The *Panch* or artisan guild had *a Patel* as its head.[12] By the sixteenth century, the guild system had consolidated itself and had become a prominent feature of the urban setting. The authority of the *Mahajan* or guild organizations over their members was vital. The organizations included Virji Vora and Hari Vaishya, among other leading Surat merchants and financiers.

Surat was a part of the "mature Mughal monetary realm".[13] The supply of monetary media was in gold, copper and silver, with preponderance on the latter. By 1600, cheap American silver began reaching Gujarat port towns in very large quantities.[14] After 1620, the minting of rupees was focused on Surat. Strict imperial regulations forced European and other merchants importing silver to convert it to Mughal coinage at the Surat mint.[15] Recent researches in Dutch VOC records establish that Mughal authorities induced merchant groups at Surat to include silver and copper among the cargo and deliver the metals directly to the mint. Many thousands of coins travelled up the valley of the Tapti river to Burhanpur and the market towns along the routes, where cloth and other commodities were purchased. By the 1666-76 decade, Surat alone was issuing 25.3 per cent of the coins of the Mughal empire.[16] In 1672 the Surat mint turned out 30,000 rupees a day for the English alone. In Surat, both the rupee and the *mahmudi* were used for commercial credit and wholesale traffic. The volume and variety of coinage, which included silver *larins* and *abbasis* from Persia *rials* from Mexico and *ducats* from Europe, indicate the level of monetary integration at Surat.

A large class of affluent merchants, shippers, bankers and money·lenders existed, engaging in trade, banking and bills of exchange transactions. Gujarati bankers performed a variety of functions. They advanced loans to Indian and foreign merchants, undertook business insurance, provided *Hundi* facilities in the different parts of the subcontinent and outside, and to some extent, accepted the deposits of their clients. Bankers also often operated as merchants, as did Virji Vora. Thus money was transformed into usurious capital. It began to be utilized more and more for speculative purposes, like insuring goods in transit, and advancing money at high rates of interest.

As a market for fully saleable *Hundis* developed, they provided a channel for investments. 'This business was mainly in the hands of the professional money changers, *the Sarrafs* who thus acquired a new and crucial role as commercial bankers, providing a specialized service as suppliers of credit.[17] Both the English and Dutch factors regularly recorded in a tone of regret their dependence on bills of exchange drawn from `shroffs'.

The penetration of merchant capital into the existing level of production occurred through the *dadni* or putting out system, which was an established practice even prior to the seventeenth century. The system of commercial advances has at times been described as an Indian version of the *verlagsystem* in Europe But the merchants almost always advanced cash sums and not raw materials under the traditional contract relationship.[18] The economy of Gujarat during the seventeenth century was a seller's i.e. producer's market. Demand was tremendous, and a large number of competitive buyers flooded the market. From the merchant's point of view, the putting out system excluded his rivals, and secured him timely delivery of the commodity in accordance with his specifications, at previously agreed rates. On the other hand, the primary producer accepted advances since he had to cope with extensive orders for which he may not have adequate money to purchase raw materials. Thus this system rendered economic services to both the merchant and the artisan. In this context, the degree of penetration of merchant capital into the production process may be assessed by examining whether the advance was in cash or in raw materials. Taking the textile industry in Surat and the adjoining areas, there is adequate evidence that advances were given in cash as more or less an established practice.

A highly specialized commercial group were the brokers, acting as middlemen between buyers and sellers. They were a link between producers, wholesalers, retailers and consumers. In all the larger markets, they were highly sought after, foreign merchants having to depend on them greatly. In 1634, the English factors wrote that "it is most usual to effect business which is at a distance by a broker".[19] Everyone who was interested in trade — professional merchants, European companies, princes, nobles, governors and even weavers — had his own broker to look after his interest.[20] They linked inland centers of production and commerce with international trade. The memoirs of the Frenchman George Roques provide a detailed account of the activities of brokers in the textile trade in Gujarat.[21]

The Surat broker features in a leading role in the narrative of the English Factory Records. Most brokers also traded on their own account, and some grew to be very rich. Three well established families are mentioned in the early Records, the Parikh family, Piru Hingola and his sons[22] and the family headed by Chota Thakur. Tulsi Das[23], Bhimji Parakh's father, was the earliest of the Parakhs. The first mention of a member of Chota Thakur's family, called Jadav, was made in 1612 when he had worked for Hawkins and Middleton. Another kinsman was Kalyanji, a broker of the English Company[24], Gourdas [25] was the brother and Deoldas[26] was the assistant of Chota Thakur. Members of such broker families worked for the European trading companies at a network of centers such as Agra, Ahmedabad, Thatta and also at Bandar Abbas, Basra etc. Ordinarily, the total commission of a broker or *dalal was* two per cent of the value of each transaction_ Brokers were also associated with the payment of customs and tolls on roads, as seen from the Factory Records. Perhaps it would not have been difficult for these broker-contractors or middlemen like Piru Hingola and others to evolve into manufacturing entrepreneurs.

Surat as a port city did not and could not operate in isolation. Along with its foreland and hinterland, it may be considered as the leading mercantile conglomeration of India in the seventeenth century. Cambay, Bharuch, Navsari, Rander, Variao, Dumas, Dumka and Olpad were closely connected with the economy of Surat. They provided commodities such as textiles, and also a variety of services such as bleaching and dyeing, transport, supplies for ships, and sailors etc. A productive and well administered hinterland was a necessary ingredient for the continuation of the processes of commerce and exchange. Communication between ports and interior markets was reasonably easy. A well organized merchant community existed not only in port towns but also in the trade marts of the hinterland. Transport of commodities from the hinterland to the port was by boats or ox-drawn carts to the waiting ships.[27] The shipbuilders of Surat were highly praised for their workmanship, and at this period were generally Konkanis or Parsis by ethnicity. In the Surat Factory Records, the advantages of building ships at Surat is clearly recorded.[28]

Surat represented an advanced urban culture. It epitomized the growth of urban centers in the early seventeenth century. Several characteristics of urban development may be discerned here, in terms of infrastructural facilities, conspicuous consumption, competitive markets and varied output of manufactured products. The major items of export were cotton piece goods, yarn and indigo. The market oriented Gujarat silk industry was concentrated at Surat and Ahmedabad. Yarn and raw silk were supplied from Bengal, especially Kasimbazar. Malabar and Kanara pepper came to the Surat market, for both wholesale and retail trade. By the late seventeenth century, the main imports of Surat were coffee, tobacco and opium, while large volumes of silk and sugar were being re-exported.[29]

One of the causes for the decline of Surat was the entrepreneurial exodus to Bombay. the alternative commercial capital on the west coast. By 1673, a considerable number of Surat merchants such as the English broker Bhimji Parakh had decided to leave Surat and migrate to Bombay. Yet Surat's eclipse was neither sudden nor total. In the memoir of Jacques Vincens written in the 1730s, 10 out of 34 folios are devoted to various aspects of trade at Surat. It was still the "richest and most trading city in India".[30] When John Henry Grose visited Surat in the mid-eighteenth century, he saw 'solid Hindu merchants' who would singly buy up the entire cargo of a European ship with half an hour's bargaining and prompt cash payments.[31]

The capacities and enterprise of Indian merchants in this period have tended to be grossly underestimated.[32] They carried on their commercial activities in the teeth of the emergent challenges. One of the reasons why the joint stock association referred to by S.Arasaratnam in the case of the Coromandel Coast[33] did not emerge in Surat was that throughout the seventeenth century, the Surat merchants competed with the English and other European traders, and never assumed the role of passive 'suppliers' or textiles or other merchandise to the Companies.

In gauging the trends of the times, stress cannot be only on impersonal factors, but on real situations, groups and individuals. However, there were complex processes and deeper trends at work which have to be examined. The period under study was witness to the regional and trans-oceanic flow of trade adjusting and redirecting themselves. The obtrusive presence of the European trading companies interrupted the independent growth of indigenous productive forces. The rise and development of merchant capital in the seventeenth century became more or less an episode in the economic history of India, and not the harbinger of an ongoing process of economic change and structural modifications within Indian society.

Notes and References

1. R. Maloni, *European Merchant Capital and the Indian Economy*: Surat Factory Records, New Delhi, 1992.
2. K.N. Chaudhari, *Trade and Civilisation in the Indian Ocean*, New Delhi, 1985. Satish Chandra, *The Indian Ocean, Explorations in History, Commerce and Politics*, New Delhi, 1987.
3. In his letter to the East India Company, November 24, 1616.
4. N. Steensgaard, *The Asian Trade Revolution of the Seventeenth Century*, Chicago, 1974, p. 307.
5. W. Foster, ed., *The English Factories in India, 1618-1669*, vol. 2, Oxford, 1906-27, p. 300.

6. Ali Muhammad Khan, Mirat-I-Ahmadi, ed., Nawab Ali, vol. II, Baroda, 1930, p. 34.
7. During Aurangzeb's reign.
8. M. J. Kaiqubad. '*Qissa-I Seth Rustam Manak*'. J. J. Modi, *JBBRAS*. New Series, VI, pp. 181-209.
9. Aurangzeb's ships, referred to in the English Factory Records as "the King's Junks", were all more than 600 tuns. His ship *Ganj Sawai* was the largest ship at the port of Surat.
10. Tavernier, *Travels in India*, tr. Ball, ed,. Crooke, vol. 1, reprint, New Delhi, 1977. p. 31.
11. *1 Mahmudi* (silver) = 1 shilling. 86 silver grains approx; less than half the value of a rupee.
12. The English at 'Broach' and 'Brodera' had some direct dealings with Patels.
13. J.F. Richards, ed., *The Imperial Monetary System of Mughal India*, Oxford Universitv Press. 1987, p. 8.
14. R.J. Brennig, '*Silver in Seventeenth Century Surat: Monetary Circulation and the Price Revolution in Mughal India*', in J.F. Richards, ed. *Precious Metals in the later. Medieval and early Modern World*, Durham, 1982, pp. 482-8.
15. R. Maloni. '*Foreign Coins in Surat:The Account of Seventeenth Century Travellers*', paper presented in 4th' International Colloquium on '*Foreign Coins in the Indian Subcontinent*', Nashik, 1995.
16. Aziza Hasan, '*Mints of the Mughal Empire*', in Proceedings of the Indian History Congress, 29th' Session, Patiala, 1967, p. 329.
17. Tapan Raychaudhari, '*Inland Trade*', in *The Cambridge Economic History of India*, vol. I, eds. Tapan Raychaudhari and Irfan Habib, Delhi, 1982, p. 346.
18. K.N. Chaudhari, '*European Trade with India*', in op. cit., p. 406.
19. Charles Fawcett, ed., *The English Factories in India*, 1634-36, Oxford, 1936, p. 79.
20. S.N. Sen, ed., *Travels of Thevenot and Careri*, New

Delhi, 1949, pp. 77-78.

21. Indrani Ray, *Of Trade and Traders in Seventeenth Century India : An Unpublished French Memoir by George Roques*, Occasional Paper No. 26, Centre for Studies in Social Sciences, Calcutta, 1979.

22. Surat Factory Diary, No. 1, Part 1,. 1660-68, Consultation 36, dated July 6, 1668.

23. Surat Inward Letter Book, vol. 1A, 1656-57, Letter 9, dated December 4, 1656.

24. *"Ancient Broker belonging to the Company" at Burhanpur.* Surat Outward Letter Book, Vol. 1, 1630, Letters 24 and 42, dated November 10 and December 6, 1630.

25. Ibid.

26. Surat Factory Diary, No. 1, Part 1,. 1660-68, Consultations 27 and 28, dated July 31 and August 26, 1630.

27. J. Davies, tr., *The Voyages and Travels of Albert de Mandelslo*, London, 1931, p. 59.

28. Surat Factory Diary, No. 1, Part 1,. 1660-68, Consultation 8, dated May 8, 1661.

29. R. Maloni, '*Seventeenth Century Surat : Cultural Interface in an Urban Environment*' in K.S. Mathew, ed., *Indian Ocean and Cultural Interaction*, Pondicherry, 1996, pp. 164-171.

30. Indrani Ray, '*India in Asian Trade in the 1730s : A discussion by a French Trader*', in Essays in honour of S. C. Sarkar, New Delhi, 1976, p. 227.

31. J. H. Grose, *A Visit to the East Indies : 1757*, London, 1920, pp. 159-60.

32. A view held by Holden Furber, Book Review, *Indian Economic and Social History Review*, vol. 1, No. 3, 1964, p. 195.

33. S. Arasaratnam, '*Indian Merchants and their Trading Methods*, c. 1700', in *Indian Economic and Social History Review*, Vol. 3, 1966, pp. 86-87.

5

Revealing and Concealing : The Business World of Middlemen and Merchants in the French Commercial Enterprise in Pondicherry (AD 1674 – 1741)

S. Jeyaseela Stephen

Writers in general, of European trade in India and the French trade in particular, during the early modern period have tended to stress their company trading character and presence. [1] But much of the European commercial activities were only linked with the Indians who performed economic functions of great significance in the ports and this feature had not been adequately covered in their writings. The possible reason attributed could be simple, to say that the European factory records do not furnish much details of these Indian businessmen, whose family records have also not survived today. But it is possible to cull information from these European documents if we look at them closely and patiently, to understand the role of the Indian traders. Therefore against this backdrop, the present paper attempts to highlight the indigenous businessmen of Pondicherry who were alone able to satisfy the French needs of cloth manufacture and their long distance overseas trade. The period chosen is from the establishment of the French settlement of Pondicherry in the year 1674 to the appointment of the French Governor Dupleix at Pondicherry in the year 1741. Manuscripts and publised documents both in French and Tamil had been chiefly used here besides the English records which throw light on the businessmen.

Middlemen

The beginnings of French trade in Pondicherry was aided by the native intermediaries. In this venture, the key role was played by Thanappa Mudaliar, of Vellala caste (alias Lazare de Mota, obtained the Baptismal name, converted by the Portuguese missionaries) who was the first to come to the aid of the French, hailing from Poonamallee (Modern Poovirunthavalli) when the French met him in Santhome of Mylapore.[2] On the invitation of the French, he settled down in Pondicherry on 14 January 1674. Although Vellala Mudaliars, an agrarian caste have not had a long history as a trading group before the advent of the Portuguese, they after becoming Christians traded in rice in Mylapore along with the Portuguese. The French appointed him as the courtier de la compagnie (broker of the company) and also wooed several other brokers and encouraged them to settle down in Pondicherry. In this regard, Francois Martin, the chief official of the French company had to be praised. After the death of Thanappa Mudaliar, his son Andre Muthiyappa Mudaliar was appointed to the post of courtier and he worked as a broker for the French company in Pondicherry. Later his son Pedro Kanakaraya Mudaliar became broker of the French company following the death of his father Andre Muthiyappa Mudaliar.[3]

Pondicherry was occupied by the Dutch in 1693 and it was handed over to the French according to the Treaty of Rijswick in 1699. But the procedure involved in the transfer of Pondicherry was completed only by 24 April 1700. Immediately after restoration of the Settlement, the French once again had encouraged middlemen to revive their textile trade. This time the response came from another caste Hindus called Pillais, who were also like Mudaliars were not traditional businessmen but shepherds by profession. In 1702, Nainiyappa Pillai who was working as a broker in Madras with the English settled down in Pondicherry along with his brother-in-law Thiruvengadam Pillai who also became another broker of the French company. According to records Nainiyappa Pillai was appointed as the chief broker of the French company in 1708 by Herbert, the French Governor. Nainiyappa was also called dubash since he served as an interpreter. We know that many of the intermediaries were also interpreters. The Jesuit missionaries objected the high post of the chief broker (courtier de la compagnie) being offered to Nainiyappa Pillai. Later several false charges were made against Nainiyappa Pillai including embezzelment of funds of the French company and under this pretext he was thrown into prison on 19 February 1716 where he died in jail on 18 August 1717.[4]

After the death of Nainiyappa Pillai, Thiruvengadam Pillai, the brother-in-law and broker of the French company had continued to help the French without leaving Pondicherry. Some Portuguese traders of Macao like Manuel de Rosa and Joao Gomes wrote a letter on 26 April 1720 approaching Thiruvengadam Pillai with a proposal to trade with Pondicherry in their ships. They had requested him to arrange for the customs duty privileges to be granted by the French Governor of Pondicherry.[5] Thus we find that brokers in Pondicherry had played a key role and the French mainly began to use their services. The death of Nainiyappa Pillai in prison had made his own son, Guruvappa Pillai to leave for France and he pleaded justice before the King. While in France he embraced Christianity and he returned from Paris after being appointed as the chef des noirs et courtier de La compagnie (The chief of the Blacks and Broker of the Company). However his Hindu uncle Thiruvengadam Pillai, (the father of Ananda Ranga Pillai, the famous diarist) was, also appointed as a deputy to Guruvappa Pillai. Thus the post of courtier of the French company became hereditary. Guruvappa Pillai remained as the chief broker of the French till his death in 1724.

Having examined the two families of Mudaliars and Pillais functioning as brokers of the French company in Pondicherry, it may be worthwhile to note why the French encouraged these brokers very much. The brokers were placed between buyer and supplier helping the French in obtaining the cloth for export to France. These brokers were essentially needed by the French for they did not have the first hand information about the manufacture of cloth, prevailing prices and supply. Further textiles of various designs, dimensions, density of threads, variety, quality and quantity produced in Pondicherry were required for their trade. Their ships in Pondicherry needed cargo within a stipulated time so that their voyages are not delayed. It was therefore necessary for the French to have the cargoes made ready earlier and not to miss the season for sailing to France. As the French did not directly want to enter into production of cloth and the brokers could control such work, the intermediaries and interpreters were needed for the French in helping their export supply of textiles. Thus non-vaisyas such as Mudaliars and Pillais began to be businessmen and it is clearly seen in this period when post of the brokers became hereditary. The family of Thanappa Mudaliar and the family of Nainiyappa Pillai continued their business throughout the Eighteenth century in Pondicherry.

Pedro Kanakaraya Mudaliar was the only broker of the French who remained in service for a long period of twentyfour years between 1722 and 1746. He was also called *dubash*. Although the role of the broker was not to supply the French company with manufactured goods, he did so. The Superior Council of Pondicherry had informed the Council of Chandernagore also not to permit their broker Indira Narayan Chaudhri to sell the goods to the French.[6] The broker was only expected to supervise the cloth manufacture, and to provide the textiles for which the contracts had been made. The broker was even forbidden to receive gifts and presents from the producers. Since I have already published an article on the role of Pedro Kanakaraya Mudaliar elsewhere, I omit here with reference to his textile manufacture and trade.[7]

It is to be borne in mind that these brokers in Pondicherry had although helped the French they had not acted as salaried officials of the French company. They were engaged in passing on the capital amount from the French to the weavers besides the textiles from the weavers to the French. Thus the relationship was between them was one that of the producer and the exporter and vice-versa. The brokers had employed several agents and so they cannot be considered as agents of the French company by taking a fixed commission on trade rather than a profit. The French in Pondicherry also never had direct contacts with the weavers unlike the Dutch in Coromandel. As the French did not like to interfere in the textile production, they heavily depended on the brokers who made direct contacts with the weavers in and around Pondicherry.

Merchants

There were merchants doing textile business in Pondicherry even before the advent of the French in 1674 at Pondicherry. It is found mentioned in a letter dated 6th February 1621 written by the Agent and Council at Batavia to the English East India Company that the Danes who had settled down at Tranquebar had built godowns and for some years lived at Pondicherry and they had established commercial contacts with the native merchants there.[8] These merchants were Berri Chettis of the left hand (Idangai) caste and they were engaged in cloth trade. The memoir of Francois Martin mentions that the Berri Chetti merchants supplied cloth to the French and the Brahmins of Pondicherry forbade the Chettis to deliver cloth to the French factory. Having known this fact the French sent their security men to the godowns of the merchants and brought textiles to the factory.[9] The English factor at Kunimedu, a port located fifteen miles north of Pondicherry always attempted to attract the Pondicherry merchants and they in their temptation to make profit supplied cloth to the English in the month of August 1685.[10] The English even encouraged the Pondicherry merchants to purchase the English goods which were stocked in their godown at Kunimedu in 1689.[11] The Pondicherry merchants in response to the invitation extended by the English factor had sent a proposal for an investment with the English company at Kunimedu to supply longcloth, salempores, beatilhas and succattums. The mode of payment was finalised with seven-eighths in ready money and one-eighth in English goods during the year 1689. Thus many Pondicherry merchants traded with the English in Kunimedu and also slowly moved to Madras. The French had no control over these native merchants in Pondicherry and they had very little to offer the traders.

Chacka Serappa, a Berri Chetti was an important trader in Pondicherry who decided to go to Madras seeking his bright commercial fortune. He worked for the English company in Madras and he was one of the successful merchants listed in the first stock joint company organized in Madras in 1680.[12] He also became the chief merchant on the request of several other local traders doing business with the English. With the Dutch occupation of Pondicherry between 1693 and 1697, many Berri Chettis migrated to Madras who were welcomed by him. Chacka Serappa at this time formed his own joint stock company in 1697 with 10,000 pagodas. However the joint stock company lasted only for four years. There was financial crunch and in the year 1703, we find that Chacka Serappa and other merchants had a commercial dispute regarding the payment of an outstanding debt to the English. Finally Chacka Serappa had to pay the debt incurred by the failure of other Berri Chetti merchants to the English company in Madras.[13] However other Berri Chetti merchants like Kalavai Chetty and Pedda Thambi Chetty had offered surety for the debts of Chacka Serappa to the English company in Madras.[14] Knowing the difficulties faced by the Pondicherry merchants in Madras, when the French resettled in Pondicherry in 1701, they invited the Chettis as they were suppliers of cloth, and true businessmen of the French during the earlier period. The crisis for the French at that time was finding merchants to cater to their business needs and credit. These Chettis were not moneylenders in Pondicherry but they could only satisfy them with textiles. It was very essential for the French to have good merchants to revive their trade. Hence they attempted to woo the merchants who served under the English. Some of them sent their gumastas (agents) initially to run their business in Pondicherry. It was at this time, the Komatti Chettis of valangai (Right hand) caste began to trade with the French. Out of the total sixteen prominent Pondicherry merchants, nine of them lived in Madras and only seven of them resided in Pondicherry itself.[15]

Among the merchants, Narasu, by name was appointed as the chief merchant "Chef des marchands malabars" by the French. Narasu, could invest the highest capital for the trade. He continued to be the chief merchant even in the year 1719.[16] His commercial activity was not only restricted to textiles supply to French but he was also engaged in rice trade. He had a share in minting pagodas and he was functioning as a money changer in Pondicherry through buying silver from the French who brought in their ships.

When there were no ships arrived from France to Pondicherry in 1719, the Superior Council appealed and promised to pay the merchants through Narasu's influence, the arrear amounts due to them before the period of expiry. Narasu was given the unique privilege to ride in a palanquin in Pondicherry.[17] He was thus very powerful among the traders and he remained as the chief merchant. He floated a joint stock company of local merchants for textile trade. On 5 April 1721, the company included twentyfive merchants. In the month of October the number fell down to fourteen. In this joint stock company of the merchants, capital was raised through subscription by the purchase of shares.[18] Joint participation in trade by the merchants using the Indian capital for French purposes was disliked by some traders. Further caste system of South India was another problem which prevented the entry of all the merchants in Pondicherry. Although they have formed a joint stock company with members of various castes, the merchants broke away as found in the French records. However, Narasu died in December 1722.

Joint Stock Company in Pondicherry

The capital of the French company was mainly tied up in advances given to the weavers. The French requested the merchants to invest in freighting, by placing their goods as freight on French ships. They also wanted merchants to invest in shipping. In 1721 a sum of 12,700 pagodas were arranged by the merchants of Pondicherry for shipping to Manila.[19] The advances made to the merchants by the French enabled them to pay for the raw materials and labour. The merchants supervised the work and collected textiles from the production centres and brought it to Pondicherry factory warehouse. There inspection was undertaken by the French company servants who accepted the cloth as per the muster roll and rejected the rest. The final reconciliation of accounts took place immediately. The joint stock company of Pondicherry merchants known as *ancien marchands* (old merchants) in French records, introduced in Pondicherry gave an opportunity to many brokers who lived there to develop an efficient form of merchant capital through the mobilization of capital from a wider network than what was already existing. Further, since there was no submissiveness on the part of the brokers to the French company it added some stimuli for functioning well. We are not sure how far the concept of joint stock company gave important lessons for the Pondicherry merchants about the French commercial ideas. Certainly the joint stock company had interferred substantially with the individual earnings of the Pondicherry merchants and so all the merchants did not like to join in it. Some merchants liked it only because they were given the monopoly status in a specific textile item such as guinea, salempores, beatilhas, etc., to manufacture and trade. As there were many too small merchants, the French also perhaps wanted to put them under different roofs to specialize in specific textile variety and to engage them in cloth trade. This also added in a way to solve the problem of the French cloth arrival in quantity and quality besides avoiding the French to buy low quality cloth at an increasingly higher price. The French who formed their suppliers into companies gained very much and it enabled them by preventing different brokers from competing against one another. Thus the weavers and merchants could not also abscond with the French capital invested in business.

Contracts were made by the Superior Council of Pondicherry with the merchants when they had sufficient money available in the month of March or April. They stipulated that 2/3 or 3/4 of the textiles should be ready by the month of September and the rest by the end of December. If there was any shortage of funds the contracts were delayed until the months of June or July for the arrival of French ships from France with bullion to pay the Pondicherry merchants. It is found in records that no contracts were made with the *ancien marchands* during the years 1726 and 1727. During March 1729 it is found in a contract that an advance of 10,000 pagodas were made which appears to be a very meagre amount on a contract of 140,000 pagodas.[20] The textile merchants who entered into contract with the French in Pondicherry on 5 May 1731 had expressed their inability to supply cloth and it was chiefly because of a dispute that arose between the weavers of different castes in Pondicherry. Further the manufacture of textiles came to a halt for a period of two months.[21] In 1736 *ancien marchands* had a contract for 1262 bales of textiles worth 114,785 pagodas which included an advance of 61,000 pagodas.[22]

Sunku Rama, a Komatti Chetti was a famous merchant in Pondicherry. He traded with the French and invested funds in shipping from Pondicherry to Manila. He floated a joint stock company of merchants in 1722 to break away the dominance of Narasu, the chief merchant. There were sixteen merchants in his joint stock company during the year 1723 and the number rose to nineteen in the year 1725. However seven merchants of the company broke away with Sunku Rama in 1727 and the company suffered very much. He was also a money changer but died in 1734. Indirani Ray, Sinnapah Arasaratnam and Catherine Manning had dealt with this merchant Sunku Rama and so I do not repeat here about his commercial activities.[23] I am interested now to highlight the role of his brother, Sunku Seshachala Chetti who conducted trade with the French company. Sunku Seshachala Chetti was welcomed by the French in 1735 and he supplied cloth to the French in 1736. Evidences suggest that the 'Superior Council of Pondicherry had ordered the increase in textile price to be given to Sunku Seshachala as an encouragement. The price increase allowed to Sunku Seshachala was credited in the book of accounts without having any consequence in the future. It is stipulated in a record dated 26 April 1736 that the bleachers who were employed under him were to be paid only at the earlier price although price increase had been given to Seshachala Chetti.[24] His textile contract of 1736 shows that he had agreed to supply 726 bales of guineas of Dutch variety, ordinary guineas of 480 bales and salempouris of 60 bales.[25] It is mentioned that he was allowed to be reimbursed by the French company the cost of transporation to the tune of 787 pagodas and 12 panams. In Tamil documents dated 3 October 1736 and 5 December 1736, we find that Sunku Seshachala Chetti was the renter of the mint in Pondicherry.[26] Further we find that Sunku Seshachala Chetti also received an advance of 71,000 pagodas on a textile contract worth of 120,491 pagodas from the French in the same year.[27] In the contract made during the year 1737 he agreed to supply

1464 bales of Dutch variety of guineas, salempouris of ordinary variety of 200 bales and fine variety of 760 bales.[28] Sunku Seshachala Chetti continued to invest his funds in textiles manufacture and supply. On 13 April 1739 we find that he was indebted for 43,000 pagodas on the previous year contract.[29] He continued to supply cloth even during the year 1741.

Finally it may be worthwhile to quote the opinion of the French officials who were the members of the Superior Council of Pondicherry about a native middleman. "He is well endowed with honesty, integrity, discernment, experience and influence. He is capable of sustained activity and of exercising full control over his subordinates and has been quite keen in informing us of the feelings and views of the Hindu population."[30] This shows that businessmen in Pondicherry followed ethics. The fact that the French also honoured the Pondicherry merchants with a gold chain of stipulated value as an award is to be noted here. During 1738 three prominent merchants like Viragu Chetti, Chittamabala Chetti, and other merchant whose name is not clear in the record were given a gold chain of each thirty five pagodas. The rest of the company merchants like Chelambara Chetti, Kalahasti Chetti, Nalla Chetti, Alagiya Manavala Chetti, Chinna Ramanna Chetti, Ragappa Chetti, Muthu Krishna, and Kulandai were given a gold chain to the value of twenty pagodas.[31] The practice of giving gold chain continued even in the next year according to a record dated 7 July 1739.[32] It is to be noted here that the practice of giving a gold chain to company merchants at Pondicherry by the French was something new and different while the English in Madras gave only rose water and some money.

It had been well recognised that several indigenous entrepreneurs had been drawn into the commerce of the French company and of whom little is known to us. To conclude we may say that the merchants in Pondicherry come into a different relationship with the French and the French were not deprived of their middlemen and so did not begin to enter into direct relations with the weavers in Pondicherry. Merchants were never over-committed to the French they had a wide range of business activities and so they were able to survive without losing their independent identity during the period of study. Komatti Chettis showed a considerable capacity to resist the French pressure. There was competition and rivalries among the native merchants in textile trade and these merchants were highly specialized in providing their elaborate services such as broking, translating, money changing, manufacture of cloth and establishing links with the weavers, dyers, bleachers and washers in Pondicherry. Thus these merchants controlled production.

Notes and References

1. I would here like to restrict myself only to the writings on French Trade in India, and not of the Dutch, the Danish or the English company writings in general since they are available in abundance. See, Philip Haudrere, La Compagnie Francaise des Indes au XVIIIe Siecle, 1719-1795, 4 vols, Paris, 1989. Indrani Ray, Les Commerciantes Francais au Bengale, 1686-1757, Paris University Thesis, 1967. Exception may be said of Catherine Manning who had spelled out the French partners and others in her work, *Fortunes a Faire*, The French in Asian Trade 1719-48, Aldershot, Variorum, 1996. The details of brokers of the Dutch company on the Coromandel coast are found in the writings of Sanjay Subrahmanyam. On Achutappa Chetti, See, Sanjay Subrahmanyam, The Political Economy of Commerce: Southern India, 1500-1650, Cambridge, 1990, pp. 300-307. On merchants see, Ashin Dasgupta, "The merchants of Surat c. 1700-1750" in E. Leach & S. Mukherjee, Elites in South Asia Cambridge, 1970, pp. 202-22 where he classifies merchants into five broad categories of shippers, merchants, brokers, shroffs and dubashies. The work of Clive had discussed the merchants as four categories such as wholesalers, retailers, transporters and peddlers. See, Clive, *A History* of *Commerce*, New York, 1921, p. 39.
2. S. Jeyaseela Stephen, "*Urbanism and the chequered*

existence of the Indo-French town of Pondicherry, AD 1674-1793" Revue Historique de Pondicherry, Vol. XIX, 1996, pp. 29-64. See also, C.S. Srinivasachari, "*The first Indian courtiers of the French EastIndia Company*", Proceedings of the Indian Historical Records Commission, (hereafter PIHRC) 1940; another article of his see "The *later representatives* of a great family of courtiers of Pondicherry", PIHRC, 1941.

3. S. Jeyaseela Stephen, "Socio-Economic Role of *Dubash* Pedro Kanakaraya Mudaliar in the French Colony of Pondicherry, 1717-1746" Revue Historique de Pondichery, Vol. XVIII, 1995, pp.15-32.
4. P. Olangier, Les Jesuits a Pondichery et l'affaire Nainaiappa, Paris, 1932.
5. Edmond Gaudart, Proces verbaux des deliberations du conseil superieur de Pondichery, 1701 to 1741 (hereafter PV) 3 vols, Pondicherry, 1912-1915, vol. I, p. 234.
6. Edmond Gaudart & Alfred Martineau, Correspondance du Conseil Superieur de Pondichery avec le conseil de Chandenagore du 30 Septembre 1728 au 10 Fevrier 1757, (hereafter CCSCCH), 3 Vols, Paris, 1915-1919. vol. I, p. 28, 65 February 1730.
7. S. Jeyaseela Stephen, "Socio-Economic Role of *Dubash* Pedro Kanakaraya Mudaliar in the French Colony of Pondicherry, 1717-1746 "Revue Historique de Pondichery, vol. XVIII, 1995, pp.15-32. See particularly pp.19-21.
8. William Foster, The English Factories in India, 1606-1621 (hereafter EFI) Oxford, 1906-I927, see details on 6th February 1621.
9. Lotika Varadarajan, India in the Seventeenth Century: Memoirs of Francois Martin, (hereafter Memoirs), New Delhi, 1980, vol. II, pt. I, pp. 1149-1151.
10. Records of Fort St. George, (Hereafter RFSG), Letters From Fort St. George to Subordinate Factories,1689, Madras, 1916.

11. S. Jeyaseela Stephen, " Historic Textiles of Pondicherry: Weaving and the Trading World under the French Flag", PILC Journal of Dravidic Studies, Pondicherry, vol.6:1, January 1996, pp.93-124.

12. RFSG, Diary and Consultation Book 1680, see the date 2 September 1680.

13. RFSG, Diary and Consultation Book 1703, pp. 24, 25, 33.

14. RFSG, Diary and Consultation Book, 1707, p. 57. See the date 29 August 1707.

15. Archives Nationales, (hereafter AN), Paris, Fonds des Colonies, C2, 25 f.180.

16. PV, tomo I, p. 214, see the date 27 September 1719.

17. Ibid.

18. Archives d' Outre-Mer d' Aix-en Provence (AOMA) Inde, p. 8. f.90, dated 5 April 1721; Inde p.20.f.630, dated 21 October 1721.

19. PV, tomo I, 290-291, dated 12 July 1721.

20. AOMA, Inde, p.35. f.156, see also, PV, tomo II, p.226.

21. PV, tomo II, p.328.

22. AOMA, Inde, p.51.ff 267, 275.

23. Indirani Ray, The Multiple Faces of the Early Eighteenth Century Indian Merchant, Centre of Studies in Social Sciences, Calcutta, 1980, p. 4. Indirani inclined to identify Sunkurama with Sunku Venakatachalam and Sunku Muthurama, chief merchants of Madras between 1711-1730. Sunkurama died in 1734. See, Arasaratnam, Merchants Companies and Commerce on the Coromandel Coast, 1650-1740, New Delhi, 1986, pp. 236-310.

24. PV, tomo III, p.26.

25. PV, tomo III, pp. 132-133.

26. Fredrick Price & K. Rangachari, The Private Diary of Ananda Ranga Pillai, 1736-1761, 12 vols. (hereafter ARP Diary) New Delhi, 1985, vol. I, p. 7; vol. II. p. 4 and 102.

27. AOMA, Inde, p. 51, ff 267, 275.

28. PV, tomo III, pp. 131-132.

29. AOMA, Inde, p.56, ff. 90,113; See, ARP Diary, Vol. I, p. 90, see the date 13 April 1739.
30. PV, tomo II, pp. 103-104.
31. Ibid, tomo III, p. 145.
32. Ibid, tomo III, p. 219.

6

Two Indian Brokers of the French East India Company in Eastern India during the first half of the Eighteenth Century

Aniruddha Ray

I

Since the beginning of the French establishment in Bengal in the second half of the seventeenth century, first in Hughly and then in Chandernagore,[1] the French did not appoint any broker. They used to buy silk, cotton piece goods and saltpetre generally from Hughli. This arrangement however did not last long. 'The prohibition in France for import of silk, the continuous European war when the Dutch had blocked the mouth of Hughly River and then the fall of Pondicherry interrupted their trade. The beginning of the eighteenth century also saw the European war when once again the French trade with India was practically stopped. This led to the fall of the French Company and the rise of a new one in 1719.

It is easier to find at Pondicherry the Indian associates of the French from the late seventeenth century. One reason could be that at Pondicherry, the French needed the cooperation of Tamil merchants who were mostly carrying on trade with the English at Madras.[2] There was no Mughal port at close proximity excepting that of Masulipatnam, then in decline. On the other hand, the close proximity of Hughli, a rich mercantile port, to Chandernagore presented no difficulty to the French. As a result, we have the incomparable diary of the broker (dubash) Ananda Ranga Pillai[3] from the 1730s at Pondicherry, while there is no such source available to us from Bengal. As a matter of fact, since the early establishment of the French at Chandernagore, thanks to the efforts of Andre-Bourreau Deslandes, the French did not have any Bengali 'courtier'. They used to have contract *merchants at Hughli* even in the days of the European war from the late seventeenth century. There is no mention of any rich Bengali merchant either at Chandernagore or associated with the French during the early eighteenth century. This could be due to the absence of the Bengali merchants trading overseas, which was controlled by the Gujratis, Armenians and even to a certain extent by the Indo-Portuguese like Cosmo Gomez. One Muhammad Ghaus used to supply saltpetre to the French in the early eighteenth century, but it was during the prohibition by the Emperor for the purchase of saltpetre for the Europeans.[4] We therefore do not get the cluster of merchants living at Chandernagore during this period as we find at Pondicherry with the Tamil merchants. Therefore the history of the growth of Chandernagore during this early period shows a trend very much different from those of Calcutta or Pondicherry. During this period, Chandernagore as a European enclave in the true sense of the term.

With the peace of Ryswick, the French in Bengal began to purchase textile and saltpetre and to pay the huge debt. The French had a peculiar problem. They needed cloth of larger width than that asked by the English and the Dutch.[5] In case of the French, the weavers would have to adjust their loom, which they were willing to do once they were paid in advance. But the French were not in a position to give such advance. They could not load the two big ships, *Mourepas* and *Toison.*[6] By that time the prohibition in France had started against the import of silk and ordinary cotton textiles. The French therefore had to buy fine varieties of *Muslin.*[7] Finally, Andre-Bourreau Deslandes could buy goods worth two lakh rupees to fill up the ship, but his fund was entirely exhausted,[8] a pattern that haunted the French till the formation of the new Company in 1719.

With severe scarcity of cash since November 1700 in Bengal, Deslandes had become desperate. He decided to contact the weavers directy, but that even with the weavers around Hughli, he would have to pay advance.[9] The only escape route was to make spot purchase with the fund brought by ships as happened in December 1700.[10] Even then the French had contract with some merchants, who of course took advantage of the lack of fund of the French as well as their peculiar demand of the textiles. These merchants were mostly those who were working with the English and the Dutch. One such was Raghunath Das, who took advance from the French of Rs. 12,000 to supply in lots and as late as possible thus preventing the French from making serious inspection.[11] The lack of fund was not limited to the French in Bengal. The French at Pondicherry had to share the same situation.[12] In Bengal, this problem was further heightened by the existence of toll stations all along the river where one would have to pay a certain amount of money. Occasional clashes occurred and the complaints to the Nawab of Bengal did not produce any satisfactory result for the French.[13] The spot purchase meant higher price and the Indian merchants were aware of it. Since the ships were bringing bullion, the French had appointed a *Saraf* from whom they would take loan.[14] He would not only change the bullion and other foreign coins but also contact other merchants for the sale of European goods and get loan for the French. The emergence of the *Saraf* in the early eighteenth century was obviously due to the scarcity of fund but also signifies to the French the need of a contact man with fund. One might say that he was nearest to a broker so far as the functions were concerned. The unreliability of the Indian contract merchants made other French dependent on the *Saraf*.

In a way, this was connected with the spot purchase of the French. After the arrival of the ship *Maurepas*, two leading merchants, Mathura Das and Ballav Das, quoted higher rates on the plea of the delayed payment of their earlier loans. This was quite justifiable from their point of view since the Company *Saraf*, who had advanced to the Company considerable fund, had maintained this rate. Paris, in the grip of scarcity of fund, refused to supply advance on such a high rate.[15] The French thus became totally dependent on the *Saraf* and on the other leading merchants who were willing to make contracts at a higher rate. The high-handedness of the Mughal authorities at Hughli and the worsening of Anglo-Mughal relation complicated the situation. The *Faujdar* threatened Mathura

Das and Ballav Das for their links with the English.[16] The French merchant at Balasore, Laurent, was arrested but Du Livier, who succeeded Deslands, managed to procure his release.[17] In 1702, Ballav Das and Mathura Das, who had supplied goods worth Rs. 2.20 lakh to the French, requested payment. Du Livier managed to get a loan from the *Saraf* to make part payment. Some other merchants practically forced the French to pay.[18] The situation did not improve within the next few years. The outbreak of the European war, the increasing demand for money from the Mughal authorities, the imprisonment of Cosmo Gomez, the Anglo-Portuguese merchant of Bengal, but the Mughal authorities, created a difficult situation for the French. In France the Company was almost bankrupt by 1706. In 1708 and 1709, they handed over the rights of Indo-China trade to a group of merchants of St. Malo, thus practically stopping their trading operations.[20]

The St. Malo merchants sent ships to India but they did not care to pay for the establishment. They demanded goods without paying for these goods, which did not improve the situation of the French.[21] The Treaty of Utrecht in 1713 eased the situation, but by then, as Du Livier commented, the commerce had gone, the reputation had fallen and the creditors could not be convinced.[22] By 1717, the French debts in India had increased to a staggering figure of more than five million rupees. Tile debt in Bengal was half a million rupees. In Bengal the *Farman* has not been renewed and the French were paying 4% custom duty instead of 2 ½ % as they used to pay earlier.[23] By 1719, a new Company was formed in France and they began to send fund to pay the debts. In 1719 the Director Hardan court had received the *Farman* of the Emperor Farrukhsiyar at Chandernagore[24] and it appears that the French in Bengal, as well as at Pondicherry, which had already become tile headquarter of the French East Indies in 1698, were on the road to prosperity. It is in this background that we would see the role of the brokers of the French East India Company at Chandernagore and Patna.

II

Unfortunately the biography of Indranarayan Chaudhuri, who became the broker (in Bengal called *Dewan*) of the French Company, is yet to be done In 1788, a letter to the French Minister Castries by Krishnaram Chaudhuri, son of Indranarayan, [25] asking for financial help for the family, stated that Indranarayan had entered the service of the French Company in 1716. Although no further details had been given on the appointment, it seems that he was referring to the appointment of a broker. 'This seems to be highly unlikely. As seen earlier the French in Bengal had no fund and the ships of St. Malo merchants did not bring any fund for the establishments in India. As a matter of fact, the situation came to such a pass that Frenchmen of thirty years of service had to beg in the streets of Chandernagore'.[26] Under the circumstances, the French in Bengal had neither the fund nor the inclination to pay for a broker. However, it is possible that a contact has been made with him or with his brother, Rasaram, for taking loans. Furthermore the later correspondences of the French showed that he was certainly not appointed at this stage, It is of course possible that with the fund coming in after 1719, Indranarayan had become a contract merchant of the French Company.

An interesting document of 14th of August 1721[27] shows that the French has just purchased 1/8th share of the village of Devipur from Rajaram (actually Rasaram), brother of lndranarayan Chaudhuri, who was later mentioned as his brother, The village was close to Chandernagore and it is clear that French, after receiving fund, has begun to expand their area of influence. But it also shows that the Chaudhuris were actually Zamindars as well. Krishnaram attests this in his letter of 1788 in which he stated that Indranarayan had influence among other zamindars as well.[28] It is not clear how they made money, but at least it was not from overseas trade. In that case, the letter would have mentioned that. Later on with Dupleix, Indranarayan did venture into overseas private trade.

It seems that till the late 1723s, Indranarayan acted merely as contract merchant, which means that he was supplying goods to the Company, although there is no mention in the contemporary correspondences. Since most of the correspondences starting from 1723 till 1727 were lost, it is not possible to ascertain his role during the period. From 1720 onwards, huge fund was coming to Bengal but there is no mention of the Company *Saraf* of the earlier years. It is reasonable to assume that during the years between 1709 and 1719, the Company did not keep any *Saraf*. How did they manage the handling of bullion and foreign coins sent to Bengal is not clear. [29] But it seems that Paris used to send fund directly to Pondicherry and the latter used to distribute this fund to the different factories. We would see this system in operation from 1728 onwards, but it is certain that the system was in full flow at least a couple of years before that date. In that case the handling of bullion and foreign coins was not that much unnecessary as Pondicherry generally used to send rupees to Bengal. But by then there was the need of the broker for contacting merchants since the investment has increased at a significant rate.

By early 1730, the Director Dirois appointed Indranarayan, obviously a 'contract merchant' as the broker. This must have happened by 1729 since the letter of Pondicherry to Chandernagore of 28 February 1730[30] showed their unhappiness over Indranarayan. While being a broker of the Company, he was still supplying contracts to the Company. They asked Chandernagore to stop it. On the other hand, they suggested that the broker Indranarayan would get 3% commission on all the goods contracted and supplied by other merchants on his recommendation and accepted by the Company. He would of course be responsible for recommending the merchants to the Company.[31] This is the usual function of the 'courtier' or *dubash* at Pondicherry and it is surprising that Chandernagore was not aware of this basic rule. This seems to suggest that there was never any Company broker at Chandernagore before the appointment of Indranarayan. The function of *Saraf* was different. He was more involved with the financial aspect of the Company than with the goods. The letters between Pondicherry and Chandernagore corrects the mistaken belief that Dupleix appointed Indranarayan and that he was the *Dewan* of Dupleix. Actually Dirois was the Director of Chandernagore then and he had made the appointment.[32]

But the rise of the power and influence of Indranarayan in the corridor of powers of the French Company could be seen with the arrival of Dupleix in September 1731 at Chandernagore. Dupleix initiated two measures which increased the position and necessarily the wealth of Indranarayan. By that time the French Company had acquired some villages around Chandernagore, but they did not have enough personnel to get the revenue or increase its potential. The French therefore resorted to the traditional Indian system of 'ijara' of farming of the revenue, which they had been practising at Pondicherry since the early eighteenth century. This revenue consisted of various taxes, including *Cohaty* or tax on marriage, right of tax from the markets, tax on sale and purchase. These also included *salamis* for different kinds of rights.[33] In 1732, Dupleix gave the 'ijara' of some villages to Indranarayan for an annual revenue of Rs. 12,000, which was increased to Rs. 13,000 in 1733. In 1734, it became Rs. 14,000 only. Besides, an entire village was given to him on 'ijara' for Rs, 12,000 only.[34] The increase of revenue in such a quick time naturally endeared Indranarayan to the Company.

But the sudden rise of Indranarayan was not smooth. An opposition began to grow against him both within the French as well as other Indian merchants associated with the French. Complaints began to pour at Pondicherry against Indranarayan and also against Dupleix for showering favours on him. Le Noir, Governor of Pondicherry, ordered Indranarayan to be kept in chains for three days for receiving complaints against him. So far there was no complaint and Dupleix had to release Indranarayan with further approbation.[35]

The other measure that Dupleix was beginning to use was to get loan from Jagat Sheth for the Company as well as for his private trade. Dupleix was in favour of giving advance for the goods for which he would require advance fund. Pondicherry was supplying fund but not to the extent he desired. Besides, private trade had been allowed by the Company in Southeast Asia and Dupleix was beginning to start his private trading ventures for which he needed funds. Even before the coming of Dupleix, the trade of the French Company in Bengal was increasing at a galloping pace. On 14th of June 1729,[36] Pondicherry informed Chandernagore that their total investment would be Rs. Four lakh for which they could contact merchants, Out of this Pondicherry approved a large portion to Chandernagar factory which already had taken two lakh Rupees for giving advance to the merchants. Therefore the increase of trade in Bengal was already there before the arrival of Dupleix and not by him alone as mistakenly held by the Indian historians.[37] Even the French biographer of Dupleix has made this mistake.[38]

Pondicherry has understood the need for higher investment in Bengal. On 3rd September 1732,[39] nearly a year after the arrival of Dupleix in Bengal, they cautioned Chandernagore not to go beyond Twelve Lakh Rupees. A few months later, they informed Chandernagore that they could send fund only when it would come from Europe.[40] Actually, Paris was eager since 1728 that Pondicherry should send more money to Bengal.[41] Haudrere's excellent study of the Company confirms the statement of Pondicherry and the rapidly increasing trade of Bengal.[42] In that case the loan from the local *Sarafs* and merchants would be necessary in which the French broker would have a role to play. Interestingly the Statistics showed that in 1729, Paris sent a large volume of bullion to India, highest quantity for many years[43] and it was from that year that the broker was appointed. Obviously Indranarayan was doing well since in 1734, the French King Louis XV presented a medal to Indranarayan for his excellent services.[44] Meanwhile Dupleix had begun his private trade in various commodities, details of which had been worked out.[45] From the private letters of Dupleix, we find that Dupleix had started the silk trade with Burat from Qasimbazar in which Indranarayan was involved. It seems that Indranarayan had invested his own fund and was involved in some other enterprises of Dupleix, which gave the mistaken idea that he was the Dewan of Dupleix. The position of Indranarayan was rather ambivalent within the structure of French trade in Bengal.

In one way, he remained under the Director and the Council of Chandernagore as a broker and *ijaradar* and on the other he was the partner in the private trade of the Director. Such ambivalent position was due to the fact that Dupleix had been expanding his private trade for which he needed fund that was supplied by Indranarayan either from his own resources or by arranging loan from other merchants including Jagat Sheth. Certain unexpected event however rudely shook the structure.

The French had been changing the bullion, which was now coming directly from France to Bengal, through Jagat Sheth after paying a *batta* that was thought to be quite high by Dupleix.[46] Pondicherry had already brought the *Farman* through the Nawab of Arcot to coin money at Pondicherry.[47] After a great deal of effort, Dupleix could get the *Farman* to take the bullion directly to the mint at Murshidabad and coin money there,[48] thus bypassing Jagat Sheth. The retribution came soon after.

In 1738, a poor Muslim woman and her boy died mysteriously at Chandernagore. A fanatic mob surrounded Burat at Qasimbazar, but Dupleix could get the matter arranged after paying an amount to the Nawab, although the guilt of the French was not properly proved.[49] The matter did not end there. A few days later, the *Faujidar* Pir Khan of Hughli arrested Indranarayan on the charge of murdering them and sent him to Murshidabad, where he was imprisoned. Pondicherry immediately cancelled the appointment of Indranarayan. Dupleix offered to resign[50] since he believed that Indranarayan was honest and that it was the machination of Jagat Sheth, who had worked through Kalicharan, the *gomosta* of Indranarayan. According to Dupleix, this was the revenge of Jagat Sheth since he believed that it was through Indranarayan's efforts that the *Farman* was obtained. From the corespondences of Dupleix, we now know that Jagat Sheth was mistaken.[51] Finally Indranarayan had to pay Rs. 35,000 to the Nawab which was advanced to him by the Armenian merchant Khoja Kamal since the Company refused to pay.[52]

Since the departure of Dupleix from Chandernagore, Indranarayan continued his service to the French. whose trade had been expanding at a fast pace In 1755, Indranarayan donated the village *Boro* to the French Company, although_the Nawab forced Indranarayan to pay 65,000 Livres. Obviously he had become a rich man and had constructed two houses at Chandernagore. In 1755, the Nawab forced Indranarayan to pay Rs. 2,50,000 and again 1,20,000 Livres. In that year Indranarayan died[53] and the battle of Plassey that followed soon, changed the fortune of the French in Bengal.

Indranarayan Chaudhuri was an ordinary zarmindar and perhaps a small trader when the French took him as a broker. His association with the French of twenty-six years, not taking into account of the earlier years when he acted as contract merchant, made him a rich man. The fortune of his family rose with that of the French and went down with the French as well. Interestingly he was perhaps the only Indian associated with the private trading operations of Dupleix, who built his private fortune in association with the Europeans, including the English and the Dutch.[54] This showed not only the ability of Indranarayan as a broker and as a merchant, but that he had enough money of his own to invest in such ventures of Dupleix, some of which did not succeed. Evidently Indranarayan did not participate in all ventures of Dupleix. He did not participate in Assam venture nor did he participate in the African venture of Dupleix, both of which failed. Indranarayan therefore acted cautiously and had not blindly followed Dupleix. The fact that the Armenian merchant offered to pay his caution money at the Court of Murshidabad would show that he was associated with some Armenian merchants as well. However his principal profit came from the official position of broker in which he used to take the commission. By 1739, on the eve of the invasion of Nadir Shah, the French trade had a turnover of more than Rupees ten lakhs a year[55] that gave him sufficient amount to become a rich man. Fortunately for him he did not live long enough to see the humiliation of the French as well as the decline of the fortune of his family as evident from the letter of his son to the French Minister Castries in 1788.[56]

III

The early life of the other Indian associate of the French, Deepchand, is not known to us. He appeared in the French horizon when the French had arrived at Patna with their fleet in 1734 to make an establishment there. Despite several complaints against him and the French supervisor. Groiselle, the French did not remove them for the obvious reason that Patna goods were fast becoming important commodities in the supply of Bengal to Europe.

It has been seen earlier that the French trade had expanded tremendously in the decade of the 1720s before the arrival of Dupleix in Bengal in September 1731. By the end of 1732, four or five big ships were coming to India and the French were then concentrating on taking saltpetre and Cauris from Bengal. In the beginning, saltpetre was bought at Hughli, mostly from the Armenian merchants, and then shipped to Pondicherry. Cauris were brought from Maldives by sending small ships there from Bengal.[57] With expansion of trade, as seen earlier, there was the problem of finding enough money for investment or giving advance to the merchants. Apart from taking loan, the French begun to sell French goods, drapes, coral, lead etc. in India to recover a part of the investment. In Bengal, the sale of such goods was limited and often the French had to barter French goods for Indian textile from the Indian merchants, which was not a satisfactory situation. Following the English and the Dutch, Dupleix decided to buy saltpetre and other goods, like opium etc. directly from Patna, where these were manufactured and therefore had a low price.[58] He therefore proposed to Pondicherry on the establishment of a factory at Patna. Pondicherry however thought that the cost of purchasing saltpetre from Bengal would be the same, if one takes the cost of the establishment there and the cost of transportation from Patna to Bengal into account.[59] But Dupleix had seen another aspect — the sale of French goods at Patna where every year the merchants from north India used to come and buy the European goods. He had before him the English and the Dutch model since they had been selling the same European goods there with profit.[60] On 16 August 1734. Dupleix sent a fleet of boats to Patna with Groiselle as leader, which anshored before The Fort of Patna on 17th of October.[61]

This was however not the first attempt of the French to settle at Patna. At the end of the decade of the 1720s the French had sent a fleet at Patna, where they had rented a house and had stayed for a few months. They had then hired the father of one Mahomdas, who had acted as a broker then.[62] It is not clear why the French did not continue since the existing documents do not reveal the full story. In case of Dupleix however, he had two other objectives for settling at Patna - to see the marketing possibilities in Nepal and Tibet for his private trade. Dupleix was certainly one of the earliest Company man to get interested in the trading possibilities in the Himalayan kingdoms.

By the middle of the 1730s, Patna had become a big commercial centre linking the markets and productions of eastern India with those of the north. The English and the Dutch were sending annual fleets from Bengal to Patna to buy saltpetre and opium and to sell European goods. Around 1734, the Governor of Nawab Nazim of Patna was Alivardi Khan, brother of Haji Ahmed, influential noble of the Court of Murshidabad. Alivardi was then residing at the Fort at the end of Patna[63] and Bihar was under the control of the Nawab of Bengal.[64] The problem of Dupleix which he probably did not foresee earlier, was that Haji Ahmed used to do private trade in saltpetre and opium in both of which he had a monopoly right given by the Nawab of Bengal.[65] He could very well be the stumbling block to the French expansion in Bihar.

IV

The French fleet left Chandernagore on 16th August 1734 for Patna headed by Groiselle. He was to be assisted by Finiel, an under-merchant and a half-caste Portuguese interpreter, innocent of Jesus. Dupleix however took the precaution of placing European soldiers and half-caste European soldiers under Lt. Maisy of the garrison of Chandernagore. The details of the journey have been published elsewhere and it is not necessary to repeat it here. It suffices to say that Haji Ahmed predictably stopped the boats, which were released only after making payments to him and the Nawab, who also stopped the boats second time near Azimganj.[66]

On the 11th of October, the fleet anchored in front of the Fort of Patna. Groiselle went into the city and found a house that had no doors or windows. Mahomdas, who had met the French in the boat a few miles before the city, perhaps reserved it for them. Besides, the Nawab of Bengal had sent word of their coming. But Groiselle changed the house and perhaps moved to a house close to the river Ganges, where the ruins were found in the early 20th century.[67]

The interest of Dupleix became clear in February 1735, when he proposed to Groiselle to form a private Society limited to two persons for private trading. Strangely, Dupleix suggested that others would not be included in this Society.[68] Given the constraint of fund, this is rather strange, This however produced negative result and later on accusations were levelled against Dupleix and Groiselle that Patna factory had been established only for the private trading of these two men. Company however did not care much for the private trading since this was allowed, but they insisted on receiving ten thousand mds. of saltpetre annually and on the sale of French goods at Patna.[69] It appears that Dupleix did not want to compete with the Company and concentrated on the purchase of opium and purchase of 800 pieces of *garras* (a kind of coarse cloth). He would also sell tin there on his own account.[70] As he saw it, Patna was a big market, which could swallow several competitors.

Around 1735, Deepchand appeared as a simple writer, one of the innumerable Indians writing the ledgers of the French Company in different parts of India. Obviously they were taken on their ability to write certainly but also on their knowledge of the 'affaires'. The process of transformation of Deepchand from writer to the 'Dewan' is not known, but he became quickly so influential as to control the entire affairs of the French at Patna. Even slaves were purchased at a cheaper rate when Alivardi Khan had brought 20,000 prisoners of war from neighbouring rebel areas. Groiselle was asked to buy some for sending to different French factories in India.[71] Perhaps in the purchase of these slaves, that the authorities noted the talents of Deepchand.

From the contemporary letters, it appears that Deepchand was involved in private trading at Patna since 1735.[72] The fleet of Chandernagore left for Patna in July 1735 with 20 boats commanded by Nehou le Mouton. It appeared at Patna in August and it had 33,963 Rupees. Out of this, Groiselle had Rs. 16,630 for his private trade and Dupleix had the rest. Burat from Qasimbazar had given to him 40 bales of silk at Rs. 703 per bale. The profit would be equally distributed between Burat, Dupleix and Groiselle. Besides these, the fleet had goods worth Rs. 60,000 only that belonged to Umichand, an influential noble of Murshidabad and goods of Rs. 20,000 for Deepchand. It was made clear that the goods of Umichand would be sold at the French factory at Patna under the name of the Company with 7½% of tax, which actually belonged to the Company. Since the goods belonged to the private merchant, it was decided that the 5% would go to the Company and Burat would get 2½% as chief of Qasimbazar and in charge of lading these goods. In case of Deepchand, it would be different. He was treated as part of the French Company and he would pay 6½% which was quite cheap since the natives would pay 10%. Obviously Deepchand had been able to influence both Chandernagore and Patna authorities and that he had plenty of money as his goods were worth more than that of Groiselle. Haji Ahmed as usual raised difficulties but the matter was resolved after a payment of 1600 Rupees. to him and after Dupleix taking a part of his goods into his account to be settled later.[73] In the beginning therefore, the cartel had not yet been formed and Deepchand had to invest on his own and pay the Company tax at Patna, which would presumably go to the coffers of the Company. Evidently, in the private Society, Dupleix had included Burat, although he had refused to allow anyone else to enter in the Society.

The other objective of Dupleix of selling French goods at Patna however materialised. By the end of 1735, Patna was able to sell drapes as predicted by Dupleix. He informed Pondicherry in the middle of April of 1736 of the success of the Patna factory. By that time the demand for saltpetre in Europe had reduced quite considerably and Pondicherry was having second thoughts on the Patna factory. They pointed out that the cost of saltpetre would be the same if purchased from Hughli given the cost of establishment at Patna and the transportation. But within a few months, Pondicherry agreed with the viewpoint of Dupleix on Patna market.[74] The letter of Dupleix had however opened up another face of Patna market and revealed the fissure within the French establishments at Chandernagore and Patna, in which Deepchand had played no mean part.

Mirailles, the favourite of Pondicherry, was the commander of the Patna detachment in the Patna fleet sailing from Chandernagore to Patna and returning there in the middle of December 1736. Like other officers in similar situation, Mirailles had taken goods worth Rs. 9000 with him to Patna for his private trading. Groiselle met Mirailes in his boat and had transferred his goods to the factory. But he could not sell his goods and finally, after three weeks, had to sell coffee and salt at a great loss. After the merchants had disappeared, Mirailles learnt that Deepchand had asked the merchants not to come to the factory and had actually bought the goods himself in the names of other merchants. Mirailles complained to Groselle without revealing the source through whom he had acquired that knowledge. Groiselle curtly asked him to leave and even threatened him. Since then Mirailles had to sell all his goods at a loss of nearly Rs. 3000. His charge was that Deepchand had purchased all these goods by an assumed name. At the same time he also complained of the under-valuation of the goods of the Company at Patna, which was a loss to the Company. According to him, in early December, Groiselle and Deepchand had made a profit of 22 to 25% by selling Company goods at a lower price to the upcountry merchants who had come in their caravans. Mirailles believed that Groiselle made an annual profit of Rs. 14,000 from such sale.[76]

After his return to Chandernagore, Mirailles complained to Dupleix who had him arrested and sent him back to Pondicherry with the recommendation of sending him to France.[77] What Mirailles implied was that there was a cartel consisting of Dupleix, Groiselle and Deepchand. It seems that the Council of Chandernagore, after hearing both the parties, had confirmed the recommendation of Dupleix. Pondicherry did not confirm it but did not take any action against the cartel members for reason not sufficiently clear.[78] It is possible that Mirrailles had failed to prove his case.

Obviously there is some truth about the accusations of Mirailles. Much later Dupleix was sore at Groiselle for giving too much power to Deepchand. But at the moment, he was fighting a case against Pondicherry. The reply of Groiselle did not touch the principal point of accusation - the sale price of French drapes at Patna as given by the French Company. Strangely, neither Dupleix nor the members of the Chandernagore Council ever asked from Groiselle such details. Dupleix however knew it well since he was having private trade at Patna, but he chose to remain ignorant for obvious reasons. By the end of 1737, the affair subsided and Mirailles faded into the oblivion. The incident however embittered the relation between Dupleix and Pondicherry and encouraged the opponents of Dupleix. Significantly enough, the French officials of the Company ventilated their frustrations and grievances through such small incidents, although they were associates of private trade that continued to flourish in India.

Dupleix was not amused and in 1737-38, he would have stopped sending the fleet to Patna if he did not have the French goods to sell there.[79] Despite such pious wishes his private trade at Patna continued unabated. He sent the fleet in August in which he had goods, mostly tin, camphor etc. of several thousand Rupees. The number of boats was reduced and if one goes by the English model, their fleet followed that of the French with reduced number of boats. The goods sold badly at Patna and at Chandernagore the Council members were disgusted by the situation at Patna. They blamed Deepchand for not allowing other merchants to come to the factory, that complaint that was raised by Mirailles earlier, excepting those who were allied to Deepchand. It was stated that he had made enough money by this process. There was of course Finiel, under-merchant, but he was kept out of all the affairs by Deepchand, obviously with the support of Groiselle. It was stated that Deepchand was at the same time the writer, cashier, seller and buyer. Dupleix had to ask for the account.[80] But the problem of saltpetre created by the Nawab obliterated all these trivial details.[81] The Maratha trouble at Agra prevented the upcountry merchants to come to Patna for the annual purchase. This was followed by the arrival of a Maratha detachment almost up to the gate of Patna. On the demand of Groiselle, Dupleix had to send a detachment to Patna, more as a symbol than as proper measure of security. Realising his vulnerability, Groiselle concluded an accord with the Dutch for the protection of the European Companies in case of Maratha attack. At the end of the year, the English also joined.[82]

Even during these bad times, the private trade of Dupleix continued to prosper. He had purchased one hundred cases of opium from Patna apart from other goods, which gave rise once again the gossip that Patna factory was established for the sake of private trade of Dupleix. This was not entirely correct since the trade of the Company had increased significantly, particularly with the sale of French goods and with the establishment of two lodges at Chapra and Singuia. Dupleix fixed the expenses of these two lodges at Rs. 1550 annually. The establishments were made on the recommendation of Groiselle who envisaged the purchase of saltpetre at low cost. The Company had not only approved of these establishments but also approved the conduct of Dupleix, which quashed the gossip as well as accusations against Deepchand.[83]

But Dupleix was losing his interest at Patna. In the fleet of 1739-40, he had some goods of his own, but it was nothing compared to the earlier years. He had even left the investment in silk to other French merchants at a small payment.[84] The cartel was breaking up. In 1740-41, after seven years of service, Groiselle retired and was replaced by Hyacinthe Guillandeau, one of the members of the Council of Chandernagore. At the same time Dupleix was nominated as Governor of Pondicherry. The factory of Patna continued even through the English blockade till the end of the century.[85] But Deepchand faded from history after the departure of two of his masters who created this establishment with much hope and vision.

The activities of these two Dewans of the French, with similar functions, show certain differences. While Indranarayan exerted great influence, yet it was under the tutelage of Dupleix, who gradually brought him into his private trading. Yet there is no accusation of Indranarayan making an undue profit through nefarious deals. In case of Deepchand, the accusation started within two years of the French establishment at Patna, assuming an importance that brought the involvement of Pondicherry. However in both the cases, the Company generally did not interfere since none of the accusations had been proved. Obviously Deepchand was out to make money as quickly as possible, Indranarayan preferred to make it through the legally constituted functions and privileges. At Pondicherry, Ananda Ranga Pillai accused, in his diary, his predecessor of amassing huge wealth that did not come through the official commission.[86] Obviously in case of Patna, it was the French official, Groiselle, who was involved, while Dupleix merely cautioned him against Deepchand. This is a kind of attitude of the French that was different from that of the earlier century and shows the difference in resources of the French that had begun to come since the third decade of the eighteenth century.

Notes and References

1. For details, see the article of Aniruddha Ray entitled "French Establishment in Bengal : Challenges and Responses, 1674-1719" in Om Prakash & Denys Lombard (ed), *Commerce and Culture in the Bay of Bengal, 1500-1800*, New Delhi, 1999, -197-220.
2. Kanaklata Mukund, *Trading World of the Tamil Merchant*, Orient Longman, particularly 103 passim.
3. *The Private Diary of Ananda Ranga Pillai* (tr. & ed.

by J.F. Price & K. Rangachari), Madras, 1904, 10 Vols.

4. For details, see the article of Indrani Ray entitled, "The French Company and the Merchants of Bengal (1680-1730)" in L. Subramanian (ed), *The French East India Company and the Trade of the Indian Ocean (A Collection of Essays by Indrani Ray)*, New Delhi, 1999, 90-111.
5. Archives *Nationales et Coloniales,* (Paris, now in Aixen Provence), (*AN* hereinafter), Colonie C (2) 65, letter from Hughli, 8 February 1700, ff 114-121.
6. Ibid.
7. Ibid.
8. Ibid; also see letter from Pondicherry, 22 February 1700 (*AN*, Colonie C (2) 66, ff 5v-6).
9. Ibid, letter from Hughli, 19 November 1700, ff 159-162.
10. *Phillipeaux* and *Pearl d'Or* were the two ships (Ibid), letter from Hughli, 1 December 1700, ff 171-171v.
11. Ibid, letter from Hughli, 15 January 1701, ff 80-80v.
12. Pondicherry sold a ship for Rs. 2800 to loan three ships (Ibid, letter from Chandernagore, 22 February 1701, ff 6v-7).
13. Aniruddha Ray, *Adventures, Landowners and Rebels, Bengal, c. 1575- c. 1715*, New Delhi, 1998, pp. 164-174.
14. The exact date of appointment is not known. It is believed to have been made after 1700, when there was acute scarcity of cash in Bengal.
15. Letter from Hughli, 15 January 1701 (*AN*, Colonie C (2) 66, ff 80-80v)
16. Ibid, letter from Hughli, 9 February 1702, ff 75-78v. The Armenian merchants left Hughli.
17. Letter from Hughli, 12 January 1703 (*AN*, Colonie C (2) 67, ff 34-37v).
18. Ibid, letter from Hughli to Pondicherry, 7 September 1702 (quoted in the letter of Pondicherry, 5 February 1703, f 37v).
19. Ibid, letter from Hughli, 24 October 1703, ff 97-103.
20. Andre Lespagnol, *Les Messieurs de St. Malo*, St. Malo,

1991, pp. 650-651.

21. Memoire sur la Compagnie des Indes Orientale (*Bibliotheque Nationale*, Paris, Fond Francais 6231, f 42v) (*BN* hereinafter).
22. Letter from Pondicherry, (*AN*, Colonie C (2) 69, f 76v), 14 February, 1714.
23. Letter from Pondicherry, 9 September 1719 (*AN*, Colonie C (2) 72, ff, 53-53v).
24. Memoire, op.cit., f 47.
25. The letter was written from Chandernagore on the 10th of February 1788 (attested by F. Nicholas and printed in full in French in *Bengal Past and Present*, 1910, July-December, pp. 157-159). Charu Chandra Ray found the letter in the archives of Chandernagore.
26. Letter of Father Baudre from Chandernagore, 12 January 1709 (BN, Nouvelle Acquisition Francaise 11168, f 82 for the ill treatment of the agents of St. Malo to the Company servants). For the condition of the factory, see the letter of Chandernagore, 6 January 1714 (*AN*, Colonie C (2) 69, f 121).
27. Memoire d'acquisition des terrains et aldees de la Compagnie (*BN*, Nouvelle Acquisition Francaise 9353, ff 1-1v).
28. The letter actually mentioned 'Rajas' (letter of Krishnaram, 1788, op.cit. p. 157).
29. The letter of Chandernagore of 6th January 1714 mentioned a big *Saraf*, who gave loans to the French. He was estimated as a very influential person. This could be none other than Jagat Sheth (op.cit., ff 120-120v).
30. Letter of Pondicherry to Chandernagore, 28 February 1730, printed in Correspondances du Conseil Superieur de Pondichery avec le Conseil de Chandernagore, Paris, 3 Vols. 1915, I, 57 (Correspondances hereinafter).
31. Alfred Martineau, Dupleix et l'Inde Francaise, Paris, 1929, 180.
32. Ibid.

33. Ibid, 180-181. Also see Harihar Sheth, Sankhipta, Chandernagar Parichay (Bengali). Chandernagore 1370 BS, 8-11.
34. Ibid.
35. See the letter of Dupleix from Chandernagore to Burat at Qasimbazar, 3 November 1738 (*BN*, Fond Francais 8981, ff 2v-4v).
36. Correspondances, I. 25.
37. N.K. Sinha, Economic History of Bengal, Calcutta, 3 Vols, 1981 (3rd ed. Reprint), II, 35-52.
38. Martineau denied any role of Indranarayan or the increasing trade of Bengal before the arrival of Dupleix (op.cit.).
39. Correspondances, I, 186.
40. Ibid, letter of Pondicherry to Chandernagore, 3rd February 1733, 198.
41. Letter of Paris to Pondicherry, 30 September 1728 (*BN*, Nouvelle Acquisition Francaise 8933, f 26v).
42. Philippe Haudrere, *La Compagnie Francaise de Indes au XVIIIe Siecle, (1719-1795)*, Paris, 1989, 4 volumes.
43. Ibid, III, Appendix : Export of gold and silver from France (II, E).
44. Letter of Krishnaram op.cit., 158, Ananda Ranga Pillai mentioned this medal given to Indranarayan (op.cit., I, 157).
45. Article of Indrani Ray entitled "Dupleix's Private Trade at Chandernagore" in L. Subramanian. op.cit., 90-111.
46. Martineau, op.cit., p. 409.
47. Memoire, op.cit., f 47.
48. Memoire D'Arrac, Dacca, 1820 (*AN* Colonie C (2) 115, f 34); letter of Dupleix to Lichterman, 19 February 1738, f 100; letter of Dupleix to Burat at Qasimbazar, 1st May 1738, ff 128-128v (*BN*, Fond Francais 8979).
49. Letter of Dupleix to Voulton at Delhi, 18 January 1740 (*BN*, Fond Francais 8982, f 227v). For the overall view of the relation between the French and the

Murshidabad Court, see the article of Indrani Ray entitled "Some Aspects of French Presence in Bengal" in L. Subramanian. op.cit. 121-143.

50. Letter of Dupleix, 25 November 1738 (*BN*, Nouvelle Acquisition Francaise 8933, ff 16-16v).
51. Letter of Dupleix from Chandernagore to Burat at Qasimbazar, 3rd November 1738 (*BN*, Fond Francais 8981, ff 2v-4v).
52. Ibid, letter of Dupleix to Burat, 18 November 1738, f 8v.
53. Letter of Krishnaram, op.cit. 158.
54. Article of Indrani Ray entitled "The English Associates of Dupleix in Bengal" in L. Subramanian, op. cit., 112-120.
55. In 1738, Paris sent to India bullion to the value of 11,244. 168 Livres Bullion was sent to China in the same year to the value of 1,400,000 Livres (Haudrere, op.cit., III, Appendix II).
56. Letter of Krishnaram, op.cit., 158.
57. Article of Aniruddha Ray entitled "Revival of French Trade in India: Pondicherry and Bengal during the pre-Dupleix period, 1719-1731" in *Indian Historical Review*, Vol. XXV, N* 2, January 1999, 58-87.
58. For the growth of Patna as a commercial town, see the article of Aniruddha Ray entitled "Changing European Views of Patna" in *Journal of Historical Studies*, Patna University, December 1998, N* 4, 1-23.
59. Letter of Pondicherry to Chandernagore, 13 March 1736 (Correspondances, I, pp. 323-327).
60. Quoted in the letter of Pondicherry to Chandernagore, 11 March 1736 (*BN*, Nouvelle Acquisition Francaise 8933, f 66).
61. For details see the Journal of Groiselle (*AN*, Colonie C (2) 75, ff 147-150).
62. Ibid, ff 159v-160v.
63. For the fort and the morphology of the city, see the article of Qeyamuddin Ahmed entitled "Patna-Azimabad, 1540-1765" in his edition of *Patna Through the Ages*, Patna, 1988, 71-87.

64. In 1733, Bihar was added to Bengal (Jadunath Sarkar, ed. *History of Bengal*, Dacca University, vol. II, 1972. reprint of 1948 ed. 423-424).
65. Martineau. op.cit., 375-376. Also see the article of Aniruddha Ray entitled "Establishment of the French Factory at Patna" in *The Proceedings of the Indian History Congress*, Calcutta Session, 2001, pp. 413-423, particularly pp. 414-415.
66. The fleet consisted of forty big boats and several other small boats (Journal of' Groiselle, op.cit., ff 147-154v).
67. Ibid, f 161v, Martineau claimed to have found the ruins in the area known as Mittenghat on the bank of the Ganges near the Portuguese Church. Nearby he found a European cemetery with the French names (Martineau, op.cit., 375-376).
68. Ibid, 377.
69. Letter of Pondicherry to Chandernagore, 10 October 1736 (*BN*, Nouvelle Acquisition Francaise 8933, f 66v).
70. Martineau, op.cit., p. 377.
71. Letter of Pondicherry to Chandernagore, 24 September 1735 (Correspondances, I, 314-319).
72. Martineau, op.cit., p. 381.
73. Ibid, pp. 381-384.
74. Letter of Pondicherry to Chandernagore, 13 March 1736, (Correspondances, I, 323-327); letter of Pondicherry to Chandernagore, 3 October 1736 (*BN*, Nouvelle Acquisition Francaise 8933, f 66).
75. Ibid.
76. Letter of Mirailles from Chandernagore to Pondicherry, 23 December 1736 (*AN*, Colonie C (2) 75, ff 252-253). It was a complicated affair as there was the problem of the payment of custom duty at Hughli (see the letter of Pondicherry to Chandernagore, 4 June 1737 in Correspondances, I, 374-375).
77. Letter of Mirailles from Chandernagore to Pondicherry, 14 December 1736 (*AN*, Colonie C (20 75, ff 252-253).
78. Letter of Pondicherry to Chandernagore, 16 March

1737 (Correspondances, I, 365-366) Pondicherry merely asked for papers from Chandernagore.

79. Martineau. op.cit., p. 388.
80. Ibid.
81. Article of Aniruddha Ray "Establishment of the French", op.cit., pp. 419-420.
82. Martineau, op.cit., pp. 388-389.
83. lbid, pp. 390-392.
84. Ibid, pp. 392.
85. Ibid, pp. 394.
86. Ananda Ranga Pillai, op. cit., I., 45.

7

The Nawab's Business: Agricultural and Commercial Practices in Eighteenth Century Bengal

Rila Mukherjee

I

Introduction

Although the term 'business' is generally used to denote commercial and industrial practices in modern times, or the business of the economy in general, as a cachet 'business history' has a long lineage; a lineage that can be traced back to the earliest attempts to early modern states to regulate the flow of peoples, goods and services for the benefit of the realm. The first states to do so in Europe were the sixteenth century mercantilist states of England, France and Spain; similarly in South Asia 'business practices' in terms of a well articulated economic policy may be said to have originated with the Mughals.

However in a wider sense of the term 'business history' may also refer to agrarian and commercial practices in any era with a well-articulated fiscal policy; used in such a sense 'business histories' may pre-date mercantilism. Think of Husain Shahi Bengal, consider Italian trade manuals of the thirteenth century, Islamic business practices in the Mediterranean or Mongol proclamations on trade in the **Bilik**. Indeed the very advantage of the term 'business history' is that we can lump together economic policies of the modern and the pre-modern, the experiences of the guild and the factory and the world of trade, industry and finance, draw upon a rich storehouse of information and thereby construct a different history[1]. The 2001 seminar on Business History organised by the Department of History, Jadavpur University, Kolkata, is particularly relevant in the current climate of globalisation that is sweeping the world.

In this paper I will focus on agrarian and commercial practices that were followed by the Nawabi state of eighteenth century Bengal in order to manage the resources of the state ; focal points in my enquiry will be: 1) the development of *grain* golas and *mandis* in Bihar and Bengal under aristocratic initiative as indicative of attempts to monitor the agrarian produce of the region and 2) business ethics as evinced by the *dadni* merchants' organization in supplying silk to European East India Companies. A third focus will be Nawabi port administration in Bengal.

The port-town is significant in that it united the market-town and the commercial town by channelising both agrarian and commercial products from the interior into a single point. The port town is emblematic, indeed the hub, of business practices in Bengal. The section on port-towns has substantial documentation on pre-Mughal business practices. This section (III.2) was incorporated to demonstrate the swing of the economic pendulum towards western Bengal, and I argue that the concentration on the west by the Bengal Nawabs actually weakened the business potential of the state.

In the long run the commercial policy was foiled therefore by an ineffective port policy on the part of the Bengal Nawabs. They could not prevent European East India Companies from establishing their own ports and thereby diverting exports from traditional Nawabi ports. The growth and eminence of Calcutta port under the English Company by the 1730s is illustrative. By the mid-eighteenth century Calcutta port accounted for the greater part of the revenues of Bengal; the diversion of the export trade away from traditional inland ports such as Patna and Kasimbazar was made possible by the control over the upcountry riverine network that was exercised by the English East India Company. In the process the sea ports - Dacca and Hugli- suffered equally. I finally argue in this essay that while the Bengal Nawabs were largely successful in garnering the agrarian resources of the Bengal *Subah* by means of controlling the distributive network of grain and essential stuffs, their failure to establish a well-articulated commercial policy centring around the silk production of

Kasimbazar in north Bengal was harmful in the long term to the business interests of Bengal in what was since antiquity a commodity of great value — silk. The article focuses therefore on three spatial categories in Bengal — the bazaar, the port and the arang town.

The story of the business history in Nawabi Bengal ultimately presents a picture of ineffectiveness and decline. Therefore in the process of elaborating this article I touch upon that greatly contested area in South Asian history - the eighteenth century with its manifold themes: a century marked by the intrusion of foreign capital and the capturing of the domestic market in Bengal as well as the collapse of central power at Delhi, the rise of regional powers and their eventual removal by the mercantilist practices of the English East India Company from 1757 onwards.

II

The Market Town in Bengal

'At this market were also many kinds of cotton goods, drugs, tobacco and opium ...the eyes were attracted by the sight of such superabundance of many things in one city.' (Manrique, **The Travels of Fray Sebastaian 1629-1643**, Luard, C.E. (Tr). 2 vols. London, Hakluyt Society, 1926-27).

The most striking feature of urbanisation in eighteenth century Bengal was the development of market-towns based on wholesale markets *(golas)* and bazaars *(mandis)* as opposed to semi-regular *haats.* The commercialization of agriculture in the late seventeenth century had led to a growing assertiveness on the part of local zamindars and chiefs in Bengal. Most of them established *haats* (semi-regular markets) within their domains in an effort to raise taxes to sustain their mini-realms. The Bengal Nawabs tried to bypass the traditional *haats* and *bazaars* established and controlled by these zamindars by putting up *golas* (wholesale markets) such as Bhagwangola in Murshidabad. They also established their own bazaars throughout the eighteenth century in an effort to divert sales from the older zamindari centres.[2] In the process a new wave of urbanisation — an urbanisation of small scale market towns-swept Bengal and

Bihar in the eighteenth century.

Establishment of *ganjs* and *golas* was obviously an essential requirement for the Nawabi state. The new bazaars *(ganjs)* or *golas* were established on rent-free lands by permission *(sanad)* from the ruler. Obviously such permission was only given to favourite courtiers, close relatives or important merchants with a presence at Court. Sometimes the markets were owned by the Nawab himself or held in the name of one of his family. The state therefore took a leading role in establishing these new markets.

Ownership of these bazaars was profitable for it was hereditary. Ownership could be transferred or sold as an asset. A bazaar was therefore a property like any other. Its owner enjoyed a limited property right in respect to these bazaars of eighteenth century Bengal. Nishatganj in the Murshidabad region was established by Shahamat Jung before 1730. It was then given to his sister Rabia Begum who in turn presented it to Muzaffar Jung when he married her daughter. Nishatganj, in effect, was treated as part of dowry and Muzaffar Jung renamed it Bairamganj.[3] But property rights were still in their infancy and because the Mughal and the post-Mughal state was the guiding spirit behind the foundation of bazaars the state also became their ultimate owner. This was made clear by the fact that often, if the owner owed moneys to the state, his bazaar was seized by the government.[4] This diffused notion of property, and its limited application, makes it difficult for us to speak of an 'agrarian business' operating in Bengal in the fullest sense.

Economic categories, and their functioning, in 'pre-capitalist' societies are often taken to be devoid of economic relationships. Anthropologists have dismissed them as gift-societies, as societies where commodity played no role. According to such readings bazaars in pre-colonial India were set up and dismissed at the will of the monarch; they were merely the theatre where the oriental monarch orchestrated his power-plays through an affirmation of social power.

It has been suggested by Sen (1998) that the pre-colonial marketplace — what is referred to as bazaar-was an ephemeral phenomenon. According to him bazaars in Mughal India were more a spectacle for the display of social prestige and power than an economic realm. Bazaars vanished or appeared at the monarchs' behest.[5] According to this reading the true market place could only come into being with the colonial reordering of the economic realm; a reordering that Sen calls a 'permanent settlement of marketplaces'.[6]

This idea, that only decisive state intervention can create a market, cannot be applied to South Asia, demonstrating as it does a blind adherence to the ideas of eighteenth century English political economy. Eighteenth century English political economy evolved out of mercantilist practices whereby *one* merchant group, *one* branch of trade, *one* overseas market was deemed superior over others and enjoyed state benefits. This state patronage, exercised by means of an exclusionist policy to other merchants, networks and commodities, ensured the beginnings of capitalism. The situation in South Asia was different where capitalism, in the western sense, did not come through state regulation. Its historical experience was different in the sense that bazaars in post-Mughal India evolved naturally out of the social demands of the economy in which all strata of the population participated; this experience was unique in that they developed further with the growth of trade and a money economy within South Asia where privileges were extended to all merchants regardless of nationality; and finally this experience was specific to the Asian context in that the market blossomed thereafter due to the participation of all categories of merchants. These were evidence of a spontaneous, unregulated growth with the minimum of state intervention; all these facts are self evident, and call for a reassessment of pre-capitalist commercial policies.

Bazaars in pre-colonial South Asia were not merely sites for the demonstration of social power (for it was a hallmark of political favour and economic status to own one); they were equally sites where various economic relations could be observed at play. The archives reinforce this impression. Often bazaars were put up as sureties or as guarantee for other commercial practices. Let us see the evidence.

When *ganjs* sprang up in the eighteenth century and became a new feature in the urban landscape they frequently combatted the role of the older urban complexes. Evidence from (Azamgarh) Bihar in Muzaffar Alam's *'Aspects of Agrarian Uprisings in North India in the early Eighteenth Century'*[7] points to a number of *bazaars* and *ganjs* established by the sons and successors of the Gautam Rajputs A'zam and Azmat Khan in the early eighteenth century. These 'neo-Muslim Rajput zamindaris' built about seven *ganjs.* Zamindari centers such as Azamgarh and Azmatgarh evolved into district *(chakla)* headquarters by 1720 with a string of subsidiary market towns attached to them — Kopaganj, Iradatganj, Sufiganj, Husainganj, Jahangirganj among others. It was evident that these Gautam Rajputs were trying to control the resources of the area by channeling the produce of the countryside into the network of markets established by them. They therefore changed the urban landscape of Bihar by setting up a string of market towns. This idea of a major market controlling a string of subsidiary markets has led scholars like Yang (1998) to apply Walter Christaller's central place theory (of a major node controlling subsidiary networks) to markets in Bihar.[8]

We have a list of *ganjs* in Bihar.[9] They are Murtuzaganj, Qazibagh, Kabutrah Khana, Alabakspur, Masallapur, Hakimganj, Dandunmandi, Arafabad, Rasulpur, Khamepur, Mandi Begumpur all established in the early eighteenth century. Others were Hindiganj (est. 1721), Begumganj (est. 1724), Hajiganj (est. 1752 by Nawab Haji) etc. Haji Ahmad was the brother of Nawab Alivardi Khan and the *de facto* ruler of Bengal and Bihar. His role as the *eminence grise* of politics in eighteenth century Bengal and the undisputed power behind the throne led him to play a powerful role in business affairs.

Similar urbanization took place in the Bhadohi region with the founding of bazaars such as Bazaar Salabat Khan, Bazzar Ruslam Khan, Bazaar Ahmadganj and Katra (market-place) Rusukhiat Khan between 1712 and 1737. We have similar evidence for Mirzapur.[10]

Again a comparable situation prevailed in Dacca and its environs where the Mughal conquest saw the establishment of bazaars by ruling subahdars. This practice continued into the eighteenth century with the Nawabs and their favourites controlling these mart-towns based on rent-free lands. For Dacca's markets we have the following data[11]: In the seventeenth century Ibrahim Khan, the Mughal subahdar, established the bazaar of Rehmat Gunge. In the eighteenth century the following bazaars came up: they are Burran Gunge established by Jesarat Khan the Naib Nazim, Emam Gunge belonging to the same family, Bazar Kartalab Khan established by Murshid Quli Khan the first Nawab of Bengal and Narain Gunge and Lakhi Gunge established by Benur Thakur during Muhammad Reza Khan's tenure in Bengal in the 1760s. Establishing bazaars was profitable and continued throughout the eighteenth century. Bazaars Jupsah, Colipara and Motibari were established before 1765; haats Sowapur and Burnah in the same period. Unfortunately we have no data as to the names of their founders or the dates of their establishment except that they were founded before the grant of Diwani to the English East India Company in 1765.

For Murshidabad we have the following data on bazaars for our period : J'afar Ganj established by J'afar Ali Khan (or Murshid Quli Khan the first so called independent Nawab of Bengal) in 1708, Maqbara Ganj established by Kasim Ali Khan the same year, Bibi Ganj established by Majum-ud-Daula in 1749 as well as the Hat Sripur established by Mughal subahdars (unknown) in 1700.[12]

What does this new type of urbanisation tell us? It denotes the prevalence of a cash economy, in a state brimming over with the commercialisation of agriculture where the ruling class and its cohorts were eager to participate in the cash-nexus that recycled wealth from the countryside into the cities and then back again through the mediation of the service gentry and the richer peasants. Such commercialisation had been going on from the sixteenth century in Bengal. This is a description of the market town of Musumabazar, situated on the Hugli opposite Baliaghata that Manrique has left us:

> 'Here there was an abundance of everything one could require, especially of eatables and of household necessities, such as corn, rice, vegetable, sugarcane, oil and many kinds of milk products. From each of these articles several vessels could have been loaded.'

Manrique's keen commercial eye, the line 'from each of these articles several vessels could have been loaded', is testimony to the commercial prosperity of Bengal's market towns in the seventeenth century. All these market towns were engaged in the sale of food grains. Manrique, Bowrey, Tieffanthaler and de Gennes de la Chanceliere tell us that the banks of the Bhagirathi and its tributaries were filled with market-towns. Finally, we have a poetic description of the market-town of Burdwan which was an important producer of coarse cloths (*garahs* and *dusutties)* in the eighteenth century:[13]

> Beyond ...the poet saw the king's market with thousands of foreign merchants sitting there. There were hundreds of traders and shopkeepers and countless gems, pearls and rubies. There were various kinds of fine and beautiful cloth such as Vanat (felt cloth), makhmal (velvet), pattu, bhunai, batadara, maldai (from Malda), daccaia (from the Dacca region), and various other kinds liked by the Amirs (nobles). There were many bilati (foreign) articles of fancy price or of fashionable designs, which were, however, heaped together for want of customers.

This description, although fanciful, is important for it indicates that English goods had penetrated the interior by 1750.

III

The Port Towns: An Export — Oriented Economy and Its Administration in Bengal

(1) Mughal and Nawabi Port Towns:

If the 'new' bazaar of the eighteenth century was expressive of the royal role in controlling the agrarian resources of the state, the new port administration of eighteenth century Bengal and Bengal was indicative of the royal desire to tap the profits arising from trade.

From the seventeenth century, with the Mughal conquest of Bengal, three major ports dominated the commercial landscape of Bengal. They were the ports of Hugli (in the west) and Dacca (in the east) as well as the riverine port of Murshidabad/Kasimbazar in the interior of the subah. From this time on port-administration came into its own as an important royal function.

We do not have exact dates of the establishment of port administration in Hugli as opposed to its foundation as port town (1580). It was probably from the time of Shah Jahan's expulsion of the Portuguese from Hugli in 1632 that port administration in Hugli started in earnest and it became designated as a 'Mughal' port.

We have however information on the administration of the port-towns in Nawabi Bengal. Murshidabad was placed under the Pachotra Bandar or Daroga as he is referred to in English records, Hugli under the Baksh Bandar and Dacca under the Shah Bandar. The first controlled the imperial dues coming into the capital, the second dues from overseas trade and the third collected duties arising out of the trade of the eastern districts.

We have seen that Hugli alone had earned the title of 'Mughal port' along with Masulipatanam and Surat. The post of faujdar of Hugli was a sensitive one; as faujdar of the only 'Mughal' port in Bengal he was entrusted to negotiate with the European ships on the river. Initially a Mughal appointee, the appointment to the post of faujdar was taken over by the founder Nawab, Murshid Quli Khan from 1711. This effectively ended the Mughal administration of Bengal's maritime trade, although the label of Hugli as 'Mughal' port continued. Kasimbazar became the 'royal' port of eighteenth century Bengal.

Kasimbazar, the chief port of Murshidabad, the base of the Pachotra Bandar's operations, rose into prominence with the shift of capital in the eighteenth century. It became the most important market-town for textiles in eighteenth century Bengal and was important enough to give its name to the Bhagirathi that flowed past its banks"[14]. Originally a seventeenth century mart-town famed for its silk mix cloths, Kasimbazar formed an island bound by the Bhagirathi, the Jalangi and the Padma and this island was covered with mulberry trees.[15] It was these that contributed to the celebrity of Kasimbazar for it was the centre of silk production in Bengal as well as the centre of all commerce in Bengal.[16]

The date of origin of Dacca as Mughal port is also obscure but it probably evolved into an imperial port with proper administration after the Mughal conquest of Bengal. An important Mughal port in the seventeenth century, the jurisdiction of the Shah Bandar of Dacca declined with the transfer of the diwani to Murshidabad and the establishment of the office of the Pachotra Bandar there. Therefore the second 'imperial' port had also been taken over by the Bengal Nawabs by the eighteenth century.

In the eighteenth century another port town came under the jurisdiction of Bengal subah. The Bengal Nawabs now also controlled an up-country port. This was the port of Patna. We do not know when the Patna port administration started in earnest; most likely it was after the river at Rajmahal had silted up in the 1660s leading to the search for a new port to conduct business with upper India. Therefore the origin of Patna as Mughal port under the Bengal Nawabs is obscure but it probably dated from the time of commercial decline of Rajmahal due to a change in the course of the Ganga. The Budrekha Bandar of Patna controlled the duties from the riverine trade with the middle and upper gangetic plain. There were therefore now four main ports under Bengal's jurisdiction : of them three were in Bengal and one in Bihar.

From this reading of the evolution of port administration we see that it started in earnest with the Mughals in the seventeenth century. In the eighteenth century there was a major shift in the hierarchy of these port-towns. Kasimbazar occupied the principal position under the Bengal Nawabs with Hugli coming a close second. Dacca became tertiary, Patna retained its importance. In addition a number of chowkis (observation posts) were set up along rivers; each subject to that particular port administration under whose jurisdiction it was situated. These chowkis were often the theatre of violent conflict between European Company ships and the darogas' officials because the state lived with the perpetual fear of its inland waterways becoming an European (especially English) highway.

A major role of the port official was to supervise the lading of each East India Company ship to ensure that Europeans only carried the stipulated amount of grain, sugar and butter that was necessary to feed the sailors (as declared in the manifest) and did not export grain for trade along the coast. Nawabi control over inland trade was still somewhat secure in mid-eighteenth century Bengal and this regulation of export items has to be seen in conjunction with Nawabi mandates over sales and distribution from the *golas* and *mandis* of the interior — or the wholesale marts— in Bengal.

(2) Pre-Mughal Ports in Bengal and Business Practices:

Other than these four main ports, three in Bengal and one in Bihar, there were other ports in Bengal. Bengal, with its extensive riverine network, was blessed with ports. All of these are in the east. We have a lot of information on these ports which gives us a glimpse of business practices in pre-Nawabi Bengal. Suvarnagram was an important port as the early history of Bengal tells us. In the fourteenth century Ibn Batuta spoke of it as a great commercial centre and port with boats destined for Java. By the sixteenth century it appears to have been less of a port and capital city and more of a manufacturing city; because both the Ain and Ralph Fitch enumerate the cotton products of Suvarnagram. Dacca too was a port.

The most important port of Bengal in medieval times was Chatighan: between the time of the eclipse of Suvarnagram and the rise of Dacca. Chatighan emerged as the frontier port of Bengal. Located at the far east of

Samatata/Harikela Chatighan lay at the mouth of the Karnaphuli river and connected two routes for merchandise: it was an entrepot for the goods of Dacca-Suvarnagram-Jugdia in the west as well as for the goods that came down from Assam and other parts of Harikela to its north. The Karnaphuli made for a safe harbour. It was navigable from the middle of October until the end of April and communicated with Dacca, Jugdia and Linepur.[17] Facing the east rather than west Chatighan's traditional trading partners were Arakan and the countries beyond. Direct sailings from Bengal to the west coast were rare but surprisingly Chatighan seems to have traded with the Malabar. At the turn of the seventeenth century Pyrard de Laval remarked that he found there a ship from Calicut.[18]

But there were even earlier market and port towns in eastern Bengal; most of which had decayed by the eighteenth century but which merit a mention in any discussion about nodes of business practices in Bengal. These — Bakla, Chandikar (Sagor), Sandwip and Sripur — were located in the deltaic zone which had experienced considerable urbanization in the early medieval period. The rule of the Chadras from Vikrampur, their commercial interests and their Arakanese lineage contributed to a new explosion of eastern trade from the eleventh century. This trade was carried by the ports in the deltaic region of Bengal.

These towns of Bakla, Chandikar or Sagor, Sandwip and Sripur were some bases of autonomous Hindu chiefs *(baro bhuiyas)* who offered resistance to the Muslims. Others well-known market and port towns were known as Hindu naval centres, lying at the heart of celebrated producing regions. The name 'Hindu' may be misleading; in actual fact these deltaic towns were essentially frontier towns displaying a bizarre mix of Muslim (chiefly Persian), Hindu, Arakanese and Portuguese elements. These were market towns and vibrant ports that carried on trade with Arakan and beyond.[19] These deltaic towns flowered from the twelfth century to the seventeenth century. Their sudden disappearance from the political and commercial map of Bengal may be ascribed to the following factors:

(1) These towns arose as a result of the commercial

policy of the kings of Vikrampur. These kings known to Ibn Batuta as the kings of Bangalah (as opposed to Lakhnawati)—based their regime on commercial activities. At a time when the economy of Gaur was land-based and there was a shrinking of coinage coins found in this coastal area indicate that commerce was flourishing in the eastern part of Bengal. At this time the rulers of Vikrampur were the Chandras. But the Chandras were rulers of a marginal area and therefore did not enjoy the same advantages that accrued to the rulers of Lakhnawati in terms of a well-demarcated territory, a substantial tax base and an agrarian core that was focussed to meet the needs of the middle gangetic plain. Moreover the Chandras were succeeded by the Varmans who were orthodox Brahmans. Like their western counterparts, the Senas, the Varmans sought to regulate society on conventional Hinduised lines. Agriculture and land based activities were therefore promoted.

(2) The commerce of this deltaic area experienced various crucial shifts during its existence. These are :

A : From the twelfth to the fourteenth centuries these towns were part of a Buddhist religio/political/commercial network straddling the northern Bay of Bengal of which Arakan was the most important.

B : From the fourteenth century the commerce of these towns was increasingly re-directed westward with the foundation of the Bengal Sultanate. Arakan however was still a priority area.

C : The Ilyas Shahis in the fifteenth century started developing the China trade. Embassies from Bengal to Yuan and Ming China were sent in 1405, 1408, 1409, 1412, 1414 and 1438-39. This concentration on the China route may have disturbed the older trading networks of the region as it meant that sailings were now diverted southward in the Bay of Bengal.

D : Husain Shahi policy in the fifteenth and sixteenth centuries cut short this network (significantly there were no more sailings to China, and Bengal textiles were no longer traded with China after the fifteenth century) and shipping lanes had to relocate themselves once again.

E: Portuguese hegemony in this region meant that from the sixteenth century trade was diverted southward to the Coromandel and Ceylon and eastward to Malacca; Arakan was no longer a priority area.

F: The Arakanese asserted their dominion over this area and captured Chatighan, the chief port in the east, by mid-century. This meant, to all intents, that Bengal was made bereft of its major eastern outlet of trade.

G: In the seventeenth century the world of Bay trade broke down. So did Portuguese domination over sea trade in the world.

H: In the seventeenth century the produce of Bengal were diverted to serve the trading needs of the overland and sea trade of the Mughal world economy radiating from Lahori Bandar and Surat and spanning Turan and Iran. Bengal goods no longer dominated the Bay.

I: In the eighteenth century English shipping took over where the Portuguese had left off. Devastated by Portuguese-Arakanese conflict for much of the sixteenth and seventeenth centuries and mauled by Mughal attacks on their sovereignty the ports of the Pratapadityas and Kedar Roys had little part to play in these new trade networks.[20] The trade channels of the deltaic ports could not constantly readjust to new routes deriving from economic and political compulsions and were thus effectively destroyed.

(3) The Arakanese (Magh) 'depredations' in this area. From the fifteenth to the eighteenth century these port-towns were fought over by Tripura, Arakan and Bengal. When the Arakanese could not retain hegemony over these tracts permanently they led frequent raids against this area and devastated it.

(4) The Portuguese factor. The Portuguese controlled much of the delta — either informally or by means of direct political control from the sixteenth century. The fortunes of these port towns declined with the fall in Portuguese fortunes in the seventeenth century in Bengal and in South East Asia.[21]

We see therefore that the economic pendulum was swinging towards western Bengal from the sixteenth century. By the mid-seventeenth century Bakla was in decline. The sovereigns of Bakla were known as the rajas of Chandradwip. We have sources affirming to the existence of Bakla from the twelfth century. The **Ain** mentions Bakla in its catalogue of important towns in Bengal, so does Ralph Fitch.[22] Manrique commented that the city contributed to the wealth of Dacca.[23]

By the eighteenth century Chandikar or Sagor was abandoned. It had been the most important maritime power of the region. Its importance at the beginning of the seventeenth century was immense, as we know from Roe and Monserrate. It was the principality of Pratapaditya who built up a strong navy and constructed ship-building yards at Dadkhah, Jahajghata and Chakvasi. This fleet became known as the Nawara fleet, later used by the Mughals to repel the Maghs; however we have no documentation as to whether the kings of Chandikar were then co-opted into the Mughal ruling hierarchy.[24] Most likely they were simply erased from the political scene of the delta.

Chandikar was reputed to be a great commercial centre and in time became an important centre for Portuguese commercial operations as well. The Jesuits built their first church here. Chandikar was also a temple town. Statues have been found here dating from the twelfth century. However by mid-century the island's coasts were menaced by the Maghs as Manrique tells us[25] but it still retained its religious importance and attracted thousands of pilgrims. It contained reservoirs of fresh water (Manrique) — a bonus in deltaic regions — and fish products were cheap and plentiful.[26]

Sandwip, at the mouth of the Meghna, too declined as port in the eighteenth century. It was under Kedar Roy. In 1602 he 'liberated' Sandwip from the Mughals and placed it under Carvalho. Cesare Frederici visited Sandwip in 1569. Lahori tells us that there was a substantial Portuguese colony there during the seventeenth century. Later in the seventeenth century the Mughal subahdar of Dacca 'liberated' it from the Portuguese Gonzales and gave it to

Arakan as *jagir*. Hamilton attests to its cheap prices (of rice, eggs and poultry) in the eighteenth century.[27]

Sripur was also a well-known port. It came under Portuguese control by the end of the sixteenth century. It was celebrated as one of the most powerful towns of Bengal. By the eighteenth century it too had fallen off the map.

These little capital towns, centres of autonomous chiefdoms were, as we saw, substantial ports. It was but natural that they evolved into market towns as well. Bakla was a great entrepot of rice, cottons and silk cloths.[28] Sripur was well known for its cotton goods. As well as these items, the deltaic ports carried on commerce in grain, oilseeds and dairy products with their neighbours.

From the sixteenth century therefore the economic impetus swung back in favour of Vanga. In 1506 Ala-ud-Din Husain Shah built a bridge connecting Triveni/Nabadwip with Saptagram, then the chief port in the west. By 1560 Nabadwip had evolved into a well-known market town; merchants were settling there and selling goods from locations as far off as Kashmir in the north to Kanchipuram in the extreme south. Saptagram silted up by 1560 and contributed mightily to the decline of Gaur. By 1580 Hugli was being developed to replace Saptagram, albeit under Portuguese aegis.

Saptagram was replaced by Hugli as chief port and mart-town of Bengal in 1580. Manrique tells us of his visit there in the seventeenth century : it appears that the town was initially founded as a mart by the Portuguese. Big '*golas*' containing trade items were divided into rudimentary rooms. They soon evolved into a permanent structure and Hugli became an emporia town. To distinguish this market from smaller markets it was called the 'great' or 'public' bazaar. This corresponds to Challes' and Luillier's observations about Hugli. There were also smaller markets which sold daily provisions, cottons and coarse cloth.[29]

It seems that Hugli had evolved naturally into a mercantile city par excellence; it had the best caravanserai in the province, many rich Muslim merchants lived here and moreover stuff from all corners of India were available here. It was a Mughal port dominated by Persians, Armenians, Turks, Kashmiris and merchants from Central Asia; despite being expelled from there by Shah Jahan in 1632 Portuguese presence in Hugli was still major in the seventeenth century.

Rajmahal rose as port and mart-town in the seventeenth century but with a difference. It connected the markets of Bihar with those of Bengal and especially those of Patna with Malda. Moreover a portion of Agra goods which came down the river to Patna were shipped onto Bengal via Rajmahal. Rajmahal therefore connected not only the markets of Bengal and Bihar through the Ganga-Yamuna riverine system but was also an important riverine port in the North India-Eastern India trade. It was also a producing centre for textiles for we have evidence of a Mughal *karkhana* there.[30] Trade must have been brisk, for Tieffanthaler has spoken of the caravanserai here. One found in its markets all the produce of the interior (Rajmahal is between Bengal and Bihar). Manrique noted that prices here were cheap.[31]

By the eighteenth century Kasimbazar became the chief port of Bengal. As port Kasimbazar experienced a riverine traffic during the monsoon whose importance and variety has been called unique in the world.[32] As the centre for commerce in all Bengal it housed the English factory (established 1658-59), the factories of the Dutch and the French (at Kalikapur) and the Armenian settlement at Saidapur at a distance.

It seems that commercial possibilities in Kasimbazar were so extensive that foreign merchants such as Kashmiris, Gujaratis, Persians and Turks had permanent residences there. Kasimbazar's location was strategic; its proximity to the Court at Murshidabad was another attraction for foreign merchants for they could then petition the Court for grievances if any. These merchants built beautiful buildings along the river. Kasimbazar was known for its salubrious climate in the eighteenth century.

In 1813 this magnificent city, emblematic of thriving commerce and sumptuous silk, died out. The changing of the course of the Bhagirathi resulted in the city being transformed into an unhealthy swamp. Like Ashin Das Gupta's Malabar this area too hides under its marshes the vanished history of a million secrets.

IV

Trade in Pre-Colonial Bengal: Kasimbazar Silk, Jugdia Baftas and The Merchants :

Textiles — silks and cottons — formed the mainstay of Bengal's artisanal production and these found ready markets all around the world. While cotton production had an ancient lineage[33] it has been speculated that silk had a more recent lineage[34] being imported from China in the fifteenth century. While wild silks were plentiful in Bengal subah and as such attested to by the **A'in-I-Akbari**, spun and woven silk in bales as well as those manufactured into 'piece goods' became an important export item from Kasimbazar from the seventeenth century[35] along with calicoes or baftas from Jugdia in the extreme east of the province.[36] Kasimbazar, Hugli and Dacca were the three port towns primarily linked with the textile business; the first two for Kasimbazar silk and the last for the Jugdia baftas.

In this section I shall speak of the organisation of the dadni merchants and dalals — that is those supplying cloth-silk and cotton to buyers and especially the East India Companies — at Kasimbazar in the west and Jugdia in the east. Dadni merchants and dalals were rarely independent merchants; for the most part they were content to be mere suppliers or middlemen between the weaver and the buyer. The term 'dadni' evolved from dadan or advance; this was a term used in Kasimbazar and in North India ; in the Dacca region the advance was called pattani and not dadan. Here merchants were called dalals.

We should however note that the 'dadni merchant' had various identities; it was not unusual to find big merchants like Coosaulchaund, moneylenders such as Gainchand, Lalchand and Anandchand, the Ray-Rayan or Chief of Ministers Alamchand, courtiers such as Ramkissen (Chain Ray's adopted son) or members of the major financial family of the Jagat Seths in English Investment lists for Kasimbazar alongside small dadni merchants from textile sub castes such as the Kapris (Copprees).[37]

In the case of Jugdia we find that the native dalals there were in the process of being displaced between 1750 and 1753 by the very powerful ring of 'Dacca Dellols' who attempted to corner the investment in baftas.[38] These Dhaka dalals were backed by the business interests at the Dacca Court who saw in a monopoly of the Dacca Dellols a chance to participate in the profits from the lucrative trade that the English and French companies were carrying on at Jugdia.[39]

We see in trade therefore the same amalgam of business and political interests as we saw in the case of agriculture, what Calkins called a regionally oriented ruling elite comprising landed, financial, commercial and political interests running the subah and which Bayly has highlighted in his study of eighteenth century India.[40] The only exception is that within the broad stratum of dadni merchants there were also those who were private brokers to English Company servants. The Catmas, Raghunath Biswas and Coosalchand were the private brokers of the chief of the Kasimbazar factory in the 1730s; the Kasimbazar Factory Record Consultations dated May 13, 1741 refer to Nimo Das, a dadni merchant, as Eyre's private broker. Ratan Manik the French dalal at Jugdia was probably a private broker for the English.[41]

How were the dadni merchants organised vis-a-vis the European companies? We notice the following: 1) Dadni merchants acted singly but sometimes formed partnerships. The latter were not long-lasting and were interchangeable. 2) Each European company had its own preferred set of dadni merchants and dadni merchants took care to nurture this 'special relationship'. 3) Dadni merchants took as much as 80% as advance and distributed it among their subsidiaries who then distributed the moneys to the weavers in the *arangs* (production centres). 4) Dadni merchants were frequently moneylenders to the European companies, helping them out with short term, but hefty, loans. 5) Dadni merchants were also the buyers of European goods; EICs regularly brought in velvets, woollens, glassware, porcelain, firearms and wines which went a small way towards supplementing their textile investments in Bengal. Dadni merchants were also dealers in European goods and they catered to a growing elite around Murshidabad (and probably also Dacca) who were used to *bilayati* stuff. 6) Finally, apart from the official *vakil* that each EIC employed to negotiate with the Court, prominent dadni merchants with connections at Court could play the twin roles of royal favourite and trusted company servant with ease.[42]

In general however the dadni merchant / dalal enjoyed an unequal relationship vis-a-vis the EICs. He went from a position of strength at the turn of the century to a dependent position by 1753 when most merchants at Kasimbazar declared bankruptcy due to a combination of Maratha raids throughout the 1740s, growing indebtedness to the English Company as a result of a permanent inability to furnish investments and rising putney (silk thread) prices from 1742. Around this time the English Company assumed overnight ascendancy among the other EICs in Bengal; taking advantage of its power it now subverted completely existing trading norms and regulations by bypassing the Nawab at Murshidabad and announcing the Agency System whereby Company servants, assisted by a 'native' gomastha, would buy directly from the arangs. Thus the Company's dream — that of penetrating into the interior and buying direct — came true. Most of the English Company's merchants at Kasimbazar had no option but to switch from an (theoretically) independent supplier of textiles to a salaried servant working for a specified wage.[43] In the east, not just the independent dalals but also the mart-towns of Jugdia and Lakhipur themselves, vanished overnight by mid-century.

What does this tell us about Nawabi trading regulations? It seems, unlike the case of agriculture, trade was very much an unorganised, indeed an 'informal' sector in Bengal. A coherent and uniform economic realm was yet to come into Bengal subah; while this was achieved partially in the case of the agrarian economy the commercial economy was completely overthrown by the increasingly ambitious mercantilist policies of the English East India Company. In trade, unlike the case in agriculture, European companies had gained a massive foothold in Bengal by the 1740s; among them the English were arguably the most powerful. The English East India Company controlled the inland waterways from the 1730s, attempted to monopolise inland trade and frequently clashed with the Nawab's officials. It channeled the produce of the interior into its port at Calcutta. By the 1750s it had completely overturned the internal market, destroyed indigenous trading networks, subverted production to its dictates and after 1754 gained an entry into the arangs of the interior — a privilege that had been its original aim when asking for trading privileges. It had pleaded for free passage from the time of the Surman Embassy to Faruksiyar in 1717. But after 1754 the middleman had been bypassed; now the whole of Bengal with its inland trade beckoned invitingly. In the face of such aggressive mercantilism, Nawabi Bengal remained a mere spectator; witness to the impotent business policies pursued by it.

Notes and References

1. See Mukherjee, Rila, 2003, *Europe Transformed 1350-1650*, Calcutta, Progressive and Mukherjee, Rila, 2003, *The Lost Worlds of Europe*, Calcutta, Progressive where pre-capitalist business practices are discussed at length.
2. See later.
3. In Sen, Sudipta, 1998, Empire *of Free Trade, The East India Company and the Making of the Colonial Marketplace*, Philadelphia,University of Pennsylvania Press : 43.
4. Karm, Abdul, 1964, *Dacca:The Mughal Capital*, Dacca, Asiatic Society of Pakistan : 112-113.
5. Ibid. : 19.
6. Ibid. : 120-143.
7. Reprinted in Alavi, Seema, 2002, The Eighteenth Century in India : 84-112.
8. Yang, Anand A., 1998, Bazaar India: Markets, Society and the Colonial State in Bihar, California Press.
9. Ibid. : 99.

10. Ibid: 94-96.
11. From Karim, Abdul, 1964: pp. 111-113.
12. From Sen, 1998 : p. 44.
13. From Dimock, E.C. and Gupta, Pratul Chandra (Tr. and Eds)., 1965, *Maharashtra Purana: An Eighteenth Century Bengali Text*, Honolulu, East West Center Press.
14. It was frequently called the Kasimbazar river by Europeans in the eighteenth century.
15. Mukherjee, Rila, 1986, *Commerce et Marchands an Bengale Autour de Kasimbazar 1704-1757*, P.D. Thesis, E.H.E.S.S., Paris. Forthcoming as *Merchants and Companies in Bengal: Kasimbazar and Jugadia in the Eighteenth Century.*
16. Mukherjee, Rila, 1986, *Commerce et Marchands* au Bengale Autour de Kasimbazar 1704-1757, Pd.D. Thesis, E.H.E.S.S., Paris. Forthcoming as Merchants and Companies in Bengal: Kasimbazar and Jugadia in the Eighteenth Century.
17. C2115, AN, Paris and Hamilton, *Walter*, 1828, *East India Gazeteer*, London, 2 vols., 2nd edition.
18. Francois Pyrard de Laval, 1887-1890, The Voyage of ...to the East Indies, the Maldives, the Moluccas and Brazil 1601-1611, 3 vols. (Tr). Albert Gray, London, Hakluyt Society.
19. See Mukherjee, Rila, *Merchants and Companies* etc. (forthcoming).
20. Ibid.
21. lbid.
22. Allami, Abul Fazl, *Ain-I-Akbari* (Tr. Jarrett and Sarkar), v.2 :147; Fitch, Ralph.
23. Manrique, op.cit.
24. Pratapaditya was defeated in 1612 by one of Islam Khan's generals Ghias Khan. It has been speculated that the Nadia Rajas assisted the Mughal general and in so doing consolidated their position in Saptagram as qanungo-a fact which later led to their confirmation as the Rajas of Nadia (Curley, David

L., 2000, '*Maharaja Krisnacandra, Hinduism and Kingship in the Contact Zone of Bengal*' in Richard B. Barnett (Ed). Rethinking Early Modern India, New Delhi, Manohar : 88-89).

25. Manrique.
26. Master, Streynsham , Diaries 1675-80 (September 5, 1676) 2 vols.(Ed). R.C.Temple, London, John Murray, 1911.
27. Hamilton, Alexander, 1727, A *New Account of the East Indies 1688-1723*, 2 vols., Edinburgh.
28. Varthema, Ludovico, The Itinerary of_ _ _ _ (Tr. R.C. Temple) , London, Hakluyt, 1928.
29. Bowrey, 1903, *A Geographical Account of the Countries Around the Bay of Bengal 1669-1679.* (Ed.) R.C.Temple, Cambridge, Hakluyt Society.: 170.
30. Karim, Khondkar Mahibubul, 1974, *The Provinces of Bihar and Bengal Under Shah Jahan*, Dacca, Asiatic Society of Bangladesh : p. 32. However he seems to confuse Akbarnagar (Rajmahal) with Gaur : p. 39.
31. Manrique.
32. Hamilton, Walter 1828.
33. Bengal cottons were traded in by the Roman Empire. Tamralipta was the port through which muslins went to the west.
34. See Mukherjee, Rila, 2000, '*Banglay Banijyik Arthanitir Udbhav o Bikash*' in R.Chakravarty, K.Chakrabarty and A.Bandyopadhyaya, eds. Samaj Sanskriti Itihas, Adhyapak Ashin Dasgupta Smarakgrantha, Calcutta, Ananda (in Bengali),
35. See Mukherjee, Rila, 1994, 'The Story of Kasimbazar.- Silk merchants and Commerce in Eighteenth century India, REVIEW, XVII, 4, Fall.
36. See 1990-91. Also see my forthcoming book Merchants and Companies in Bengal.
37. See Mukherjee, Rila, 1994.
38. Mukherjee, Rila, 1990, The Chandernagore - Jugdia Letters : A Look at the FEIC's East Bengal Trade

from 1750 to 1753, Calcutta, Centre for Studies in Social Sciences, Occasional Paper 122; Mukherjee, Rila, 1990-91, 'The French East India Company's Trade in East Bengal from 1750 to 1753: A Look at the Chandernagore Letters to Jugdia', Indian Historical Review, XVII, Nos. 1-2 : 122-135.

39. Ibid.
40. Calkins, Philip A., 1970, 'The Formation of a Regionally Oriented Ruling Group in Bengal 1700-1740', Journal of Asian Studies, Bayly, C.A., 1983, Rulers Townsmen and Bazaars: North Indian Society in the Age of British Expansion 1770-1870, Cambridge.
41. Mukherjee, Rila, 1990, 1990-91.
42. Data from Kasimbazar Factory Records. See Mukherjee, Rila, 1994.
43. The bankruptcy of the dadni merchants of Kasimbazar, and their subsequent plight, has been dealt with extensively by Mukherjee, Rila, 1994.

8

The Salt Merchants of Bengal : 1757 - 1800

Balai Chandra Barui

The activities of the salt merchants of Bengal can be studied in two phases viz., from 1757 to 1780, and again from 1781 to 1800. Each period had distinct characteristics of its own. In the first phase the Indian merchants were involved in production as well as in distribution. In the second phase Indian merchants had nothing to do with production which was monopolised by the Company under the agency system. But the distribution of salt was entirely handled by the Indians. P. J. Marshall has suggested that after Plassey Indian participation in the salt trade did not decline appreciably.[1] In the first phase there was considerable collaboration between the Europeans and the Indian salt merchants. Some Indians entered into a formal partnership with the Europeans by becoming their banians. Marshall also thinks that on the whole Bengal's trade was not seriously affected by British competition. Even when the British merchants were actively involved they usually acted merely as wholesalers, who sold off their merchandise in bulk, which was then redistributed by a chain of Indian merchants.[2] Marshall concludes that "there was a considerable degree of continuity between the independent merchants of the early 18th century and the collaborators of a later period".[3]

Position of the Salt Merchants before 1757 :

Salt trade was fairly well organised in pre-Plassey Bengal. The Nawabs of Bengal used to handle the trade in salt as "a matter of favour or as a source of revenue".[4] In the later years of Mughal rule they generally assigned it as a monopoly to a favourite or favourties or sold it to the highest bidder. Monopolies were usually granted to the Muslims and the Armenians.[5] Under the Nawabs the salt trade of the frontier areas was also subject to government monopoly. Generally the Foujdars and private Indian merchants were authorised to handle this trade.[6] The Foujdar of Rangamati (Assam) controlled the salt trade of his area.[7]

The principal Mughal monopolists had the title of *Fakhar-ul-Tujjar* (pride-of-merchants) or *Malik-ul-Tujjar* (King-of-merchants).[8] The Indian salt merchants did their business under these monopolists.

The monopolist in Mughal times, however, had neither the ability nor the organisation to make his monopoly exacting.[9] Before 1757 salt trade was open to all on payment of duty of 2½% to 5%.[10] The profits of the business went to them. It was impossible for a single trader to monopolise the trade. This was because salt was produced over a wide area by many malangis without restrictions.[11] The trading merchants received salt from the priduction-merchants, who had the commodity produced with the help of the local zamindars and through the labour of the malangis. The selling merchants, in their turn, distributed the commodity to different markets. There were not only the Bengalee merchants but quite a number of rich traders and *saudagars* (one kind of merchants) who came down to Bengal from Punjab, Kashmir, Multan, Gujrat and other places to buy salt, and import it to their respective provinces and districts.[12] Thus before Plassey the Indian salt merchants traded openly and freely under the Nawab's monopolists. There was also a smooth and regualr inter-provincial trade in salt.

Before 1757 private Englishmen were also involved in the salt trade of Bengal on a limited scale. At first they tried to secure exemption from customs duties by extending the privileges of dastak to inland trade but the Nawabs refused to grant it. Though it was laid down in the farman of 1717 that 'all goods and necessaries' which the Company's factors '......... bring or carry away either by land or by water' should be exempted from customs, the Nawabs and their officials made a distinction between articles for import or export by sea, which they argued, were covered by the farman, and 'inland' articles, moved from one part of Bengal for sale to another, which were not.[13] Since the Company did not participate in inland trade in this sense, the chief sufferers from this distinction were English private traders.[14] In 1731 the last hopes of the Englishmen were belied when the Nawab denounced the English for trading 'in all the country merchandise besides what are proper for the European markets, as well salt as every other commodity'.[15] Curiously enough, this distinction between 'inland' and 'import and export' commodities was not rigidly followed by Nawabs in cases of sugar, food grains and certain kinds of piece goods. The Court of Directors also ordered that Englishmen should not deal in 'inland' articles. But the restrictions were not effective. Salt was being smuggled up to Patna in 1741.[16] This was done by Englishmen under the cover of dastaks and under a Muslim name, paying duties at rates fixed for Muslims.[17] The Nawabs were infuriated. They blockaded the Company's trade at several points and seized English boats but the illicit trade in salt by private Englishmen could not be totally stopped before 1757.

The Situation between 1757 and 1765 :

The situation changed substantially after Plassey. A number of privileges granted by the Nawabs to the Company placed the English private traders in a favourable position in repect of salt trade. The traditional Indian merchants were gradually pushed out of this lucrative trade. The exercise of political power by the Company after Plassey helped the private traders a great deal. The English private traders wanted to claim exemption from customs and local duties and to maintain control over producers to whom large sums had to be advanced.[18]

The acquisition of the Diwani by the Company in 1765 gave the private traders a good opportunity to extend their salt business. Civil servants were sent out to these places to set up a new administration but they lost no time in setting up their private trade there. Extension of English administration meant the extension of the network of English private trade.[19]

The exemption from duties after Plassey and particularly after an agreement with Mir Jafar (1763) which gave the private traders an additional advantage to compete with their Indian rivals. A review in 1763 showed that salt-duties were paid only in Dacca, Lakshmipur and Calcutta. The Englishmen paid nothing at Chittagong or Kashimbazar, Patna or Malda.[20] On top of all this the misuse of dastak continued unchecked. Large investments were made in the salt trade by the senior servants of the Company. Factories were established in districts and villages. Moreover, the violent and arbitrary activities of the private traders and their gomastas had a seriously dislocating effect on the indigenous salt trade. The old independent Indian merchants, connected with production as well as distribution of salt, and the zamindars progressively lost control over salt. The old structure of Bengal's salt, trade broke down under the new pressure and in the situation created by the expansion of British private trade in salt.

Chevalier, a private trader, enjoyed protection from Samuel, the Chief of Dacca.[21] They were secretly connected with each other in the salt trade. Vansittart's share in the salt trade was said to be 'equal to that of all the other servants of the Company put together'.[22] A joint concern by John Johnstone, William Hay and William Bolts, three senior servants, had at least three Europeans working for it in northern Bengal and Bihar.[23] Warren Hastings, whose trade was usually managed by his partner, the surgeon Tysoe Saul Hancock, was involved in salt trade, employing five Europeans in 1763.[24] In 1761 it was rumoured that Vansittart had obtained 'an exemption for the country duties' for a large consignment of salt to Patna in which he had a half share.[25] He also ordered the Nawab's officials to release boats with a Company's dastak which were carrying salt, on which they presumably had not paid duties.[26] In June 1762, he admitted that he had issued dastaks for salt. Thus by exercising administrative influence, the Company's senior servants earned great fortunes from the salt trade. It brought ruin to the Indian salt merchants as the Nawabs failed to protect them against the Englishmen's misuse of dastaks and evading of duties.

However, the major damage to Bengal's traditional salt

trade was done by private traders and gomastas. They began to sell the commodity not only in Calcutta but throughout Bengal. Salt was transported to the Company's factories and to other places where private traders wanted to sell it. Large shipments of European-owned salt were moved to palces lke Patna in 1758. Under Vansittart, many more Europeans took part in the salt trade. The volume of transactions also grew larger. Archibald Keir had 7,00,000 maunds of salt awaiting sale at Patna by 1765.[27] All these were examples of direct defiance of the Nawab's monopoly. Hastings himself wrote to the Chief of Dacca on 13 January, 1759 that "we have not, I believe, any right to trade in salt".[28]

The private traders and the gomastas evolved their own methods to invade the salt trade of Bengal. First, they tried to capture the trade of a particular area by establishing factories there. The factories really formed the base of their business operations in the neighbourhood. They safely carried on salt trade in remote parts of the province through these factories. In May, 1762, Mir Kasim complained to the Governor of Bengal that "in every Pargana and every village, they have established ten or twenty new factories, and setting up the colours and showing the 'Dustaks' of the Company, they use their utmost endeavours to oppose the ryots, merchants and other people of the country".[29] In the pargana of Dinajpur, besides the old factory, twenty new ones were established in one ganj. They also forcibly established new markets, built new houses and employed men who role-acted as sepoys and at the orders of private traders detained and harassed the natives.[30] Many haats, ghats and parganas were ruined as a result of their violent activites.

Secondly, they also obstructed and paralysed the business of the indigenous salt merchants. Mr. Chevalier, a private trader, had forcibly taken undertakings from all indigenous merchants of Chilmari (Dacca) and Corigam by which they were not allowed to sell any salt till his goods should all be disposed of.[31] Mr. Chevalier practically established a monopoly of salt there. The gomastas and private traders also advanced their business by exploiting the producers and consumers. They took away by force salt from the malangis and indigenous merchants for a fourth part of their value and through violence and oppression obliged the consumers to give five rupees for goods which were worth just one rupee.[32] English gomastas and private traders brought a large quantity of salt to Sylhet which ruined the business of Durlavram, an established Indian merchant. They forced the ryots to purchase the commodity at an exorbitantly high price.[33] The Company's gomastas and officers captured the salt farms, golas and ganjs at Sandwip. They forcibly collected salt from the malangis at the lowest price possible and sold it to the consumers at a price of their own.

The activities of the English traders led to the displacement of the Kashmir merchants from salt trade at the Sundarbans.[34] The ryots of Bazargamedpur (Dacca) were compelled by the British traders to purchase salt at a high price.[35] Private traders penetrated deep and wide into the salt trade of Bengal. At Rangamati, Goalpara and Jugigopa, in Assam, they were engaged in bitter conflict with the Nawab's Foujdar at Rangamati.[36] The Foujdar had the sole right to trade in salt with the hill people. But after Plassey, Mr. Chevalier forcibly secured the right for himself. He remained on the Assam border until 1762 and carried on the salt trade with extreme ruthlessness. In many areas oppressive activities of the English private traders forced the indigenous merchants, paikars and producers to migrate elsewhere.

The private traders also refused to pay salt duties. They misused the dastaks frequently. The Nawabs informed the Governors about the affairs of the gomastas and private traders. But the indigenous merchants got no redress. After Plassey, the private traders were filled with a sense of power. In a letter to Mir Ata Ullah, *wadadar* (collector of the revenues) of the pargana Bakarbund (Dacca), Chevalier wrote, "If you want to be informed, who I am, and who sent me, send a man to the Chief, who will answer you. If the people of your pargana are guilty of any violence to mine, I shall chastise them handsomely for it. Forbid your people, that they enter no quarrels with mine; if they do without reason, they shall be punished".[37]

The Salt Trade of the Europeans and the Bengalee Merchants (1765-71)

The emergence of Bengalee banians as salt merchants was an interesting development after the formation of the Society of Trade in 1765. The society put no restraints on the Europeans either in making or in trading in salt. Its activities, however, placed the traditional Indian merchants in a difficult position.

The Society was committed to supply salt to the natives at a reduced price. It usually obtained salt in three ways – from the Company's servants in the districts where salt pans were situated near the Company's factories, like Dacca or Midnapur; from other Europeans in the Calcutta area; and from the Foujdar of Hooghly for the Tamluk and Hijli districts.[38] In distributing salt, the Society followed two systems. It introduced auction system for indigenous merchants for selling salt in Calcutta. For distribution outside Calcutta, the commodity was transported to thirteen centres throughout Bengal, where the Society's European agents were responsible for selling it to the indigenous merchants. The agents received a commission of 5%. The Society controlled prices at two different stages – when salt was sold by the Society to the midigenous merchants, and when it was sold by the latter to the consumers. In the areas outside Calcutta the agents of the Society were instructed to sell salt at 15% below the average price.[39] In Calcutta, the Society sold the salt to the indigenous merchants at Rs. 215 per hundred maunds in 1765 and at Rs. 200 in the next year. The merchants were asked to sell the commodity to the consumers at a fixed price of Rs. 230 per hundred maunds. Those who purchased salt from the Society made a profit of 15% if they sold it on the spot, and made about 17½% if they could transport it from where they purchased it to other places.[40]

The system of disposing of salt by the Society put the indigenous merchants at a disadvantage. It was hardly possible for them to make profit by selling salt at the high rate fixed by the Society. They had little incentive to trade for fixed profit. Secondly, as private trade was allowed to continue, the European traders had the chance of selling salt at a price lower than the one fixed by the Society. The regular indigenous merchants could thus be easily undersold.

By 1771, Clive admitted in private that 'the price to the natives was too great and so was the advantage to the servants'.[41] But all these years the question of advantage to the servants was uppermost in his mind. No wonder that when the Company's Secretary told Clive that 'the natives' had 'a natural right to an open trade' in salt, or when in November 1767 orders was sent to Bengal forbidding participation by Europeans in salt trade, he did not show much concern. It was only after the Society had completed the third year of its operations in 1768, that the instructions of the Directors were complied with.

How did the indigenous salt merchants react to the fixing of a high price by the Society? At Midnapur they did not buy salt at the enhanced rate of Rs. 200.[42] Mir Muhammad Ashruf an indigenous merchant was able to sell only 23,596 maunds of salt out of his stock of 50,929 maunds. When he was questioned for his failure to dispose of the entire quantity, he replied that "in many places there was salt belonging to English gentlemen, and it was not in his power to stop the sale of their merchandise, in order to dispose of the Sircar's; and that notwithstanding the obligation entered into by the merchants of the city, the officers of several of the neighbouring places did not put a stop to the business of other merchants, so that it was possible he should sell Government's salt at an advanced price, while they sold their's at the former price".[43]

Not only was the price fixed by the Society, strict watch was maintained over the retailing of salt and offenders against the regulations were severely penalized. One of its regulations provided that if salt should be sold at any of the bazars for one cowri above the stipulated price, the vender should not only forfeit all the salt then found in his possession, but would also be liable to a penalty of Rs. 1,000 for every 100 maunds of salt so sold. Half of the salt and money, so forfeited, should go to the informer and the other half to the government.[44] Kasinath Sen and his partners

(Sovaram Basak of Kolutola and Madan Dutta of Bowbazar) sold the Society's salt to the retailers of Calcutta and Kulberia at a price higher than Rs. 200 per 100 maunds, the rate fixed by the Society. The excess money detected was Rs. 41,525. The merchants were compelled to hand it over to the Society.[45]

Though the Society of Trade was officially abolished in November 1767, it continued its operations till November 1768. In November 1768, by a government declaration the salt trade was closed to the Company's servants, free merchants and to all Europeans. Henceforth, the salt pans were to be worked by Indians who would sell their salt to the Indian merchants. It was one thing to exclude the Europeans from salt trade by a government decree and quite another matter to enforce the prohibition. Though salt trade was open to the native traders alone, this was only nominal. At factories and residencies where the Company's servants were well established, such as in Dacca, Midnapur and Burdwan, they clearly had no intention of giving up this lucrative business. They continued to participate in it under Indian names. But this was for a short time. In 1770 the Court of Directors reconsidered the matter and instructed that manufacturing salt and dealing in it should be open to all, Europeans as well as Indians.[46] In fact, during the period between 1768 and 1771 the salt trade of Bengal was largely in the hands of the Company's servants working through their native banians and gomastas.[47]

The difficulties of the Indian salt merchants remained unresolved. The ex-members of the Society interferred with the merchants by selling their old stock at a reduced price. They smuggled salt into the interior of the province by evading duties. The indigenous merchants were often compelled to pay a duty called *gully mangum* at certain chowkis in Hooghly, Burdwan, Krishnagar, Mushidabad, and Katwa.[48] The salt merchants of Chittagong were directed to pay 30% duties within the district. But it was the custom that the merchants of eastern Bengal would pay duties only at Rajabari in the Dacca district.[49] Sometimes the government failed to supply salt to the merchants in due time. In 1768, four Calcutta merchants, who contracted for large quantities of Hijli salt did not get more than 1,26,635 maunds.[50]

Salt Merchants of Bengal (1772-80)

In 1772 Warren Hastings created the 'great monopoly' in salt by introducing the five-year farming system. It was a monopoly for the benefit of the Company rather than for the benefit of its servants. The Company's servants were excluded from salt production. They were, however, free to deal in salt, sold at the Company's auctions for another year or so, until the Regulating Act of 1773 finally stopped Europeans from being 'concerned directly or indirectly' with salt trade.[51] But the new regulations too proved ineffective. European participation in salt trade seemed to be declining by the late 1770's. This was partly the result of a thorough enquiry by the Council in 1775 and partly due to fall in the salt prices throughout Bengal caused by importation of cheaper salt from Orissa and Madras. By 1780, the Europeans had left the salt business. The prohibitions of 1772 and 1773 were at least effective.[52]

Apart from the competition of the English private traders, the indigenous merchants had other problems like deficiency causing irregular supply of salt to the merchants. The following table would illustrate the point :

Table 1

DEFICIT SUPPLY OF SALT TO THE MERCHANTS

Names of the Merchants	*Quantity of deficit salt*	*Areas fallingin deficit*
1	2	3
	Maunds	
Gokul Ghosal	3,38,349	Hijli, Tamluk
Kasinath Sen	24,992	Tamluk, Jalamuta
Syam Charan Dutta	49,233	Mahisadal

Source : Progs. of the Revenue Board Consisting of the whole Council, vol. 6, 30, July, 1773; Prog. No. 19; 27 July, 1773; Prog. No. 16; 3 Aug., 1773; Prog. No. 9.

Merchants were sometimes compelled to pay *rahdari* (transit) and ganj duties.[53] Servants of the Company's revenue department interferred in the business of the regular traders. The Company's Diwan at Midnapur and

Jessore forced the dealers of that areas to puchase salt from him.[54] Bostom Das Sarkar, as a representative of these traders, complained to the Board of Revenue that Bipra Prosad Ray, the Diwan, had stopped selling of their salt until all his own salt was disposed of. Mr. Archdekin, an officer of the Company, sent a large quanitity of salt to Moyachoura, which also threatened the interest of these traders. Actually, Archdekin was permitted to sell his salt only at Hijli. Gokul Ghosal and his partners (Kashinath Babu, Lokenath Nandi, Sridhar Saha, Darpanarain Tagore) purchased a contract from Messrs. Grant-Francis-Charlton-Huzurimal at a high price.[55] In accordance with this contract, the merchants were to receive 135 maunds of Banga weight, in lieu of 100 common Bazar maunds, that is to say an excess weight of 35 maunds. Furthermore, the authorised Indian salt merchants suffered as a result of the smuggling of salt by the salt farmers and the English private traders who sold it at a reduced price.[56] The delay in weighing the salt affected the traders, as the salt dried up and was reduced in weight.

Thus during this period the private traders participated extensively in the salt trade of Bengal. Interestingly enough, it was recorded in the proceedings of the Calcutta Committee of Revenue that some Europeans purchased salt in 1774 and 1775 at the same time when Gokul Mitra, Madan Dutta, Baranasi Ghosh, Kasinath Sen and other Bengalee merchants were purchasing it. Mr. Dacres bought more than 32,000 maunds of salt. Mr. Charles Child also purchased above 31,000 maunds.[57]

Mode of Business of the Salt Merchants of Bengal (1765-80) :

After 1765, the indigenous merchants had to collect salt by a procedure fixed by the Company. At the beginning of the manufacturing season, the merchants were asked by the Company to declare the quantity of salt they intended to purchase. The purchasing price of salt was also fixed. Then, they had to pay to the government, in advance, a fixed sum of money for the quantity they had asked for. They were required to pay nearly the whole amount. Out of this money the government paid advance to the farmers, who then supplied the stipulated quantity of salt to the merchants.

There was also the system of *neyafte* contract. It literally signified 'not got'.[58] This form of contract was used by a merchant who dealt directly with the zamindar, the supplier of salt. *Neyafte* contract usually worked in the following manner. A merchant made a contract with the zamindar, for say, 50,000 maunds of salt, but ultimately was unable to pay for more than 30,000 maunds. A second merchant then offered to pay the balance of the purchase money and thereby secured the contract for the remaining 20,000 maunds.

The big merchants supplied salt to their under-merchants and the beparis, who had also to enter into prior contracts with them. There was a chain of distribution. The system had certain limitations. Once a merchant failed to collect the contracted quality, it followed that the under-merchants would not get their expected amount either. The whole chain would thus be disrupted. The shortfall in supply usually created a serious problem. All the traders from big merchants to the lowest buyers, made advances by borrowing money from the creditors at a high rate of interest. In case of insufficient deliveries, the traders failed to pay the creditors in full.[59]

An interesting feature of the business operations of the Bengalee salt merchants was their joint venture. Big merchants often conducted their business jointly. Kasinath Sen had two partners — Sovaram Basak of Kolutola and Madan Dutta of Bowbazar.[60] Sometimes Gokul Ghosal, Kasinath Sen, Lokenath Nandi, Sridhar Saha. Darpanarain Tagore, the big salt merchants of Calcutta, often worked in common. Transfer of contract from one merchant to another was also quite common. Kasinath purchased such a contract from Gokul Ghosal when the latter was in difficulty owing to an uncommon scarcity of money in Calcutta caused by the withdrawal of the gold mohurs.[61] The big merchants usually appointed agents or gomastas to supervise their business in different parts of the country.

Salt of the Bengalee Merchants' Trade in Salt (1765-80)

Though private traders and the Company's servants largely controlled the salt trade of Bengal during this period,

Bengalee merchants, who collaborated with the British, had some share in it. Under the Society of Trade, Kasinath and his two partners sold about 1,13,700 mounds of salt to the retailers.[62] From the following table one can form an idea of the extent of participation of Bengalee merchants in the salt trade of Bengal.

Table 2

VOLUME OF TRADE OF THE BENGALEE MERCHANTS

Year	Name of Merchants	Quantity Purchased	Quantity Contracted for	Places of Manufacture
1	2	3	4	5
		Maunds	Maunds	
1768	Lokenath Nandi	2,200,022	-	Hijli
1768	Anandaram Naik	2,34,415	-	Hijli
1768	Shridhar Saha	90,750	-	Hijli
1772	Kashinath Sen	1,74,820	- Sujamutra	Hijli, and Tamulk
1772 Sarkar	Ghanashyam	80,572	- Sujamutra	Hijli, and Tamulk
1772	Shridhar Saha	1,65,600	- Sujamutra	Hijli,
1773	Lokenath Nandi	-	62,444	Sujamuta and Hijli
1773	Anup Narain and Chand	-	62,976	Mahisadal
1775	Anup Narain and Chand	-	1,26,482	Mahisadal

(Fractions Omitted)

***Source*:** Comptrolling Committee of Revenue Progs. Vol. 1, 25 April, 1771, F-130; Progs. of the Revenue Board Consisting of the Whole Council, vol. 8, Part I, 19 Nov., 1773; Prog. Nos. 1A, 1B, 4D; Calcutta Committee of Revenue; Progs., Vol. 2, Part I, 2 March, 1774; vol. 6, Part III, 22 May, 1775, Consultn. No. 3.

Apart from examples of individual enterprise, the extent of business transactions of Bengalee merchants can be surmised from the amount of salt they purchased or contracted for.

Table 3

CONTRACT OF SALT TO BE PURCHASED BY THE BENGALEE MERCHANTS

Year	Amount	Place of Manufacture
1	2	3
	Maunds	
1772	1,50,000	Mahishadal
1772	16,02,743	Hijli
1772	1,16,596	Sujamuta
1772	3,18,596	Tmaluk
1773	2,54,712	Mahisadal
1773	3,49,650	Hijli
1773	71,344	Tamluk
1775	3,79,430	Mahisadal

(Fractions Omitted)

Source : Prog. of the Revenue Board Consisting of the Whole Council, vol. 2, 6 May, 1774, Consultn. No. 5; vol. 8, Part I, 19 Nov. 1773; Prog. Nos. 1A, 2B, 4D; Calcutta Committee of Revenue; Progs., vol. 2, Part I, 2 March, 1774; vol. 9, Part II, 1776, Appendix; vol. 6, Part III, 22 May, 1775, Consultn. No. 3.

Table 4

SALT SOLD BY THE GOVERNMENT TO THE BENGALEE MERCHANTS

Year	Amount	Place of Manufacture	Number of Merchants
1	2	3	4
	Maunds		
1773	1,50,000	Mahisadal	20
1774	16,02,743	Mahisadal	30
1774	1,16,596	Jessore	-
1774	3,18,596	24 Pargans	-
1774	2,54,712	Tamulk	-
1776	3,49,650	Mahisadal	20

(Fractions Omitted)

Source : Calcutta Committee of Revenue. Progs., vol. 9, Part III, 1776; vol. 15, Part II, Dec., 1776, Appendix.

The activities of the Bengalee salt merchants during the period 1765 to 1780 were not confined to salt only. Many prominent salt merchants had large interests in land. They often stood as securities for the ijaradars of estates or the zamindars.

Salt merchants also stood as securities for the salt farmers. Gokul Ghosal, a big salt merchant, became a security for Syed Pir Muhammad, salt farmer of Sandwip. Many salt merchants were the banians of the Company's senior servants. Krishnakanta Nandi, Kasinath Babu and Munshi Nabakrishna were notable among them. Moreover, salt was not their only business. They had interests in other types of business also. Many big salt merchants were actually banian-zamindars.

During the five-year farming experiment (1772-77) forty-two parganas of Midnapur were given to Krishnakanta Nandi of Kashimbazar who was the banian of Warren Hastings. Two parganas were given to Kasinath Babu, a Calcutta banian.[63] Krishnakanta Nandi was also a banker of Murshidabad[64] and engaged in silk trade. Nabakrishna too, had other interests apart front salt. He was granted the talukdari of Shovabazar.[65]

Madan Dutta, a prominent salt merchant, was a ship owner in Calcutta. Darpanarain Tagore, a big salt merchant of Calcutta, served the French Company as Diwani.[66] Mosts of the salt merchants of the later period (during tile agency system) were also zamindars.

Krishnakanta Nandi - A Typical Banian-Merchant of this Period :

Krishnakanta Nandi came from a family of dadni merchants who were in the silk trade before 1757. He seems to have been tile first person in his family to have entered the salt trade around 1764. Official records show that in that year he was a salt contractor in Hatiagar in the 24 Parganas.[67] In that period of indiscriminate private trading in salt, before the Society of Trade was formed by Clive, Kanto Babu, who was closely associated with the Company's senior officials, apparently had little difficulty in securing salt contracts. Francis Sykes became Collector of salt duties in 1768. In that year Kanto Babu as the banian of Sykes was able to take lease of salt mahals in Hijli in the names of his younger brother Gokul Chandra Nandi and his four-year old son Lokenatth Nandi. He also farmed thika khalaris in the name of Gobindaprasad Babu of Kashimbazar. Krishnananda Sarkar was engaged as his gomasta. In 1769-70, Kanto Babu was second only to Gokul Ghosal as a salt contractor. Before he left salt manufacturing in 1774, Krishnakanta had become the leading salt manufacturer and had controlled more than 400 khalaris. After 1774 he took to wholesale trading in salt and gave up manufacturing altogether. S. C. Nandy suggests that Kanto Babu must have relinquished his salt khalaris, somewhat abruptly in 1774 on the advice of Warren Hastings, his chief benefactor. He must have done it to save the Governor-General from being harassed by the majority in the Council.

As a wholesale trader in salt Krishnakanta continued his activities only for two years. He finally withdrew from salt trade in 1776. During this period and afterwards he carried on business in silk, and at the same time built up landed estates.

The story of Krishnakanta's involvement in salt is instructive. It shows clearly how his close connection with senior officials of the Company, which helped him to emerge as the leading salt manufacturer in Bengal also served to limit his business career. With all his affluence he could not operate as an independent merchant.[68]

Bengalee Salt Merchants under the Agency System: Formation of Sub-Monopolies :

With the introduction of the agency system in 1781, the Bengalee merchants became relatively free to trade in salt. There was no problem of interference by the English private traders. The Company's officials seemed to have lost interest in the salt trade. The Company limited its monopoly-control only to production. Salt production, in this phase, began to be controlled directly by the government. The agency salt was sold, without any restriction of the quantity, to the indigenous merchants at a stipulated price. In 1786, however. Cornwallis introduced the system of periodic auction sale of salt and this imposed a restriction on the quantity. It gave the more affluent merchants an opportunity to control the sale of salt in Bengal. They formed sub-monopolies and began to dictate prices of their own to their under-merchants and retailers.

One noticeable feature of the salt trade of this period was that the inland trade of salt passed almost completely into the hands of the Bengalees. The banians mostly withdrew from the salt trade along with their masters. Most of the pre-1780 merchants gave up trading in salt and a new group of merchants emerged. A few of the banian families such as the Tagore family and the family of Madan Dutta, however, continued to trade in salt. Many new merchants came from very poor families. They rose to prominence by trading in salt. These families played a vital role in the early 19th century Bengal.

Classification of the Salt Merchants

The introduction of periodic auction sales in 1786 by Cornwallis created opportunities for the rise of various groups of indigenous salt merchants. In the official documents they have been grouped into six classes :[69]

1. First Class Dhuratia.[70]
2. Second Class Dhuratia
3. First Class Bhanga
4. Second Class Bhanga
5. Third Class Bhanga
6. The Assamees (Paikars)
   - i) First Class Assamees
   - ii) Second Class Assamees

The first class dhuratias were originally employed as agents by some persons for their superior knowledge of the custom and mode of transacting business in Bengal. The agency represented by the dhuratias changed its character over time when the agents took advantage of the new opportunities to become salt purchasers themselves. Hence arose that large class called 'dhuratia mahajans' or the purchasers of *chhars* [71] and *rowannas*.[72] They had no intention of transporting salt to the markets of the interior but they purchased and hoarded it to be sold again to real mofussil dealers.

When the government established the system of public auction sales of salt in 1786, men of large capital like the first class of dhuratias came forward and engaged in salt trade. Almost simultaneously, a class of petty dealers called the first and second class bhanga merchants emerged.[73] They purchased salt at the public sales and also the chhars from the first class dhuratias on a premium and disposed of it in the interior.

The first class dhuratias, finding themselves threatened by the keen competition of another class of lesser capitalists, were no longer satisfied with eight or ten per cent return of the capital and started to deliver salt to the bhanga merchants on credit at a larger profit. The immediate consequence was the rise of the third class bhanga merchants, who purchased salt from the first class dhuratias on credit and sold it to the paikars in the mofussil at an enhanced price and waited till the time when they could receive in return mofussil crops like grain, sugar and cotton from the paikars, at eight or ten per cent lower than the market price, on the system commonly called bari trade.[74] Then they brought the commodities for sale in the Calcutta market.

Modes of Business of the Different Classes of Merchants :

The first class dhuratias were not, strictly speaking, salt merchants, but speculators in the Calcutta salt market. Many of them were shroffs in the Barabazar.[75] If the speculation of the dhuratias happened to fail, they had to mortgage their chhars and rowannas.[76]

The second class dhuratias or the persons of limited capital purchased salt at the public sales, having made the deposit of the required amount, and resold it to other merchants. When they found the market prices falling below the price they had paid, they even preferred to lose by reselling the chhar to other merchants at a lower price, rather than collect the salt from the Company's golas and export it into the interior oil their own account.

The first class bhanga merchants were small capitalists, who purchased salt at the public sales according to their limited capital and immediately cleared it away at the Company's golas. If after the public sale, they could command a capital, they purchased salt from the dhuratias at the best advantage and immediately cleared it from the Company's golas and despatched it into the interior, where they owned golas and retailed it in small quantities for ready money.

The second class bhanga merchants were in every respect the same as the first class except that they occasionally purchased salt chhars from the first class on credit and also sold it by retail to their regular customers on credit, usually of one or two months, but received the return in ready money.

The third class bhangas were also the same as the second class except that they delivered their salt to their paikars on credit at an enhanced price, and waited till they received in return crops like grain, sugar, cotton etc. at eight or ten per cent discount on its market value, which they sent down to the Calcutta market.[77]

The bhanga merchants usually purchased salt through agents residing in Calcutta, but their payments through those agents were regular. They were mofussil traders in their habits and appearance; apparently rude, but cautious businessmen. They did not, in general, buy large quantities of salt (only two or three lots, while the dhuratias bought fifty or sixty lots), and what they did purchase, they paid for without making deposits. They did not get themselves involved in the complicated machinery of the system of resales for deposits or resales for the principal amount, gola rent, wastage, postponements and petitions to government. These merchants cared little for the state of the Calcutta market. They cared only for the demand which they knew existed in the interior, and for the price of the produce they intended to bring back in return for the salt and to provide the means of purchasing more.

The assamees or paikars were sub-divided into two classes. The first purchased salt from the bhanga merchants for ready money. They were by no means dependent on the bhanga merchants for any pecuniary considerations. The second class assamees were entirely at the mercy of the third class bhanga merchants. These petty dealers sold their salt to the *mudis* (grocers) and large families. The latter purchased it for family consumption and the mudis sold it to consumers.

Most merchants carried on their business through their gomastas and moktars (representatives) who had separate *gadis* (shops) at Hatkhola, Jorabagan, Pathurighata, Barabazar, Chitpur and Tollygunge.[78]

Almost all the bhanga merchants had zamindaris or landed properties in the interior.[79] They did not speculate exclusively in salt. Most of them were engaged in trade of other commodities like rice, sugar, oil, ghee, cloth, gur, mustard seeds etc. But some bhanga merchants, like Rajkrishna Roy, Bholanath Kundu, Premchand Ballav Saha, Baisnab Charan and Guru Dayal Kundu, Ramananda Saha, and Debnath Kundu traded exclusively in salt.

Formation of Sub-monopolies :

There were two types of sub-monopolies. One was formed by the big dhuratia merchants who resided in Calcutta. Another type was organised by some bhanga merchants in a particular tract of the country. But the opinion of the Company's officials varied about the existence of sub-monopolies in the salt market of Bengal. While the Board of Customs, Salt and Opium did not recognise such type of monopoly,[80] the Superintendent of Bhulua agency confirmed its existence in eastern Bengal.[81]

The quarterly auction sale, introduced by Cornwallis in 1786, offered a big opportunity to the dhuratias to form a sub-monopoly in salt. Huge quantities of salt were disposed of through these auction sales. Thus in 1789, at the auction taking place on 30th and 31st March, about 3,51,000 maunds of Tamluk salt were sold for Rs. 12,28,980. Another 1,00,000 maunds were sold for Rs. 3,18,260 on 8th June,1789.[82] Under the agency system the Company's monopoly in salt was limited to production only. Their responsibilities ended after selling it to the merchants through auction. At these auctions a few dhuratias who commanded large capital, purchased the entire amount and monopolised its sale. Thus sub-monopoly was formed within the larger framework of the government monopoly. This was a natural outcome of the system of sale through public auction in Calcutta.

The dhuratias easily made their own terms with the secondary purchasers who came to them from tile mofussil. Some dhuratias jointly controlled the public sales. They did not usually bid above the upset price. They were speculators and generally belonged to a group of rich bankers of Calcutta. For the sake of securing sub-monopoly they did very often run up prices to an extravagantly high pitch.

Cornwallis was strongly opposed to a combination among merchants which tended to eliminate competition.

With a view to re-creating conditions for competition, in 1786 he introduced quarterly auction sales of limited quantities, divided into large lots, in the places of existing system of regular sales of unlimited amounts at fixed prices.[83] As it was, the dhuratias conspired to prevent any outside broker from purchasing, and actually hustled out those at the public sales who attempted to bid. A similar situation was noticeable at the tea sales of the East India Company during the close monopoly. Such incidents unmistakably showed the organisational power of the sub-monopolists. It was Mr. T.L. Peacock who made the perceptive remark that, "In all trades there is something in the nature of combination. Political economists speak of competition; I think combination is stronger than competition".[84] A crucial element in the operation of the sub-monopoly was the time which was allowed to the purchasers to hoard the salt in the golas. By holding salt at a nominal gola rent these merchants controlled the selling price of salt.

The bhanga merchants also had scope of forming sub-monopolies. There is evidence to show that in the first half of the nineteenth century, the whole salt trade of eastern Bengal was brought under a sub-monopoly by seventeen merchants, who transacted 12 lakh maunds of salt annually. The second class traders, the retail dealers and the consumers were entirely at the mercy of this small body of merchants, whose nature of business was combination and not competition. Interestingly enough, all the seventeen of them were connected by blood, marriage and caste.[85] There was no competition in the selling price at the various markets controlled by them.

Most of the petty traders were in bondage to big merchants, to whom they paid a high rate of interest. This additional burden ultimately fell upon the consumers. Salt was sold at Narainganj at about 7 rupees per maund.[86] In 1823, salt was bought at the Company's sales by an Association of Calcutta baboos, who formed a sub-monopoly. As a result the price of salt rose to 12 rupees per maund where it was generally sold for Rs. 5, and in many places it was not procurable at any price whatsoever.[87]

Some Important Merchant-families of Bengal :

During the years 1786 to 1836, the salt merchants of Bengal did flourishing business. Many of them started from almost nothing, but built up large fortunes through successful trading. This period witnessed the spectacular rise of some new merchant-families.

PAL CHAUDHURI's OF RANAGHAT (NADIA)

The Pal Chaudhuri family of Ranaghat was founded by a reputed salt merchant, Krishna Chandra Panti and his brother Sambhu Chandra Panti. They were Tilis, a traditionally trading caste. Their original family title was 'Pal'; but as they were petty dealer of *pan* (betel-leaf), they came to be called 'Panti'. The title 'Chaudhuri' was conferred upon Krishna Chandra by Maharaja Sib Chandra of Nadia who borrowed money from Krishna Chandra.[88]

In those days Hatkhola was a big trading centre of Calcutta before the rise of Barabazar. It was particularly famous for salt trade. Krishna Chandra purchased some land in Hatkhola, and built a small house. Having followed the business scene carefully, he rightly picked up salt as a suitable trade for investing his capital. With the little money in his hands he was not in a position to trade all by himself. He therefore joined hands with others. Within a short time, however, he built up a capital of 30,000 rupees and felt confident enough to start business on his own.[89] In course of time, he became one of the prominent salt merchants of Calcutta. As a big dhuratia merchant he took part in the Company's auction sales. It is said that when he was absent the auction remained suspended for the day.[90] He was also known as *'Kartababu'* (the lord and master) of Hatkhola. He set up salt golas in various towns of Bengal, Bihar and Orissa. In Bengal these were located in Dacca. Murshidabad, Narainganj, Sirajgunj, Hanskhali, Nalhati, Kanchannagar, Bhadreswar, Kalna, etc.[91]

Deys of Serampore (Hooghly)

In the late eighteenth century, the Dey family of Serampore rose to prominence through the salt trade.[92] The founder of the family was Ram Chandra Dey, a famous salt merchant of Calcutta. He was born in 1763 to a poor family, and died in 1823, a zamindar. He belonged to the Tili caste. His grandfather belonged to Rishra, a village two miles south of Serampore. Ram Chandra's grandfather, Ram Bhadra and his father, Sefaliram, were petty dealers at Rishra. But Ram Chandra by dint of sheer talent, industrious, perseverance and honesty acquired an immense fortune and earned for his family unique distinction and fame, and a high position within the Hindu community.

The rise of Ram Chandra Dey makes a fascinating story. The story goes that once rebuked by his father, the young Ram Chandra was weeping by the banks of the Hooghly river. Just at that moment an Englishman was passing by in a boat on his way to Calcutta. The sympathetic Sahib brought the child along with him to Calcutta and got him a job under a merchant of Hatkhola. In a short time, Ram Chandra proved his worth. Once he purchased a big lot of salt at an auction in the name of his master, who was ignorant of it. In a few days the price of salt shot up, and Ram Chandra's master made an enormous profit. Realising that the credit belonged to Ram Chandra, the generous merchant handed over the profit to his young and intelligent employee. This amount formed the initial capital of Ram Chandra's business. He soon "established a private sub-monopoly of salt".[93] Apart from opening a warehouse in Calcutta, Ram Chandra established a number of golas and offices at Kalna, Murshidabad, Bhagwangola, Amta, Tamluk, Ghatal and other places, where salt and other commodities were stocked. His gomastas and clerks were constantly kept busy discounting every bill he drew, and regularly conducting all kinds of mercantile transactions on his behalf. In twenty years' time he is said to have built up property worth almost 20 lakhs of rupees.

After Ram Chandra's death, his third son, Raj Krishna, was entrusted with the task of running the family business. Raj Krishna was known as the 'Prince' among the salt merchants of Calcutta. He died in 1846 leaving 21 lakhs of rupees. Raj Krishna Dey's name occurs in the list of the bhanga merchants who purchased Company's salt in November, 1834, where he is reported to have bought 12,500 maunds of salt.[94]

Motilals of Bowbazar (Calcutta)

The Motilal family of Bowbazar was founded by Biswanath Motilal, a renowned salt merchant of Calcutta. He was born in 1779, and rose to prominence working his way up from an ordinary position. He had entered the salt trade in partnership with Rammohan Mallick of Barabazar. But Biswanath was unsuccessful in business. Then he became an ordinary *muhuri* (a clerk) in the Company's salt gola at Shalkia on a monthly salary of Rs. 8 only. From this position he eventually grew into big salt merchant. He died in 1844 leaving behind property worth 15 lakhs of rupees.[95]

There were many other families in Bengal who grew rich in salt trade. Among these were the Mallicks of Barabazar and the Duttas of Hatkhola. There were the Mitras of Baghbazar, a well-known member of which family was Gokul Chandra Mitra. Besides one could also refer to the Kars of Mahanad (Hooghly), the Kundus of Itachuna (Hooghly) and the Nandis of Jamgram (Hooghly).

A remarkable feature of the Bengalee salt merchants was their simultaneous interest in business and in their landed estates. They were capable of continuing it for at least three generations. But how was it possible? The existence of the joint-family system must have been an important factor. The Deys of Serampore, for example, followed a healthy tradition in their family which was congenial to the maintenance of the twin business. It was customary to make the eldest son the *Karta* (head) of the joint family. He was to live in the ancestral home at Serampore, managing and supervising the vast zamindari, while the next son looked after the business in Hatkhola.

An interesting feature of business operations of the Bengalee salt merchants was their close association or combination. Before 1780 they used to combine themselves in the salt trade. The best example of it can be seen in the formation of sub-monopolies. Sometimes combination was formed among three or four merchants.

In some cases there was solidarity based on caste. The salt trade was generally conducted by persons of various castes like the *Tilis, Tamlis, Sadgopas, Basaks* and *Sunris.*[96]

It is a striking fact that a large section of them belonged to the Tili caste. The Pal Chaudhuris, the Deys and the Nandis of Kashimbazar belonged to this caste. A list of the names of dhuratia and bhanga merchants, who purchased Company's salt in 1834, shows that out of fifty two traders at least twenty possibly belonged to the Tili caste.[97] It has already been mentioned that the seventeen merchants, who established a sub-monopoly in the salt trade of eastern Bengal, were closely related by caste, blood and marriage alliances.

Notes and References

1. Marshall, P.J., *East India Fortunes*, 1976, 264.
2. Ibid., 266.
3. Ibid., 268.
4. Sinha, *Midnapur Salt Papers*, 2.
5. Marshall, op.cit., 109. Khwaja Wazid, a great Armenian trader who was granted a monopoly in salt, agreed to pay to the Nawab nearly £ 2,00,000 per year.
6. J. Newbey (ed.), *Tansactions in Bengal* 1759-64. Papers sent by Mr. Vansittart to some of his friends in England, London, 1765, vol. 1, 203. Durlavram was granted monopoly of salt trade in Sylet for a yearly revenue of 40,000 caouns (a measure of quantities) of cowries.
7. Marshall, op.cit., 122.
8. W.W. Hunter, *A Statistical Account of Bengal*, vol. 3, London, 1876, 151.
9. Sinha, *Midnapur Salt Papers*, 2.
10. Majrul Huq, *The East India Company's Land Policy* and *Commerce in Bengal, 1698-1784*, Dacca, 1964, 232.
11. Ibid., 233.
12. J.K. Nag, *Modern Review*, Sept., 1939, 300.
13. Marshall, op.cit., 111.
14. Ibid.
15. Ibid.
16. Ibid., 112.
17. Ibid.

18. Ibid.
19. Ibid., 114.
20. Newbery, op.cit., vol. 2, 75.
21. Ibid,. vol. I, 7.
22. Marshall, op.cit., 115.
23. Ibid.
24. Ibid.
25. Ibid., 121.
26. Ibid.
27. Ibid.
28. Newbery, op.cit., vol. I, 5.
29. Ibid., 198-99.
30. Ibid., 206.
31. Ibid., 5-6.
32. Ibid., 199.
33. Ibid., 203.
34. Ibid., 230.
35. Rev. J. Long, *Selections from Unpublished Records of Government 1748-67*, Calcutta, 1869, vol. I, 408. The vakil of the zamindar of Bazargamedpur wrote a petition that "The Purgunnah of Buzzoorgamedpoor & C., is the Zamindar of my Master. By reason of the oppressions of the Factories of the Company and many other English traders all the inhabitants are fled; the people of the Factories take from the Merchants what they please at half price; cut down Bamboos and Trees belonging to the inhabitants and take them away by force; if any one complain they punish him for it. They press the inhabitants and carry them, in the woods of Soonderbun, paying them only half their wages. They take possession of land in the Soonderbun and make Taffals of salt for which they pay no rent. They seize the salt of the Taffals of the pergunnah and of the inhabitants. They force the inhabitants to take Tobacco, Salt and other articles and refuse to pay the legal duties on the trade which they carry on.

If we demand a sight of the Company's Dustack they beat us with Bamboos."

36. Marshall, op.cit., 122.
37. Newbery, op.cit., vol. 1, 7.
38. Marshall, op.cit., 131.
39. Ibid., 132.
40. Select Committee of Revenue Progs., vol., 2, 15 Aug., 1766, F. 137.
41. Marshall, op.cit., 135.
42. W.K. Firminger (ed.)., *Bengal District Records, Midnapur 1763-1767*, Calcutta, 1914, 47.
43. Newbery, op.cit., vol. 1, 236.
44. Select Committee of Revenue Progs., vol., 2, 3 September, 1766, F. 204.
45. Ibid., 15 Aug., 1766, F. 137.
46. Marshall, op.cit., 142.
47. Watter Wilkins, Collector of Chitagong, was engaged in the salt trade.
48. Comptrolling Committee of Revenue Progs., vol. 1, 24 April, 1771, F. 115.
49. Ibid, vol. 2, 5 Dec., 1771, Prog. No. 3.
50. Ibid, vol. 1, 25 April, 1771, F. 130. The mechants were Loknath Nandi, Sridhar Saha, Anandaram Nag, Darpanarain Tagore.
51. Marshall, op.cit., 143.
52. Ibid.
53. Proceeding of the Revenue Board Consisting of the whole Council (henceforth P.R.B.C.C.), 10, Part I,1 March, 1774, Prog. No. 21.
54. Calcutta Committee of Revenue (henceforth C.C.R) Prog. 22 April, 1776. LR No. 141.
55. P.R.B.C.C., vol. 3, Part II, vol. 5, 27 July, 1773, Prog. No. 17.
56. C.W. Forrest, (ed.), Selections from the Letters, Despatches and other State Papers preserved in the Foreign Department of the Govt. of India, 1772-1785, Calcutta, 1890.

57. C.C.R.Progs., vol. 9, Part III, 2 Jan., 1776, Consulation No. 1.
58. Ibid., vol. 19, Part III, 22 Dec., 1777, I.S. No. 423.
59. Ibid., vol. 14, Part III, 10 Oct., 1776, Prog. No. 24.
60. Select Committee of Revenue Progs., vol. 2, 15 Aug, 1776, F. 137.
61. P.R.B.C.C., vol. 6, 27 July, 1773, Prog. No. 15.
62. Select Committee of Revenue Progs., vol. 2, 15 Aug., 1776, F. 137.
63. N. K. Sinha, *The Economic History of Bengal*, vol. 2, Calcutta, 1962,
64. Ibid., 224.
65. Ibid., 127.
66. Ibid., vol. 2, 221.
67. Miscellaneous Records, Revenue Department, Proceedings of W. Young and D. Anderson on the salt khalaris in the 24-Parganas, 17 Dec, 1774; 6 Feb, 1775, F. 105.
68. In a recent work entitled *Life and Times of Cantoo Baboo, The Banian of Warren Hastings*, vol. I , *The Early Career of Cantoo Baboo and His Trade in Salt and Silk*, Calcutta, 1978. Somendra Chandra Nandy has produced a well documented account of the life and work of Krishnakanta Nandi, the banian of Warren Hastings. The book carries voluminous documentation from the official papers of the East Indian Company as well as from the family papers of Krishnakanta Nandi of Kasimbazar, See S. C. Nandy, op. cit., 93, 94, 99, 104-5, 110-11, 115, 117, 120, 126-127.
69. *Appendix to the Report from the Select Committee on Salt, British India*, 1836, 100.
70. Dhuratias literally mean those who take premium.
71. Chhar is a delivery order.
72. Rowanna means a pass or certificate from an official authorizing goods to pass without payment of further duty.
73. *Appendix to the Report from the Select Committee*

on Salt, British India, 1836, 101. The name of this group of merchants has been variously spelt in the records as Bomga, Bauga, Bhanga etc. Here the last mentioned form has been used.

74. Ibid.
75. Ibid., 67.
76. *Appendix to the Report from the Select Committee on Salt, British India*, 1836, 68.
77. Ibid, 101.
78. Board of Customs, Salt & Opium (Salt) Progs., vol. 430, 15 July, 1844, Prog. No. 42.
79. Ibid.
80. *Appendix to the Report from the Select Committee on Salt, British India, 1836*, 66. Letter from the Board of Customs, Salt & Opium to W. C. Bentinck, Governor-General of India, 19 Nov, 1834.
81. Board of Customs, Salt & Opium (Salt) Progs., vol. 424, 18 Jan, 1844, Prog. No. 36, Report of Mr. J. Baker, Superintendent, Bhulua agency, 17 July, 1843.
82. Sinha, Midnapore Salt Papers, 172.
83. Parimal Roy, 'History of Taxation of Salt under the Rules of the East India Company', Calcutta Review, 1930, Jan-March, 35.
84. Minutes of Evidence taken before the *Select Committee on Salt, British India*, 1836, 118, Evidence of T.I. Peacock, 7 July, 1836, No. 1077.
85. Board of Customs, Salt and Opium (Salt) Prog., vol. 424, 18 Jan, 1844, Prog. No. 36.

1.	Guru Prasad Kundu	Same caste and related
2.	Chaitan Krishna Pal	
3.	Nityananda Saha	Brothers
4.	Raychand Saha	
5.	Golap Goup Nury	Partners and Related
6.	Atit Pandit	
7.	Sashi Mohan Saha	Related
8.	Addi Chandra Saha	
9.	Hari Pada Mohan	

10.	Rajchand (surname not known)	Related
11.	Ram Hari (surname not known)	
12.	Adwaita Balaram (surname not known)	Related
13.	Madan Mongal (surname not known)	
14.	Jiban Krishna Poddar	
15.	Krishna Mongal Pal	
16.	Gaur Poddar	
17.	Seluk Ram Mohan	

86. These merchants were located in Dacca and Bakarganj and carried on their business operations from these centres of trade in eastern Bengal.
87. Ibid.
88. Minute of Evidence taken before the Select Committee on Salt, British India, 1836, 116. Evidence of Peacock, 7 July, 1836.
89. Subodh Chandra Gangopadyaya, Krishna Chandra Panti, Calcutta, N.D., 14.
90. Gangopadhyaya, op.cit., 19.
91. Ibid., 20.
92. Ibid., 29-31.
93. I owe the information regarding Dey family to Sri Samar Chandra Dey and Sri Sunil Kumar Chatterjee, Librarian, Carey Library, Serampore. Other information regarding this family can be found in the *Friend of India*, vol. 3, Dec. 1823; Calcutta Review, vol. 7, 1845, the article being 'Right Bank of Hooghly'.
94. L.S.S.O' Malley (ed.), *Bengal District Gazetteers, Hooghly*, Calcutta, 1912, 316.
95. *Appendix to the Report from the Select Committee on Salt, British India*, 1836, 105.
96. Satish Chandra Motilal, Bahubazarer Motilal Bansha, Calcutta, 1935, 75.
97. Board of Customs, Salt and Opium (Salt) Prog., vol. 430, 15 July, 1884, Prog. No. 42.
98. *Appendix to the Report from the Select Committee on Salt, British India*, 1836, 105.

9

From Artisan to Merchant: Looking From Below*

Smritikumar Sarkar

Conventional notion based on early European evidence states that traditional production organization in India was characterized by its rigidity depriving the artisan of an opportunity to change his economic position. Pelsaert's (1626) oft-quoted remark perhaps remains its best illustration. He observed, '... scarcely anyone will make an effort, for a ladder by which to climb higher is hard to find, because a workman's children can follow no occupation other than that of their father.'[1]

This notion of traditionalism and social immobility has been forcefully reinforced in the *Cambridge Economic History of India*. It has been held that 'the artisan acquiring wealth and emerging as a capitalist was rare and atypical. The institutions of society and government exerted a downward pressure on the producer, holding him firmly to his place on the lowest rung of the social and economic ladder. His self-perpetuating poverty had reinforced a culture of hopelessness hardly conclusive to innovative effort.'[2] Though a good deal has been written against it, the notion of immobility has continued to influence scholars, who have worked in this field.

Tirthankar Roy has thus referred to 'social barriers to the artisan's taking up capitalist roles', thereby concluding that 'social and cultural backwardness ... did contribute to

---

* This paper is a part of the chapter entitled 'Social Organization of Artisan Production in India: Changing Role of the Market, Technology and Merchant Creditor: 18th to 20th Centuries', I have contributed to B.B. Chaudhuri (Ed.), *Economic History of India: 18th to 20th Centuries,* which is a part of the *Project of the History of Indian Science, Philosophy and Culture,* sponsored by the Centre of Civilization, New Delhi. *Forthcoming.*

economic backwardness in India'. He argued that 'Colonial India began with a crippling initial condition that changed too slowly. By and large pre-colonial Hindu society had no notion of literacy or scientific knowledge as a commonly shareable resource. Notions of welfare were not intrinsic in the caste-divided society. ... Every village in India had tanners. But only a small percentage among them could become merchants or industrialists. The conversion of craft skills into industrial and innovative capacity required an induced social revolution in India, the conditions for which were not created.'[3]

However, the evidence made available by recent research does not support the well-known Weberian position of the cultural determinist.[4] Contrary to the conventional notion, the point I would like to emphasize here is that a mechanism of economic and social mobility had been very much inbuilt into traditional organization of industrial production in pre-colonial India. The existing social and cultural systems did not stand in the way of an enterprising artisan to promote himself by dint of a better utilization of his occupational skill. Although the artisan's motivations and standards suffered enormously under British rule, the system more or less continued till the end of the nineteenth century. British rule brought in its train a whole range of 'new systems' that had further encouraged this mobility process.

Traditional Organization of Artisan Production in India

Traditional organization of artisan production in India was based on caste/community and not unusually the tool technique used by the particular workgroup. A case in point is the *Hath Gade* potter of the early nineteenth century Maharashtra. A subdivision of the larger caste cluster of potters, the group had derived its name from their technique of turning out pots simply by their hands without using the ubiquitous wheel. Originally a cluster of artisans of the same occupation, arising out of their co-existence, uniformity of interests and working arrangement, the social organization of artisans exercised significant control over both the production and marketing of industrial goods. Eventually, the unorganized cluster hardened into a close-knit group, a corporate body of artisans as if, having a set of cultural-behavioural norms of its own. Each group also had a mechanism, a *Panchayat* usually consisting of elders, which enforced the convention of their social and occupational behaviour.

Variously known in different parts of India, the social organization of artisans appears to have close similarities with the craftsman's guild of medieval Europe. Both had actually emerged out of their compulsion to reduce competition within the craft, as also to prevent outsider - the person not belonging to their workgroup - from poaching into their occupation. In reality, however, the craftsman's guild of Europe was widely different from the artisan's organization, as it existed in India.[5] The European guild was primarily a body of master craftsmen, an economic organization in the main to buttress their interest in monopoly. The guild of medieval Europe was a highly organized body with rules clearly laid down and recognized by the state. A clearly demarcated territory of its own also distinguished the European guild, while the right of membership was most often denied to ordinary craftsmen following the same craft even within its jurisdiction.

In India, artisans were only loosely organized into caste or community; or similar other group based on territory, tool-technique and their product. Societal in nature, the artisan's organization was governed by customs and conventions, unwritten yet largely inviolable, which varied widely from one artisan group to other. Each group had a hierarchy of leadership determined by the artisan's craft skill and seniority, often represented by the *Panchayat,* literally an association of elders. Gradually, the hierarchy representing this organization came to be identified with a hierarchy of control. Early evidence refers to the artisan/merchant guild also having a legal status, sometimes, an exclusive right to produce and sell a certain product within a territorial limit. The system is perhaps best exemplified by the Bhil robber king Raghoji Naik granting a monopoly of silk weaving at Yeola in Maharashtra to a group of *Gujar Vanis* at Yeola leading to the origin of the famous Yeola silk; or the Peshwa chartering out a similar right to a group of migrant *Momin* weavers at Pune.[6]

As a corporate body, the social organization of artisans had developed some measures of collective action regulating occupational and social life of their members. There must have been important variations in the nature of this control — urban-rural, craft-specific, regional/ethnic and similar others. The ways and means by which this control was actually exercised still remains largely unknown, since conventional sources dealing with these organizations are hard to come by. Nevertheless, some of the areas of this control can be clearly identified.

The exclusion of outsiders from their specific craft was one such area. Keeping the technique of production a closely guarded secret among members of the group did this. Hence, Dutch attempts to produce 'the Gujarat-type cloth' in Bengal failed because of the Gujarat weavers' refusal to divulge their secrets to their counterparts in Bengal.[7] The community organization of artisans also tried to control the quality of production and labour hours. The *Asur/Agaria* myths and legends regarding the use of iron-ore, the variety of logs to be used in the furnace for smelting, and the whole range of rituals relating to the *Kansari* craft-technique were actually intended to standardize the quality of production.[8] Some nineteenth century evidence also refers to the artisan guild regulating labour hours. Thus in 1873, Ahmedabad brick-potters' *Panch* (guild) finding that some of their members not getting work hastily decided, '... as there was not enough work for all, no member should be allowed to work extra hours'. In all probability, this was in pursuance of the practice traditionally followed by them.[9]

The artisan's organization also enforced the exclusion of women from craftwork similar to what guilds in medieval Europe had done in the period from fifteenth to seventeenth centuries.[10] Resorted to mainly as a security device, this happened only occasionally in India, *Kansaris* and *Sankharis* of Bengal, the *Chitrakar* of Rajasthan being some of the important examples of similar exclusion. In the changing social environment of the nineteenth century India, some artisan groups rigidly enforced the exclusion of women as a means of claiming a higher social status - a point, which remains out of the scope of the present discussion.[11]

In the urban manufacturing centre, the social structure of control over production and disposal of artisan goods was more clearly defined.[12] Sometimes, those at the top of this hierarchy, in addition to their usual authority over artisans, also had a kind of economic control; acting as their agents, receiving orders from the merchant and distributing the work among fellow artisans. Smaller the group and more skilled its work, the more well organized and efficient was the control. Evidence of similar control was found among the urban-based small artisan groups even in the mid-eighteenth century. Hameeda Hossain informs us that the headman of *Rafugars* in Dhaka was a powerful man with important control over his fellow craftsmen exercised through the distribution of work against orders that he received from the merchant.[13]

In their pristine form, these organizations were run on the basis of *panchayet,* the headman assisted by elders. With most of the artisan's caste being endogamous, most important form of control exercised by the *panchayet* was marriage. Everyone had to abide by the decision of the *panchayet* for the marriage of his daughter / son. Even when not settled, every marriage had to be formalized by the *panchayet,* which also arranged the feast on payment of the customary *(riti)* fee to it.

Eventually these organizations passed under the control of a coterie of powerful members, with headship becoming hereditary. Thus the headman of the weaver's *Mahanadu* of Kanchipuram, known as *Mahatmana* or *Senapati,* was the highest executive authority, whose jurisdiction spread to seventy-two *nadus.* Even in early nineteenth century, the hereditary chief of the *Jadera* weavers, called *Shittigar,* with the assistance of a Council settled all disputes and levied fines on 'those who transgressed the rules of the caste.' *Jiyamana,* the hereditary chief of the *Togotaru* weavers, also had a similar authority.[14] Similarly among *Gadulia Lohars,* a backward cluster of nomadic blacksmiths of Eastern Rajashtan, the powerful five or the *panch* were also the most prosperous persons of their community.

Early European traders, in their notion of decadent urban guilds of contemporary Europe, failed to realize the importance of these caste/occupation-based artisan organization in India. In order to buy cheap, therefore, they tried in vain to forge a direct relationship with the primary producer - a move opposed by both weaver and the traditional merchant already in that trade. Hence, early European records refer to the organized opposition of weavers to European merchants operating in the urban manufacturing centers, largely dominated by their Indian and other Asian counterparts. Sometimes, the weaver-merchant combine even tried to dictate terms to early European traders. In 1630, for instance, Gujarat weavers had refused to sell cloth to English traders until they stopped buying thread from the local market, which pushed up the supply price of their most important raw material causing difficulties to weavers in general.[15] What Europeans had ignored was that a merchant-outsider had to approach through a rigid hierarchical structure of the caste/locality/product/technique based artisans' social organization. Although the size of this structure varied from one centre to other, there was some kind of uniformity in the character of their organization.

Studying weaving villages of Coromandel in the late seventeenth and early eighteenth centuries S. Arasaratnam thus argued, '... Companies had no direct access to the weaving village and that the agent of the movement of goods from the loom to the port was the merchant - and through a variety of persons he used to achieve this.'[16] In reality, this was a continuation of the earlier system, widely followed even by the Mughal official willing to procure bulk goods that were not readily available in the market. Abul Hassan thus directed Mughal officials concerned to contact the artisan's headman. He states, 'Officers of the Imperial Government have reports that 210 *kudi* of cloth of the *sahan, barabarah, dosuti* and *thati* varieties ... are required. Urge the officers of Jaipur, Bhadrak, and other *mahals* (areas) in your *faujdari* (an administrative unit) to get them ready quickly. The price of these things should be deducted from the amount due from the *Amlas*. The *Amlas* should advance to the weaver ... money for the things ordered. First, settle the price with the help of the brokers. Then take bonds with the attestation of the brokers for the delivery of goods in time.'[17] The broker belonged to the weaver's organization, often the most well-off member of the particular group like the *Coppudarudu* or *Kopdar* of the Tamil weaving village or the headman of Dhaka *Rafugars,* already discussed earlier. Writing on the early nineteenth century Gujarat, Shireen Mehta also referred to 'a variety of organizational patterns in the case of the artisan *panch*', also identifying 'intermediate artisans between great merchants and petty artisans.[18]

Process of Mobility and the Question of Leadership

A mobility process thus distinguished the pre-colonial production organization. This is clearly indicated by the way it responded to market expansion. In order to produce more, traditional organization always inducted unskilled labour at the lower level. It generated a kind of mobility, with the existing artisan concentrating on skilled work, while leaving the production of coarse and bulk goods to the new entrant, who eventually hardened into a separate group. A continuous process of sub-caste formation within the larger caste cluster of the specific artisan group thus worked in all major industries affected by market expansion, complicating the simple scenario - the much-hyped unchanging character of the caste-based production organization.

Another important source of this mobility was the leadership process indigenous to the artisan's organization. Leadership in a similar situation required four important attributes - industrial skill, enterprise; a little accumulation of capital and trust of the fellow artisan generated through social affinity and interaction. An enterprising artisan stepping into the role of a petty merchant was logical to the exclusiveness of the caste-based production organization, which discouraged the artisan's direct dealing with a merchant outsider.

More often than not, therefore, an enterprising artisan could become a trader, disposing of goods produced by others in addition to his own, and in the way could eventually assume the petty-capitalist functions; subordinating his one-time craft fellows to financial control they could not foresee earlier. Far from being an impediment, social institutions by ensuring a sort of occupational monopoly had in fact created conditions for the powerful artisan to scale the ladder. The person, who succeeded in achieving material prosperity through his enterprise, yet keeping himself attached to the group of his origin, was readily accepted as its leader.

For medieval South India, we have a number of temple inscriptions referring to the weaver making land and other forms of donations to the temple.[19] This is indicative of two things - that a group of weavers owned a sizeable amount of land, which was by itself a measure of social status in medieval society, and that weavers had felt an urge to socially validate their material achievements.

Who were these weavers and what was the actual size of this group are some of the questions that need to be answered. It seems these weavers actually refer to a small group of what may be called improving weavers emerging from the rank through the process of evolution of 'petty mode of production', and gradually attaining the status of weaver-merchant with capitalist production functions. This process was closely intertwined with the question of caste leadership.

Significantly, an important change in the nature and volume of the temple donation made by the weaver took place in the late medieval period. The donation made by the weaver in the Chola period was mostly nominal in nature, while those made by weavers in the later period (Vijayanagar) were major donations such as 'the gift of land, the setting up of deities or the construction of temples'.[20] The changing nature of donation by the weaver to the temple over fairly a long period, therefore, seems to suggest a consolidation in the position of the weaver-merchant. From the rank of 'improving weavers', therefore, there emerged a few immensely rich weavers, thus assuming the role of the merchant capitalist with extensive control over a large number of weavers.

An indirect evidence of this change is the use of the title *Chetty* or *Nayakar* by weavers, as one comes across in some of the late medieval epigraphic records of South India. Admittedly, both the term point to the weaver attaining merchant status, weavers used the latter title only during the Chola period. The title *Chetty* was used both by the *Kaikkola* (i.e. the group of coarse weavers) and *Devangulu* weavers of South India, indicating a fairly large and 'a more rapid movement among the weavers to mercantile occupations.'[21] V. Ramaswamy has argued that 'The title *Chetty* affixed to the names of weavers shows they must gradually have risen to the rank of merchants.'

Similarly, a sixteenth century record found in Chingleput describes the *Kaikkolar,* originally a weaving caste, as one of the leading merchant communities of the region.[22] By the late seventeenth and early eighteenth century, *Kaikkola* weavers in Coromandel thus used titular names of *Mudali* and *Nayanar.* This was an attempt on the part of the '*Kaikkolar* weavers, who had moved to merchandising' to claim a distinct identity. The *Devangulu* weaver had similar sub-groups.[23] The *Diary* of *Strensham Master* (1680) thus referred to one Kunna Cundala Chengama acting as a chief merchant for the Company at Masulipatnam, who had assumed the title of *Chila Sevappa.* 'The prefix *Chila Sevappa* literally means cloth dyer and indicates that the dyer had risen to the status of chief merchant for the Company'[24]; clearly comparable with the finisher-merchant of Europe during the early phase of proto-industrialization.

Shifting attention from the great merchant operating at a major port city to the local level, we often come across a group of artisans acting as the fulcrum between the market and the community of artisans they were socially attached to. A case in point is *Kopudarudu,* or *Copdar* in early records of the English East India Company. Originally a weaver, the *Kopudarudu* 'had gradually risen up the economic ladder' and was the weaver's linkman with the Company.[25] Similarly, the weaver's *Panch* (guild) of Ahmedabad used to sell cloth to foreign merchants only through *Karidia,* a weaver-turned-trader.[26]

In the Andhra region, *Nattavar* of the weaving village usually came from the category of the head weaver. The term *Nattavar* derives from the word Natta - the person who controls an authority - and *Var* means the great, also used as a form of salutation. Collectively, the term *Nattavar* implies the most notable of influential persons, thus comparable with the similar term *Mahattama* as the chief of each guild was called in ancient India.

The promotion of a head weaver to the office of the *Nattavar* was in reality an outcome of his acquiring a status higher than his fellow weavers, usually by virtue of his enterprise. The head weaver 'had drawn themselves away from the mass of weavers by their ownership of land and / or loom into a position of caste leadership. The *Nattavar* and head weaver were the leader of weavers, looking after their general interest vis-a-vis the merchant and the state.' [27] Here was, therefore, an increased opportunity for the enterprising person to further expand his activities.

Perhaps the best evidence of the artisan acquiring merchant status comes from the late pre-colonial Bengal. Here we have a caste cognate called the *Kayet-Tanti*, literally the *Kayastha*-weaver. The *Kayastha* switching to weaving was in reality extremely unlikely. Primarily a literate caste, *Kayasthas* in Bengal held a ritual rank next only to the Brahmin with whom they shared their social habits and customs. Hence, the *Kayastha* could hardly take to weaving in a group sufficient to form a distinct sub-division of their own within the larger caste-cluster of weavers. The more so, because in the *Kayastha* caste tradition an illiterate *Kayastha* or the one not pursuing a clerical occupation, which they were very proud of, was often looked down upon as 'a creature with no right for existing whatsoever'.

Hence, a *Kayastha* taking to weaving would mean sacrificing his high social position in favour of the low ritual status of the weaver, always an object of mockery and ridicule to the literate class. It is likely that a section of prosperous weavers (*Tanti*) had improved their social position by virtue of their material achievements, hence assumed titles traditionally used by the *Kayastha*. In fact, this was a dominant trend widely found among lower social groups. In order to justify their social aspiration, lower social groups always tried to appropriate to themselves attributes of the higher group and slowly dissociated themselves from their not-so-well-off caste-craft fellows adhering to their ancestral occupation.

In Dhaka, a group of weavers (*Tantis*) had given up weaving to concentrate on trade in capital, raw cotton and textile goods; also working as the collaborator of European companies. Assuming the title of *Seth* and *Basak*, they had eventually hardened into the highest sub-caste of the *Tanti*, called *Barobhag* or the elder. The so-called *Kayet-tanti*, described in the weaver's caste tradition as *Chotobhag*, literally the Younger, stood just next to the *Seth* and *Basak*. The two groups were distinguished by their relative distance from weaving; while the former had fully dissociated itself from the loom, the latter was still directly involved in weaving; indicating a process of social mobility of the small group of improving weavers; similar to those in the medieval South India referred to above. Significantly, the *Barobhag* and *Chotobhag* sub-divisions also existed among *Sankharis* or the conch-shell worker of Dhaka possibly for the same reason.

On the whole, the rise of a group of merchants from the artisan's rank had been an outcome of the pressure in-built into the traditional production system. In an expanding market condition, the simple scenario of the artisan combining in him all the functions of procurement of raw material, manufacturing and marketing the product could not continue for long. The pressure for diversification in the context of the compulsion of the social system had thus eventually encouraged intermediary functions from among the more enterprising members of their own caste/ community or technique based group of artisans.

Some Case Studies

(i) Artisan-turned-great merchant: Gurucharan and Taraknath Pramanik of Calcutta

A classic example of the artisan's rising to merchant status through expansion of family trade was the Pramanik family of Shimla-Kansaripara of the nineteenth century Calcutta. Taraknath Pramanik (1816-1883) was the most notable person of this family. Known as the *Kangsabanik-kula-tilak* or the Glory of the *Kangsabanik,* he has been described in the *Kansari* caste literature as the richest and hence the most powerful man of their community. Not only among the members of his own caste, Taraknath was well known and a highly respected person in Calcutta of his times.

Significantly, the use of the title *Pramanik* by itself refers to a process of social mobility of lower occupational groups. Used by a cluster of potters located in Pabna, the title *Pramanik* actually denotes a particular group of potters known as the *Daspara ghar,* a *Gain* or a sub-caste of the larger caste cluster of the *Kumhar or Kumor,* as the potter was traditionally known in Bengal.

In reality, however, *Pramaniks* were an off-shoot of the much larger conglomerate of heterogeneous occupational groups such as the *Tanti, Teli, Napit, Kumhar, Goala. Bauri, Bagdi* and *Dom,* literally the weaver, oil-presser, barber, potter, milkman, bird-catcher, sweeper and basket-maker; as also similar other nomadic groups at the bottom of traditional occupational structure. The title *Paramanik* was used by all of them. Unspecific of occupation and hence a misnomer, the term was actually a calling - a formal way of addressing the low-born by his high caste fellow. Slow and unnoticed, the term *Paramanik* came to be used as a suffix to the name of the person belonging to large number of lower occupational groups - a convention, which the later-day census enumerator gave an official approval to.

Hence the *Pramanik's* manufacturing copper utensil, which in Bengal was the caste specific occupation of another workgroup called the *Kansari,* holding a somewhat higher social and occupational status than the *Paramanik* or *Pramanik,* is indicative of a fairly long-drawn process of their vertical migration; in course of which they might have changed their occupation several times before finally settling for the *Kansari's* job. When did the ancestor of the *Pramanik* of Shimla-Kansaripara switch from the potter's work to copper working cannot be stated. In their oral tradition, as recorded by Panchanan Roy Kavyatirtha in the early 1930s,[28] Pramanik claimed their descend from one Babulal, who lived at Mirkala near Shahaganj in Hooghly. It further adds that an unknown ancestor of Babulal had shifted from Saptagram to Hooghly, formerly a small Portuguese outpost. The latter had replaced Saptagram as the port city after its adjacent river Saraswati got silted up. What emerges, therefore, is an obscure account of the migration of a group of potters from Pabna in the north to Saptagram in central Bengal and their eventual separation from their traditional occupation to take to utensil manufacturing.

Necessary evidence to cross-examine the oral tradition of the *Paramanik* family is hard to come by. Nevertheless, two important points can be cited here in support of the Pramanik's account. Firstly, the utensil manufacturing, as I have analyzed elsewhere, underwent a significant transformation at Saptagram. What had been earlier a migratory craft of an essentially marginal group of nomadic *Kansari* coppersmith was slowly transformed into a sedentary industry catering to a fairly large and stable demand. A change in the *Kansari's* tool technique and their process of manufacturing utensil following the fusion of an essentially local craft with that of the north Indian coppersmith did this. Consequently, the demand for labour in the utensil manufacturing increased to such an extent as to make it impossible for the hereditary *Kansari* artisan to meet; thus creating an opportunity for the cheap non-*Kansari* worker to join the utensil industry at its lower level.[29]

How is it that potters had come from far away Pabna to join the *Kansari's* industry at Saptagram? Favourably located, Pabna and much of the adjacent areas of northern Bengal were closely interconnected with the central-western Bengal through their river systems. Boatloads of agricultural products, notably paddy, thus moved to the rice deficient areas of the *Rarh* or south-western Bengal, particularly the eastern fringe of it and on their return journey collected raw cotton, textiles, raw silk and silk goods, salt, iron, copper, brass and bell-metal utensil, conch-shell and etc. There were innumerable small trading networks based on local circuits and manned by what could be called *a la* Marika Vicziani 'men of straw' or small entrepreneurs.[30] Similar networks could be found in almost all major branches of trade in the early nineteenth century Bengal.

Referring to two such networks of local trade could be relevant here. Small groups of *Kansari* traders from Nabadwip, Khagra and Malda used to go on seasonal selling tour in Bagura, Pabna, Rajsahi and Jessore in large boat, called *Kisti*, laden with all sorts of copper/brass and bell-metal utensils; selling these articles partly for cash and partly for the old scrap ware, as and when the occasion emerged. Usually their business trip commenced immediately after the rainy season and continued throughout the winter months, making one or two bouts of trade as the market situation demanded. A lesser group of potter-traders from northern and eastern Bengal, made similar trips to the western and central Bengal districts fairly at the same time of the year. They carried with them small and sundry pots in their boats. The usual practice was to sell the pot in lieu of the quantity of grain, mostly paddy, it holds to its brim - a practice known among the potter of eastern Bengal as the *Ganoal* or selling direct to the user of distant village.[31]

Since the nature of trade changed only too slowly in earlier times, these local networks of trade existing in early nineteenth century, actually indicates the commercial tradition prevailing in Bengal long since. The point to note is, at lower levels of commercial organization these groups were interconnected and often complementary to each other. Contrary to the conventional notion of insularity of the village-based production organization, there was, therefore, a scope of inter-sectoral exchange of information, goods and services, brought about over fairly a large space. All these encouraged movement of labour from the surplus sector to the deficient one, promising higher returns. It was in this context of the intermeshing of a backward hinterland with a large market centre, that a group of Pabna potters' joining the *Kansari's* industry at Saptagram does not seem incredible.

Not much is known about what happened to the potter-turned-brazier Pramanik at Hooghly. The Pramanik family resurfaced again with one Madanmohon, who had shifted from Hooghly to the Company's Calcutta sometime in the 1730s, possibly in search of security during the recurrent Maratha raids of south-western Bengal. Madanmohon relocated his family at the southern end (Shimla) of the *Basak's* Sutanuti and started his factory (*Saal*) for manufacturing copper/brass and bell-metal utensil. Here, the family flourished and Madanmohon died as a well-off artisan of the colonial Calcutta's *Kansari* cluster called Shimla-Kansaripara.

As in similar other trade, Calcutta in those days had been rapidly developing as a market for traditional utensil to cater to the demand for cookeries of its newly emerging urban class. The industry was further encouraged by the increasing availability of cheap ingots of copper/brass from overseas through various channels of foreign trade. Madanmohon's more enterprising son, Gurucharan Pramanik, had seized this opportunity and soon combined his family occupation with wholesale trade in the traditional metal ware. To the family manufacturing activity, therefore, he had added a number of shops - two at Chandni and one at the Bara Bazaar - selling copper and brass utensil. However, the real test of enterprise lay in his launching a ship-repairing firm called Caledonia Dock on the western side of the river Hooghly at Salkia in the Howrah district. Established long before the development of Calcutta's cluster of dockyards, Gurucharan's firm was certainly one of the few early enterprises, if not the Bengali pioneering one, in this wholly non-conventional branch of trade.

Born in a family of brazier-artisan, Gurucharan's establishing a ship-repairing business deserves attention. The name of the firm suggests a European influence, although nothing is known about the collaboration, if any. In pre-steamship days, bottom of the ship's keel sailing high seas had to be covered with copper/brass sheet to ward off the possible hazards of submarine magnetic rocks. After two or three voyages, the metal sheet had to be replaced - an exigency encouraging regular imports of similar sheet of copper into Calcutta from Europe. Initially, Gurucharan was interested in procuring cheap scrap sheet that he recycled in his utensil factory and then decided to go in for a dock of his own. He concentrated on sheet replacement, which gave him a steady supply of scrap sheet. A pioneering enterprise, Gurucharan's dock brought him immense fortune, encouraging him to gradually extend its facilities. A wholesale timber trade at Nimtala, in collaboration with one Gangadhar Sarkar, followed soon.

The Pramanik family really made a tryst with the destiny under its next head - Taraknath Pramanik, Gurucharan's only son. He had extended the family trade in manufacturing and marketing of copper/brass utensil, thus considerably adding to the number of shops that he had inherited. He had organized these shops into a sort of corporate, entrusting management of each shop with the seniormost person associated with it and thus encouraged a spirit of competition among managers in charge of different shops. He also allowed them a share of the profit earned by a shop manager in addition to his usual salary. He had also initiated trade in imported brass/copper sheet, which he began to send to different parts of Bengal, Orissa, Central Provinces, north and western India. The major port for the whole of eastern and northern India, Calcutta during this period had been importing large amount of metal sheets, which railways catered to as far as Punjab.[32]

In 1852-53, Taraknath upgraded the dock his father had established at Salkia to a dock with latest facility, which eventually became the primary source of his minting money. To cope with the increasing volume of his trade in copper and brass sheets he had also started direct import of metal sheet from Europe, particularly Austria, while purchasing two ships for the same. His trade in timber also expanded in consequence. A close friend of the Parsi merchant, Rustomji Manikji, Taraknath had been one of the leading merchants of contemporary Calcutta. As a result of all these, Taraknath had amassed immense fortune in his lifetime; most of which he had spent in charity. In those days, Burra Bazaar, the great market of Calcutta, was divided into a number of *chowk* and *patty*, literally quarter and locality localizing specific branch of trade. A good number of these belonged to this *Kansari* merchant. The Taraknath Pramanik *chowk*, which still exists in the present day Burra Bazaar, bears a testimony to his achievements as a merchant.[33]

(ii) Artisan-turned-great merchant: Gurudas Das of Nabadwip

A near contemporary of Taraknath Pramanik, Gurudas Das of Nabadwip is an identical case of a *Kansari* artisan rising to the rank of the *mahajan* of *mahajans*, or the great merchant. A former capital, Nabadwip was a holy city and a centre of classical learning of medieval Bengal, which attracted wide popular attention as the cradle of the neo-*Vaishnava* movement launched by Sri Chaitanya. Like similar other artisans, the city had a cluster of *Kansaris* long since primarily catering to its steady traffic of pilgrims from different parts of Bengal, Assam, Orissa and northern India. Nabadwip *Kansaris* were a mixed population consisting of a number of sub-castes of territorial nature originating from different localities in Bengal. Sometime in the late 1780s, a group of *Kansaris* called *Kalighati*, named after the place of their earlier localization near the Kali temple at Calcutta, had migrated to Nabadwip.[34]

However, we do not know which of these groups did Gurudas actually belong to. Unlike the Pramanik of Calcutta, his antecedent is shrouded in obscurity except the fact that he was born in a poor family of hereditary *Kansari* artisan. The poverty of his early childhood had forced him to try his luck in Calcutta, then the El Dorado of the east. Here, he got the secret of his later-day commercial success. He had amassed in his lifetime a fortune enough to carve out a position of pride in contemporary society. His business networks covered nearly the whole of eastern and northern India, including Bombay, where he had a number of business establishments. Understanding the nature of his enterprise one has to take note of the changes affecting his hereditary occupation, namely, copper, brass and bell-metal manufacturing since the early nineteenth century Bengal.

The most important development, which helped the Indian brazier to expand his trade during this period, was the introduction of the imported machine-made metal sheet of brass and copper sometime at the end of the nineteenth century. By simplifying the traditional process of utensil manufacture, hence reducing its prices, the use of metal sheet had greatly encouraged its demand to expand. The effect could be compared only with the kind of impact mill-made yarn had generated in handloom weaving.

Significantly, this was yet another case of the Indian artisan's exemplary dynamism and innovativeness, largely ignored by earlier scholars in this field. Thus Tirthankar Roy has argued, 'Foreign trade did not expose brassware to any significant competition but it did substitute scrap by imported sheets wherever possible.' The important point he missed out is that brass and copper sheets had been brought to India in the beginning not for the use of the brazier, but for some other purposes. Its subsequent use by the brazier largely added to its demand in India, and had introduced a whole range of new specifications to diversify its uses.[35]

Two points need to be considered here. Unlike the mill-made yarn, which exactly looked like the hand-spun variety it had replaced, the metal sheet hardly resembled with the raw material braziers had been traditionally using in India. Secondly, there was also no organised initiative whatsoever, public or private, to popularise its use in the traditional metal ware industry; as it was done in several other cases since the early days of European trade - the filature technique and fly-shuttle loom of the earlier period and the use of aluminium ware of the later days are some of the more important cases in point.[36] Also important to note is the context in which the metal sheet came into use in traditional metal ware industry. From the closing decades of the nineteenth century, the price of copper in India had been rising as a result of the increasing diversification of its uses - electrical and industrial. In 1915, the Datta Committee on prices in India had recorded forty per cent rise in the price of copper in the Calcutta's wholesale market.[37]

Going by the large amount of evidence we have on this industry since the late nineteenth century, it was the enterprise of a few *Kansari* artisans of Bengal who had first tried this substitution. Incidentally Bengal, by the end of the nineteenth century, had been the largest centre of copper and brassware manufacturing in India. The latter was the largest industry of Bengal second only to the handloom weaving, both in terms of its localization and the size of the labour force involved. The railways, which made the transport of the low-value bulk utensil relatively cost effective, had further encouraged it.

Gurudas Das of Nabadwip[4] was one of the innovative artisans to have successfully applied metal sheet to the manufacturing of traditional utensil. Born in a poor *Kansari* family, he had moved to Calcutta to seek sustenance outside the family trade. Caste affiliation brought him to Bhabanipur, which had a sizeable *Kansari* population in those days. Here, working in a horse carriage workshop, Gurudas had been introduced to the use of imported brass/copper sheets, widely applied in the inlaying of the carriage walls.

After a few years of apprenticeship, when he also became aware of the Calcutta's trade in imported metal sheet, Gurudas returned to his hometown, took to family occupation once again; and for the first time started making traditional utensil from imported sheets of brass and copper, cheaper scrap sheet in particular. His experiments paid him good dividends, thus encouraging him to extend his trade; so much so that he himself started importing brass sheets from Europe. Eventually, he assumed the role of finisher - distributing metal sheet to *Kansari* artisans in and around Nabadwip/Burdwan, collecting unfinished ware from them in lieu of the wage and finished the unfinished ware in his factory. His son had fitted these factories with electrical lathe and polishing machines to further add to the volume of their work.

When he died in the early twentieth century, Gurudas Das had 360 warehouses and nearly 800 retail shops selling metal utensil of copper/brass/bronze and trading in scrap ware and metal sheet. Spread all over eastern and northern India, Gurudas is stated to have an average daily income of five thousand rupees from his trade in traditional utensil alone. Like Taraknath Pramanik, he had a cluster of shops in Burra Bazar (the Great Market of Calcutta), located in the *Nadia Patti,* thus named after the famous *mahajan* of Nadia - Gurudas Das. He had diversified his business, made huge investment in landed properties, indigo manufacturing, urban housing, wholesale trade in rice and oilseeds; and money-lending to boot. His landed properties, including a *Neelkuthi* (indigo manufacturing factory), were located mainly in Burdwan and Nadia, while he had his urban properties in Nabadwip, Shantipur, Dhaka, Calcutta, Benares and Bombay. At Bombay, he had wholesale trade in rice and linseed oil. We do not know whether Gurudas had any business link with his near contemporary, Taraknath Pramanik. However, there are considerable similarities in business activities between these two artisan-turned *Kansari mahajans* of the early colonial Bengal.[38]

If the local tradition of Nabadwip is to be believed even *dewans* (commercial agents) of Gurudas Das used to travel on elephants. Control over capital apart, he had also succeeded in enlisting the support of a wider community of *Kansari* artisans through a skilful combination of business enterprise with an ambition of caste leadership. The most powerful merchant of contemporary Nabadwip, the holy city owed most of its early urban development projects to this enterprising *Kansari* merchant - its municipality, the first layout of municipal roads and drains, electricity, embankment of its treacherous river. Besides he had, constructed hostels for poor students, *dharamsalas* for the ascetic, bathing *ghats* and temples in Nabadwip, Benares and at other religious places.[39]

(iii) Artisan-Turned-Petty-Merchant: Barmans of Matiary

Together with the artisan-turned-great merchant, there are similar references to the petty merchant rising from the artisan's rank and operating at local level. One such case could be the Barman family of Matiari. Matiari on the eastern bank of the river Bhagirathi in Nadia had a large cluster of *Kansari* artisans, who had shifted to that place in phases - from the erstwhile Gaur, when people abandoned the city due to the outbreak of recurrent epidemics, from Karanjal, Dainhat and Katwa in the Burdwan district probably in the early eighteenth century during the period of recurrent Maratha raids; and in the post-Partition period from the adjacent eastern Bengal districts that went to East Pakistan. Barmans were just one of several such groups of *Kansari* artisans, who had settled in Matiari and had been living on their hereditary occupation - making of utensil by traditional casting method. The adjacent river offered them excellent opportunity to ferry their ware to remote parts of eastern and northern Bengal and procure raw material and agricultural product in the way already referred to above.

Like similar other traditional center, the industry at Matiary began to decline in the early twentieth century in competition with the cheaper utensil made in Calcutta from the imported metal sheet. Hard pressed, the *Kansari* youth of Matiary thus began to move to Calcutta in large numbers to work in the utensil workshops of the city. Barmans followed the suit. After a few years of hard toil, Barmans managed to have a shop of their own in Calcutta. They combined manufacturing with small trading activities in utensil produced by their fellow artisans - an achievement, which they shared with many others.

However, a real turnaround in the situation came in the period following the Second World War. The outbreak of the war had dislocated supplies of metal sheets from Europe, encouraging the growth of a few units recycling metal scrap into sheet for utensil manufacturing. A similar unit was the Gyllinder Company near Deoghar with an outlet at Howrah, frequently visited by Barman. In the post-Partition period, when the Gyllinder Company closed its business in Bengal, Barmans somehow managed to get their Howrah unit on lease. They had initially concentrated on recycling the metal scrap into sheet and sold the same to the open market; but could not make much headway for want of capital. At that time, Ashutosh and Ajit Barman shifted some of their unit first to Dainhat and then to Matiary mainly to take advantage of cheap labour. At Matiary, their enterprise not only flourished but had also changed the traditional structure of the industry. Barmans began to produce metal sheet for their fellow *Kansari* artisans of the village, who turned them into utensil; thus reviving the old trade. The example of the Barman brothers encouraged others; the rolling and recycling units thus multiplied at Matiary. By the late 1960s, the sleepy village had been slowly transformed into a hub of commercial-industrial complex of urban nature.[40]

(iv) Weaver-Turned-Petty-Merchant of Sonamukhi

Before we conclude, reference may be made to similar other evidence of the artisan-turned-petty-merchant in the handloom sector, the most extensive industry of Bengal. Kanairudra Das was a weaver by profession and his caste affiliation, who lived at Sonamukhi, an important centre of textile manufacturing in the Bankura district of Bengal. Kanairudra started his life as an ordinary weaver producing coarse cloth. He also possessed some land, which we do not know if he had inherited from his father. Nevertheless, possessing of agricultural land had made his life easy compared to his other craft fellows. Combining weaving with small trade in textiles, he had eventually risen to the rank of the head weaver, working as an agent of the English East India Company at Sonamukhi *aurang* or collecting centre. His association with the Company made him more powerful, which eventually led to his election to the post of *mandal* or the chief spokesman of the village *panchayet*.

A similar other case was Brajamohon, *Gandhabanik* by caste, who was also a head weaver and a *mukhia* or the chief spokesman of weavers' village. Brajamohan acted as a surety of the Company's weavers in Sonamukhi and in the way became immensely rich. Anyone familiar with the nature of their activities must know that people like Brajamohan earned at the cost of both the Company and the weaver. It is interesting to cite the Board of Trade's remark on the head weaver's influence on his craft fellows. The Board of Trade argued, 'It may be proper to explain the nature of the head weaver's influence over others, which arises principally from their being able to write and read for which reason the others of whom very few had this advantage almost constantly apply for their assistance whenever involved in distress.'[41] Not always so, perhaps. Their power emerged from their position in their respective caste organization. Brajamohan had later on constructed a temple in his native village by way of justifying his claim to a higher social status.

Conclusion

The available evidence is fairly conclusive on one point that there was some amount of mobility among major artisan groups. Neither society nor the political system appears to have blocked the prospect of an enterprising artisan's promoting himself to the higher rank. If the majority of artisans in India had failed to scale the ladder and improve their lot, their failure could hardly be attributed to the so-called social and cultural barriers.

Our case studies also tend to substantiate yet another argument that artisan-turned-great merchant had failed to extend the frontier of their economic activities - shift to industrial manufacturing, similar to developments that were so common in proto-industrial Europe. Instead, they wasted their time and energy in extending putting out operations: thus, Gurudas Das having 360 warehouses and 800 retail shops spread over large parts of India. They had also wasted their scarce resources in buying up landed properties and in promoting religious and social activities at a time, when the caste/community and the technique based social solidarity of artisans had lost much of its earlier force.

Hence, both Taraknath Pramanik and Gurudas Das of our case studies more or less followed the same trend. Brought up in the liberal environment of colonial Calcutta - hub of economic activities for nearly the whole of northern and eastern India closely integrated to the metropolitan economy of England; they had failed to look beyond their immediate social environments and aspirations. On the face of it, that seems to take us closer to the position of the cultural determinist. To my mind, however, that would be an oversimplification of a complex phenomenon - a point that remains an agenda of future research.

Notes and References

1. For observations of Pelsaert and similar other contemporary European authors see Jagadish Narayan Sarkar, *Mughal Economy: Organization* and *Working,* (Calcutta, 1987), p. 99.
2. Tapan Raychaudhuri & Irfan Habib (Ed.). *The Cambridge Economic History of India,* Volume: I: c. 1200 - c. 1750, (Delhi, 1982), p. 307; Hereafter CEHI (I).
3. See his *Traditional Industry in the Economy of Colonial India.* (London, 1999), p. 60.
4. Max Weber's notion of the Hindu world view discouraging the early growth of capitalism in India. For counter arguments, read Dwijendra Tripathi, *Historical Roots of Industrial Entrepreneurship in India and Japan, A Comparative Interpretation,* (Manohar, 1997), pp. 14-17.
5. Smritikumar Sarkar, 'From autonomy to subordination : a study of the changing organization of artisanal production in colonial Bengal : the cases of the *Kansaris* and the *Sankharis*' in *The Calcutta Historical Journal,* 16:2, July-December, 1994, pp. 105-151.
6. Smritikumar Sarkar, 'Social Organization of Production etc.' in B.B. Chaudhury (Ed.), *Economic History of India,* Op.cit.
7. Tapan Raychaudhuri in *CEHI,* Vol. I, p. 285.
8. Smritikumar Sarkar, *Social Roots of Craft Technique: Blacksmiths of Colonial Eastern India,* (a research project sponsored by the Indian National Science Academy, New Delhi), Forthcoming.
9. W. W. Hunter, *Brief History of the Indian Peoples, (? 1903),* p. 98.
10. P. Kriedte, H. Medick, J. Schlumbohm, Op cit, pp. 94-95, 270-271.
11. See H. R. Sanyal, *Social Moleility* etc., Op cit: See

also Smritikumar Sarkar, 'Caste, Occupation and Social Mobility: A Study of the *Kansaris* in Colonial Bengal' in Bandyopadhyay, Sekhar *et al* (Ed.), *Bengal Communities, Development and States,* (Delhi, 1994), pp. 65-89.

12. For an interesting discussion of the point see Shirin Mehta's 'The Mahajans and the Business Communities of Ahmedabad', in Dwijendra Tripathi (ed.). *Business Communities of India.* (Delhi, 1984), pp. 173-184.

13. See Hameeda Hossain, *The Company Weavers of Bengal,* (Delhi, 1988), pp. 49-50.

14. F. H. Buchanan, *Journey from Madras* etc. Op.cit., Vol. I, p. 316; Vol. II, p. 242.

15. Surendra Gopal, *Commerce and Crafts in Gujarat,* (New Delhi, 1975), pp. 196, 202; E. W. Foster, (Ed.), *Factory Records in India,* 1661-64, Vol- I, 1618-21, (London, 1923), p. 192, Vol – II, (London, 1936), p. 208.

16. S. Arasaratnam, *Merchants, Companies and Commerce,* (Delhi, 1986), p. 265.

17. As cited by Jagadish Narayan Sarkar, Op.cit, p. 81.

18. Shireen Mehta, *Op.cit,* p. 178.

19. V. Ramaswamy, *Textiles and Weavers in Medieval South India,* (Delhi, 1985), pp. 13, 54, 97-98, 120-121.

20. V. Ramaswamy, *Textiles and Weavers in Medieval South India,* Op.cit., pp. 97-98.

21. S. Arasaratnam, *Merchants, Companies and Commerce,* Op.cit., p. 266.

22. V. Ramaswamy, Op.cit., pp. 84, 142; See also her 'Weaver Folk Traditions as a Source of History' in IESHR, 19:1, January-March, 1982, p. 48. Chicherov has also referred to the wealthiest weaver gaining the title of *Chetti* during the Vijaynagar period. A.I. Chicherov, *India : Economic Development in the 16th-18th Centuries,* (Moscow,

1971), p. 166.

23. S. Arasaratnam, *Merchants, Companies and Commerce*, Op.cit., p. 266.
24. V. Ramaswamy, 'Weaver Folk Traditions as a Source of History', Op.cit., p. 49.
25. S. Arasaratnam, 'Weavers, Merchants and Company' etc., Op.cit., p. 200.
26. Shireen Mehta, *The Mahajans and the Business Communities of Ahmedabad*, in Dwijendra Tripathi, op. cit., p. 178.
27. See his *Merchants, Companies and Commerce* etc., Op.cit, pp. 267-268.
28. Editorial note on 'Late Taraknath Pramanik' in *Mahajanbandhu, (A* monthly journal published in Bengali from Calcutta for the benefit of the Bengali merchant). Vol. I, No. 5, 1307-1308 BS. (1899-1900), pp. 113-119.
29. Smritikumar Sarkar, 'From autonomy to subordination : a study of the changing organization of artisan production in colonial Bengal, the cases of the *Kansaris* and the *Shankharis'* in *The Calcutta Historical Journal,* (University of Calcutta), 14:2, July-December, 1994, pp.105-151.also `Caste, Occupation and Social Mobility: A Study of the *Kansaris* in Colonial Bengal' in Sekhar Bandyopadhyay *et al* (Ed.), *Bengal Communities, Development and States.* (Delhi, 1994), pp. 65-89. `Indian Craft Technology: Static or Changing - *A* Case Study of the *Kansari's* Craft in Bengal 16th to 18th Centuries', *Indian Journal of History of Science,* Vol. 33 (2), 1998; pp. 131-142.
30. Marika Vicziany, 'Bombay Merchants and Structural Changes in the Export Community 1850-1880 in K.N. Chaudhuri and Clive Dewey, (Ed), *Economy and Society: Essays in Indian Economic and Social History,* (Delhi, 1979), p. 186.
31. For the *Kansari* trading networks see Smritikumar Sarkar, 'From autonomy to subordination : a study

of the changing organization of artisan production in colonial Bengal, the cases of the *Kansari* and the *Sankharis'*, op.cit. For the potter-trader seeJames Westland, *A Report on the District of Jessore: its Antiquities, its History and its Commerce*, (Calcutta, 1871), pp. 212-215.

32. In 1882-83, for instance, Punjab imported nearly forty maunds of brass and copper from Bengal by railway-, 'the greater part of this supply was in the form of sheets, ... and was used for domestic purposes'. See J. L. Kipling, 'Brass and Copper of the Punjab and Kashmir', op. cit., as cited by S. Sengupta, Op.cit, p. 205.

33. Panchanan Roy Kavyatirtha, *Taraknath Pramanik*, (Calcutta. 1937), in Bengali. Incidentally, Panchanan Roy belonged to a family of great scholastic tradition of Krittibas Ojha and Roy Gunakar Bharatchandra on the paternal and maternal side respectively. Krittibas Ojha and Bharatchandra were two noted Bengali poets of the late medieval Bengal. Panchanan's father was a great Sanskrit scholar, whose merit was recognized by Pandit Iswarchandra Vidyasagar himself. See also editorial note on 'Late Taraknath Pramanik' in *Mahajanbandhu*, op.cit., pp. 113-119.

    I am grateful to Mrs. Basanti Nandan of Calcutta for allowing me to use the book by Panchanan Roy Kavyatirtha in her family collection.

34. Smritikumar Sarkar, *'Bhabanipur: Prak-Upanibeshik Kolkatar Pratham Shilpakendra'* in *Itihas Anusandhan, VI*, (Calcutta, 1991), pp. 218-227, in Bengali.

35. Tirthankar Roy, *Traditional Industry*, op.cit, p. 131.

36. E. W. Collin had observed that the Indian brazier's knowledge of metallurgy is too good to warrant any further technical demonstration.

37. K.L. Datta, *Report on the Enquiry into the Rise of Prices in India*, 1915, (Calcutta, 1915), p. 37.

38. Interview of Sri Narayan Chandra Das, President, Gurudas Das Trust in Nabadwip, held on 23 February 1996. Letter of Sri Narayan Chandra Das to Smritikumar Sarkar, dated 25 Nov, 1997.
39. Smritikumar Sarkar, 'Caste, Occupation and Social Mobility', op.cit., p. 78.
40. This is entirely based on the data collected from Matiary, personal interview of Arun Barman, S/o Ajit Barman in particular, during the *Survey of Rural Industries in West Bengal: Matiary Chapter* under my supervision in collaboration with the Department of Cottage and Small-scale Industries, Government of West Bengal, 18-20 July 2001. I am grateful to Shri Amalendu Sarkar of Nederpara, Krishnagar and Shri Naren Mondal of Matiary for their kind assistance and my students - Shubendu Pal, Gopal Saha and Saikat Guha, who worked as field assistants, during the survey.
41. Prabhat Kumar Saha, *Some Aspects of Malla Rule in Bishnupur, 1590-1806,* (Calcutta. ?), pp. 108-109.

10

The Brown Ships in The Indian Ocean : The American Merchants and The Bengali Banians 1790-1880

Ranjan Chakrabarti

I am writing this essay because silences and slippages in history writing strike me. The closing decades of the 18th century saw a rapid expansion of America's trade with the world's major ports. The seafarers of New England started undertaking voyages to distant lands discovering trade routes and returning home with stories, gifts and souvenirs. During this period India-trade came to occupy a special place in American maritime experiment. Calcutta, in particular, became a favourite haunt of the Yankee merchants. Both the Indian and the American sides benefited from this early commercial interaction. It advantaged some of the aspiring Indian banians to collaborate directly with the American ship-owners and supercargoes. Ramdulal De, one of the leading banians of the city, turned millionaires by tying up with early American business. Again Elias Hasket Derby, the Cabots, the Crowningshields, William Gray and others amassed vast wealth by embarking upon this trade. But this particular branch of economic history remains as one of the least explored areas of history. This slippage has encouraged this researcher to venture into this particular subject.

The paper has three major focuses and each of these has been placed under a separate section. The first section notes the broad pattern of the trade. The second section concentrates on one particular family, namely the Browns of Providence. This section attempts to present a blow-up account of the Providence-Calcutta trade. The final section brings to light the role played by the Bengali banians in this trade.

Cut off from the West Indies, their traditional market, the newly independent US began to look elsewhere for new and profitable markets. If circumstances at home compelled the early Americans to leave their newly independent country in search of trade, the situation largely created by the Napoleonic Wars, gave them an opportunity to replace Europe's East India trade.[1] Napoleon's global war on the U.K. taxed Britain's naval strength so severely that England was forced to master all her ships to save the Empire. India was not a seller's market for America. Mostly the European population in Calcutta was interested in American products. The merchants of Salem, Boston, New York and Philadelphia brought rum, fish, spermaceti candles, Madeira wine, mackerel, beef, beer, ice etc. On their voyage homeward the Americans took tea, sugar, silk, cotton, linseed, saltpeter, and gunny bags.[2]

Section I: Broad Pattern of the Trade

It is difficult to bring out the broad pattern of this early American trade. The nature of the trade was not very well-knit. It had no fixed form. The ships would visit various ports for various purposes depending on the market or the freight rates. The ships would touch upon ports like Canton and might go as far as Australia. Besides engaging in carrying trade, Americans found a rewarding preoccupation in coastal trading in India (Bombay-Madras-Calcutta, Coromandel-Mauritius-Ceylon-Rangoon-Batavia).[3] There are plenty of instances in which the vessel could be sold off. We learn from Brown Family papers for example that the Brig Providence owned by the Browns, which visited India in August 1790, was advertised for sale.[4] There was no fixed destination for ships. The purchase and sales of cargo depended to a large extent on the condition of the market and the freight rates at both the American and the Indian ends. The following extracts of a letter to Captain William Rodman of Ship Hamilton, which visited Calcutta from Providence in the month of May 1795, would bring out this uncertain character of Indo-American business of the period. The Browns of Providence who were conducting a booming India-trade at that time sent this letter. "............China goods probably will be very less as long as the European War lasts we could wish to have a handsome property vested in them and suggest for your Government that in case you are obliged to proceed to Calcutta and can't hit upon a good arrangement for your return cargo that you employ the ship afreighting in India and proceed to Canton the very first of the next season either from Bombay with a load of cotton on freight from some other part of India. Probably you can get a freight from Calcutta round to Bombay when you can take on board the cotton and be ready to sail as soon as the monsoons changes also as to be in Canton by the first of August or September 1796 ....". If you can get a moderate freight from Calcutta to some other part of India and go to Bombay and load on freight for Canton we think it will be much the best arrangement for you and we hope greater freight for cotton will be given than what Dennison had".[5] Instances like this are many.

American merchants always lacked working capital because few ships could be fitted out for less than $50,000 and ports east of the Cape of Good Hope would accept nothing except Spanish milled dollars and specie. We find some instances however, when bills of credit drawn on London were accepted on the recommendation of the rich Bengali Banians who operated as American agents. The American vessels sailing towards India were usually packed with dollars and bullion. To cite just one example the Calcutta account book of ship Arthur owned by the Browns of Providence shows that an amount of Rs. 1 Lakh 36 thousand was raised by selling gold bars, Spanish dollars, Dutch guilders etc. This amount was used to purchase the return cargo.[6] One remarkable thing about the Americans in India was that they never established a commercial house here as they did in China. Nor did they use the European agency houses. Instead they made use of the services of the Indian brokers who were willing to work on two or two and a half percent commission.

An 'East India merchant' in New England enjoyed more social prestige than even the cotton millionaires. To have an office in India Wharf, Boston or at India Point, Providence conferred a special distinction. Among sailors, the men who had made an East India voyage had a special place in society.[7] It was commonly said of a pretty well-bred girl "She is good enough to marry an East India Captain". In Salem there was a Marine Society called the East India Marine Society. It's membership was restricted to Salem shipmasters or supercargoes "who shall have actually navigated the seas near the Cape of Good Hope or Cape Horn". It was an exclusive club, a patent of nobility. Small adventurers varying in amount from a box of codfish to several thousand dollars in specie were carried both by China and East India traders. On the brig Caravan of Salem, captain Augustine Heard took 200 silver-dollars for his father, the same for each brother, and from 20-100 dollars for sundry maiden aunts and retired sea-captains. Numerous friends requested him to purchase for their wives, Indian silk and muslins. Another trader Henry Pickering wanted a Sanskrit Bible and three children gave him a dollar each to invest in Calcutta. It was a very profitable trade and according to one estimate it was possible to earn $300 by investing $100 in India trade. There is no wonder therefore that 'To the farthest gulf for the wealth of India' was the appropriate motto on Salem's city seal. As feudalism had been a fact of culture in Medieval Europe (Marc Bloch), similarly, India trade had been a fact of culture in colonial and post-colonial New England. The popular story from Cohasset is illustrative of this culture. The story runs like this: One Spring evening (somewhere in New England) young Southward Pratt, farmers bare foot boy, goes out as usual to drive the cattle home. There was no trace of the lad. Something called him from the sea. He had obeyed the call. A few years later Pratt returned with bronzed face and with lot of wealth (understandably from the Indies) to marry Martha, his childhood girlfriend. Thereafter they lived happily forever.[8] Such Pratts were many in nineteenth century New England. One gets a graphic account of this maritime culture in Melville's Moby Dick too.[8a]

The early profits of the trade attracted more people and the trade grew to a vast proportion between 1790 and 1815. The period between 1815 and 1860 saw a gradual decline of the trade as the merchants of New England turned to cotton spinning. Indo-American trade however, went on till the

1880s. When the American trade began India was still anchored to medieval commerce. India was then selling her cotton to the World and raking in a large amount of silver. This trade also demonstrated how the traffic changed into colonial trade during this period, from cottons for export and silver for import we switched to raw materials like leather, oilseeds and jute and contented us with money bills instead of silver.[9]

Section II : The Merchants of Providence

Next we turn to focus on the initiative of the merchants of Providence in India trade. Providence today is the capital of Rhode Island situated about 50 miles north of Boston. The city of Providence has an enormous history It remains as one of the most colonial towns in the United States. The streets and mansions in this city are older than the American Revolution. The streets, in particular, bear the names of those merchants who were engaged in the India trade: Ormsbee, Sheldan, Brown etc. etc. After the Revolution, Providence entered on an era of great prosperity. This was brought about by her shipping trade, and especially by the trade with China and the East Indies. If we could transmit ourselves to Providence of the late 18th Century and take a look at the Providence River we could find it much wider than it is today. We could see the river crowded in sailing ships of all kinds of brigs, sloops, schooners etc. We could see around them, in them, on them, great number of men working, wearing trousers and shirts of soil canvas, lifting bales, boxes and kegs. Some are using carts and wagons pulled by horses and a few oxen. The traveller to the Providence of the past could smell the stench of salt, sweat and fish, tar and horses. You could hear a hubbub of shouting, hammering, even singing, noises punctuated by the neighing of horses, the crack of whips, the barking of dogs, the ceaseless cry of seagulls swooping above. Providence is not an ordinary city; even today there are stone posts on curbs for tying up horses, blocks to mount for climbing into carriages. There was lot of sea-favoring activities in colonial and post-revolutionary Providence.[10] The merchants of Providence too along with their counterparts in Boston, Philadelphia, Salem and New York embarked upon the profitable India trade. Particularly noteworthy in this connection is the initiative taken by the Browns of Providence. John Brown's house is now on 52 Power Street. The old counting house of Brown and Ives is No 50 South Main Street and is still used by the descendants of the Browns. In the good old days the bales and packages were brought on board ship to the wharf just across the street. The John Brown House was constructed in 1786 and referred to by John Adams as one of the magnificent houses of the continent. The Browns had wider area of business. From 1753 onwards the Browns were manufacturers as well as merchants and ship owners. The character of their business came more and more to be shaped and influenced by the fact that they were seeking markets not only for goods purchased at home and abroad, but also for the products of their own making in their Rhode-Island plants. In 1750 Obadiah Brown began to manufacture and sell spermaceti candles, laying the groundwork for a business, which was in later years to become one of the most successful and far reaching of all the Brown enterprises. The Browns were also drawn into the marine insurance business. In 1765 the Browns went into the iron business. Their early maritime contact with the West Indies help them to secure capital for setting up their manufacturing units. Between 1783 and 1860 the Brown family ran more than five business companies or partnerships in Providence. Their India trade was mostly carried on by the Brown and Ives and Brown and Francis.[11]

The firm of Brown and Francis of Providence sent the 1000-ton General Washington (Jonathan Dennison, Master) to India in 1787. The General Washington, typical of those to be used in New England's India trade, cleared Providence on December 27, carrying anchors, sail cloth, munitions of war, claret, proper, cider, hams, chocolates, cheese and spermaceti candles. General Washington went first to Madeira, thence to the Cape of Good Hope and the coast of India, where it engaged in coastal trading with Pondicherry and Madras, much to the annoyance of the officials of the East India Company, and on to Malacca. Finally, from Madras the vessel went to Canton and returned to Rhode Island via the West Indies.[12]

The return cargo of the General Washington was valued at $99,848, one dollar invested in the Eastern venture brought three dollars to the firm. Encouraged by the handsome profits, Brown and Francis sent two ships to India in 1789. One was the General Washington, which sailed for Bombay on December 30, and the other was the brig Providence (Richard Low, Master), which sailed on November 20 for Madeira, Tenerife and Bombay. Another the brig Hope (Benjamin Page, Master), left for Bombay on January 09, 1790.[13] Thus John Carter Brown entered into the India trade to a greater extent than had merchants in Philadelphia, New York or Boston. Having realized huge profits from the several Indian voyages of General Washington, the Browns decided to use a second ship for their trade in India.[14] In the Providence Gazette of October 11,1794 we find the following report: 'Wednesday morning last was launched a new, strong and elegantly built ship belonging to Browns, Benson and Ives,. ...A number of smart able bodied seamen, belonging to the town of Providence and its vicinity - also a few stout, young raw hands, who are desirous of going to sea - are invited to ship on board the new ship John Jay bound for the East Indies".[14] The John Jay under captain Olney sailed from providence in December 1794 with captain Samuel Snow as the Super Cargo. A Super cargo was the representative on shipboard of owners and consigners. He took no part in navigation. A captain may act as super cargo especially when he was a relative of the owners. The voyage of John Jay was very profitable. The Browns continued with their Indian business until the 1820s. That their Indian trade was growing in size is evident from the fact that they continued to engage more vessels in the business. Between 1800 and 1820 the ships either directly owned by the Browns or in which they had interest, which visited the Indian ports like Calcutta, Bombay, Madras were Stephen, Arthur, Hamilton, Rambler, Providence etc. The contemporary Providence newspaper, the Providence Gazette throws ample light on the great demand of Indian products in the USA. Among the earliest is one dated May 22, 1790, which announced a public sale of Indian products like printed calicoes, muslins of all sorts etc. In the *United States Chronicle* of July, 09, 1789 we find the following bit of news : "On Sunday last arrived here from the East India, the ship General Washington, Captain Jonathan Dennison, with a valuable cargo of the Productions and Manufactures of that Quarter of the Globe. The General Washington was fitted from this port in December 1787, and made her voyage out and home, in 19 months and a few days, having been at the following ports - Madeira, Madras, Pondicherry, Canton, St. Helena, Eustatia; - and what is very remarkable has brought home, in good health, every person she carried out, except a black boy, who was by Accident lost overboard. In the General Washington came Samuel Shaw, Consul for the U.S.A. at the port of Canton etc."[15] The usual method followed in India trade by the Providence firm of the Browns was to start off with the mixed Cargo assembled from the West Indies and New England, peddle it out at the Cape of Good Hope, Mauritius, and various ports in the East Indies, picking up assorted staffs here and there, taking freight when occasion offered, before returning home. In 1800, the Browns imported from the East India goods valued at $726,924, in 1804, the value was $ 887,000 and in 1806 it was $ 662,000. In 1806 the Arthur alone brought to Providence from Calcutta cargo worth Rs. 181,693.14.5, and Brown firm realized $ 158,627.78 from the sale of the import. The record of the first voyage from Providence to India and the China seas is completed by the manifest of the cargo brought back to Providence by the General Washington. This manifest, which antedates the Federal administration of the customs revenue in Rhode Island, is found in the State Import Book for 1788-89, and is especially valuable because it is apparently the sole instance where a valuation of the entire cargo is given. From this manifest we learn that General Washington brought to her owners a cargo valued at $99,848.The principal items were: 240,000 pounds of tea (25 cents per pound), silk valued at $1400, cotton goods $3,650, cloves and flannels, China $1800.[16] It is difficult to ascertain the exact volume of profit but it is certain that the owners of the ship were not disheartened by the results. This was why on December 26, 1789, the ship Washington sailed again for India, and from this time onwards there was a steadily increasing number of such clearances. The fleets of the East India traders make a peculiar appeal to the imagination. One reads in their tonnage and in the records of their builders something of the economic history of the struggling young nation. Most of the ship was very small in size. General Washington, which opened up the frontier of India trade to the Browns, was only 360 tons, though it could stow 600 tons. Again the Brig Rambler of Providence, which visited Calcutta in April 1816, was only 317 tons. Ship Arthur owned by the Brown and Ives and made voyages to Calcutta was only 263 tons. We are not to believe that this tiny ships were selected for the Indian trade in preference to larger craft. There use bears witness to the problem of capital shortage. With few exceptions there were no American vessels anywhere near 1000 tonnes in the East India trade until the arrival of the famous Mass. built Clipper ships in the 1840s.

The India trade of the Browns dried up after 1820s. The trade of Providence appears to have been better supplied with capital at the outset than either New York or Mass. The growth of the trade had limitations because Providence was a poor distributing point.[17] After the War of 1812 the Browns gradually withdrew their capital from the trade and turned to spinning industry. Secondly, in 1813 British merchant and shipping interests wrested the monopoly trade with India from the East India Company, and increasingly thereafter drove American vessels out of Eastern waters. Also the United States suffered a financial crisis between 1818 and 1819 that temporarily affected the shipping industry. High tariffs that were in effect between 1816 and 1842 further restricted America's profitable imports from the Orient. Silver also became scarce because the British Government had given an order "excluding America from furnishing our West Indian Colonies with supplies". In New Hampshire, Massachusetts, Rhode Island, and Connecticut, for instance, mills were producing great quantities of woollen goods. As a result of the shift to industrialism, ports such as Newburyport soon abandoned their tradition of shipbuilding and foreign trade, as did other New England towns - Beverly, Gloucester, Ipswich, Marblehead, Salem and Providence and Philadelphia. New

York, however, began to emerge as the leading port of the United States; within a few years it had outdistanced Boston, Philadelphia, and Baltimore. On the whole Indo-American trade declined considerably between 1815 and 1860. American imports from Calcutta had collapsed under the tariff of 1816. But still, the American business went on till the 1860s and even beyond. It did not stop as Amales Tripathi[18] thought, with the entry of European free traders after the Charter Act (1833) ending the East India Company's monopoly. I have shown elsewhere how Frederick Tudor's ice came just in time to save Boston's India business from ruin. The ice business increased to such an extent that by 1841 although pushed by 15 competitors, and forced to lower the retail price to one cent a pound, Tudor was able to pay off a debt of a quarter-million dollars contracted by his early experiment.[18a]

Section III : The Bengali Banians

Finally, we turn to explore the role of the Bengali banians in this early American trade. The Yankees carried on the bulk of their trade through the Indian brokers because this was a cheaper way of conducting the business. This way of conducting the business fostered some kind of a cultural intercourse between the two cultures. It also advantaged some of the aspiring Indian banians to collaborate directly with the U.S. merchants. Ramdulal De and his nephews, Asutosh De and Pramathanath De, Rajindra Datta and Kalidas Datta, Rajkrishna and Radhakrishna Mitra are some of the early Calcutta banians who carried on big business with the Americans. The early Americans had treated the Indians with informality, humour and respect. Ramdulal became a household name among the contemporary American business houses. The grateful American merchants gave him a full-size portrait of George Washington in appreciation of his services. The Washington and Lee Universities still have a Ramdulal society to cherish his memory. An American ship owner named a vessel after him.[19]

The American merchants who came to India came largely to Calcutta. It is a fact forgotten now that the Calcutta trade was one of the important American trades anywhere.

There is a tendency to ignore the role played by India in general and Calcutta in particular in the American imagination of these times, but the mariners carefully collected such artifacts as the area they visited and these artifacts found their way to the United States. The foundation of the East India Marine Society in Salem in 1799 was illustrative of America's deep interest in India. Out of the collection of East India Marine Society grew the Peabody Museum of Salem (Mass).

The Browns of Providence too conducted their trade through the Bengali banians. The Brown family papers, which I had the privilege to consult at the John Carter Brown Library, are packed with instances in which the supercargoes of the vessels owned by the Browns, were assisted by Bengali banians in the loading and unloading of cargoes. The Providence firm of Brown and Ives had regular contact with Bengali banians like Ramdulal De, Ramdhan Ghosh, Ramchandra Mitter and others.[20] We have enough evidence to show that the Bengali banians were ever ready to offer credit to the Browns whenever such credit was needed. Here is an example Letter from Ramchandra Mitter to the Browns of Providence dt. December 1819: "I offered to advance them what they wanted on the same terms and advance Peabody and Tucker of Salem and Mr. Thorndike of Boston, for whom I have done business for many years. The very high character of your house in this place forbid my hesitating to advance guarantor which ever might promote the interest of the voyage".[21] Again on another occasion Ramtanu Das, another Bengali businessman wrote the following to the Browns (letter dt. November 30, 1819) from Calcutta: "We have the pleasure of sending by Captain Stanhope two Kashmiri shawls of Gown piece one for Mrs. Brown and the other for Mrs. Ives. We hope that this poorly present be acceptable to them".[22] There are many such instances. Thus, besides economic history, the Indo-American interaction, their reciprocal ties and bonds friendship are also worth looking into. What is important is the fact that the growth of this trade added a new dimension to the cultural and commercial milieu of the city of Calcutta. But maritime historians of the subject like K. W.

Porter and others tend to underestimate the importance and volume of this trade and play up China trade as bigger draw for the Americans. But as Bhagat has shown this was not the case between 1790 and 1815 when the merchants of Providence were present in the Indian Ocean. The decline set in later.

To conclude, I will argue that the American trade in India was important for a number of reasons. To begin with, the early commercial intercourse between India and America illustrates how the Mughal commerce gradually changed into colonial commerce. When the Americans landed in India, she was still anchored to medieval commerce. She was then selling her cotton to the wider world and taking in a large quantity of silver. This trade shows how the traffic changed into colonial trade during this period, from cottons for export and silver for import, the Indians had to turn to raw materials. Secondly, this intercourse opened up a fresh frontier for both the sides. We have seen how quite a number of New England families turned millionaires by tapping the Indian resources. Again the Bengali banians too, were elated to see the merchants of a new nation who were, unlike the British merchants, relatively free from racial prejudice. Thus both sides benefited from the interaction. Thirdly, the capital accumulated from the India trade later helped the Americans to begin the cotton manufacture. The Browns, in particular withdrew from the India trade to set up the earliest cotton mills in New England. Fourthly, the American trade remained as a source of bullion to the Indian economy for quite some time. The economic historians who probed into the history of Indian commerce, in particular, have acknowledged this point. Finally, the growth of American trade added a new dimension to the cultural and commercial milieu of the city. The Yankees carried on the bulk of their trade through the Indian brokers. This way of conducting the business helped to foster some sort of a cultural intercourse between India and America. Although the early consular relations between the two countries ended in a failure, yet, the presence of the Americans in India at that stage of history is particularly significant. The Americans landed in Calcutta and elsewhere charged with the emotionalism of Common Sense, the revolutionary pamphlet that had laid down in flashing phrases, the idea of anti-colonialism. While the British had pursued a policy of racial discrimination, the Americans by their presence had helped to disseminate the message of democracy. But it requires a different approach to understand this. It has to be dealt with separately.

Notes and References

The essay is chiefly based on the private papers of the Brown family preserved at the John Carter Brown Library, Brown University and the Rhode Island Historical Society (Providence, USA), which the author had the opportunity to consult as a Senior Fluorite Visiting Scholar attached to the History Faculty in Brown University.

1. G. Bhagat, *Americans in India*, New York, 1970, p. VII.
2. Ibid.
3. Ibid.
4. Brown Family Papers .John Carter Brown Library (hereafter cited as JCB).
5. Ship Hamilton Papers(JCB).
6. Ship Arthur Papers (JCB).
7. S.E.Morison, The *Maritime History of Massachusetts* (1783-1860), Boston, 1921, pp. 79-89.
8. Ibid.

8a. Herman Melville, Moby *Dick,* Vols 2, New York, 1963, passim.

9. G. Bhagat, op.cit.
10. James B.Hedges, *The Browns of Providence Plantations : Colonial Years*, Cambridge (USA), 1952, Vol. I, pp. 7-9, see also G.S.Kimball, *The East India Trade of Providence*, Providence, 1896 and Providence in Colonial Times, Boston,1912.
11. Ibid.
12. Ship Washington's Invoice Book (JCB).
13. Brown Family Papers (JCB).

14. *United States Chronicle*, July 9, 1789.
15. *Providence Gazette,* May 22, 1790.
16. Bhagat, op.cit.
17. Dennett Tyler, *Americans in Eastern Asia,* New York, 1979, pp. 9-10.
18. Amales Tripathi, *Trade and Finance in the Bengal Presidency,* Calcutta,1978.
18a. Ranjan Chakrabarti, Frederick Tudor and the Ice Trade in India, 1833-1870, A.Mukherjee (ed.), *Studies in India's Maritime Trade,* Calcutta,1999.
19. This discussion is based on the Brown Family Papers (JCB), Girish Chandra Ghosh, Ramdoolal De: The Bengali Millionaire, Calcutta, 1868, Susan Beane, Rajindar Dutt : Merchant of Calcutta, Span, 1989, Ashin Dasgupta, Akrur Datter Paribar (in Bengali), *Desh,* Special Number, 1990 and G. Bhagat, op.cit.
20. Brown Family Papers (JCB).
21. Ramtanu Doss & Sons, Calcutta to Brown and Ives dt. 8/11/1819, Brown Family Papers (JCB).
22. Ramtanu Doss & Sons to Brown and Ives dt. 3/11/1819, Brown Family Papers.

11

More about Swadeshi Economic Thinking: Bengal in the Late 19th and early 20th centuries

Amit Bhattacharyya

When we speak of the swadeshi period, we generally keep in our mind the period which is directly associated with the anti-Partition political campaign of 1905. In a broader sense, however, it embraces a larger period, i.e., which started from the second half of the 19th century - from the 1870s - and continued till 1947. This period particularly that embracing the late 19th and early 20th centuries - was one of the most creative periods in the history of modern India. During that period, swadeshi ideas of different strands took shape, handicraft industries showed signs of revival, new and modern industries were set up, technological education was disseminated through the newly-constructed technical institutes, the Bengal National Chamber of Commerce and indigenous banks and insurance companies were set up and many shipping companies were floated. The aim of the present paper is to examine, in brief, the nature of swadeshi economic thinking, particularly of those who were entrepreneurs themselves.

The birth and growth of swadeshi economic thought had its roots in the changing objective condition of the time. The colonisation of the country brought with it the destruction of traditional handicrafts along with their technical know-how, drainage of wealth through direct plunder and revenue extraction, and the transplantation of the western type of industrial capitalism in India. It also brought about the transformation of the country from a feudal into a colonial and semi-colonial one and the conversion of the Indian economy into a material-supplying appendage to metropolitan Britain. This fact of industrial ruin undoubtedly influenced swadeshi thinking very profoundly during that period.

Dadabhai Naoroji, M.G. Ranade, William Digby, R.C. Dutt and others argued that the contrast between the prosperous, industrialised West and the poverty-stricken India was the result of deliberate British policy. The British had used the "arm of political conquest" to destroy the traditional dependence on agriculture; agriculture was ruined by exorbitant land tax; and the crisis was exacerbated by a crippling "drain of wealth". These doctrines were explained also by Sakharam Ganesh Deuskar in his book *Desher Katha.* [1]

Those swadeshi thoughts had been taking shape in many areas, particularly in Bengal, and the process of the accumulation of capital in the hands of some Bengali entrepreneurs had also started. They could at best be categorised into the small and medium sections of the Indian bourgeoisie. One can refer to *C.K. Sen & Co.*(b.1878), the manufacturer of 'Jabakusum' hair oil; *P.M. Bagchi & Co.*(b.1883), the producer of ink, perfumes, hair oil, almanac and many other products; *Oriental Hosiery Manufacturing Co.* (b.1893); *Pioneer Glass Mfg. Co.* (b.1890); *Sukea Mfg. Co.* (b.1895), which sold umbrellas; *Sikdar & Co.* (b.1876), which made cooking pans, water pipes etc. These apart, a number of artisan centres manufactured iron-nails, cutlery goods, locks and keys and surgical instruments in places such as Chandannagar, Kanchannagar, Sodepur, Howrah, Tripura etc.[2]

There was a lively controversy at the turn of the 19th century over the type of industrialisation that was most suitable to India. It involved not only economic but also social and ideological issues. By degrees, intellectuals became aware of the social evils produced by large-scale machinery in the capitalist West - the two poles of wealth, at one end and misery at another, and class antagonism that necessarily followed. A serious quest had been going on for a peculiarly 'Indian' path that would preserve the virtues of traditional society even while solving the problems of the country. From 1898 onwards, *Dawn* - the nationalist magazine - warned against the uncritical transplantation of western industrialisation. Satish Chandra Mukherjee referred to the book by Engels entitled 'The condition of the working class in England' as an evidence of the horrors caused by the industrial revolution in England. He advocated a kind of 'dual economy', with capitalist organisations only where these were absolutely necessary (such as railways, mines, chemicals), while small-scale organisations would be encouraged in other sectors of the economy.[3]

Some people raised their voice against the growth of big capital. A *Bengalee* correspondent deplored the starting of large mills, as this would inevitably produce "antagonism between the wage-earner and the capitalist".[4] In an issue of *Swadeshi,* it was stated: "Machines enhance the suffering of the common people, and benefit only the rich handful. Independent professions are destroyed, labourers increase in numbers, become victims of drink and immorality, and in time totally debased. Handicrafts provide food for everyone, preserve the freedom of all and produce worthy and religious men."[5] Sumit Sarkar writes that such ideas became fairly common after 1905, largely because they could be easily integrated with the general current of Hindu nationalism.[6]

There is no doubt that the anti-Partition political campaign of 1905 and the boycott campaign associated with it provided a stimulus to the process of the shaping of swadeshi economic thinking as also to the development of swadeshi industries. Bholanath Chandra was the first in Bengal to champion the idea of boycott in an oft-quoted article entitled 'A voice for the commerce and manufacturers of India' in *Mookerjee's Magazine* in the 1870s. It was a call for national regeneration along independent lines and the non-consumption of the goods of England. His voice was clearly anti-colonial. "To strip naked the disguised truth, the English want to reduce us all to the condition of agriculturists... let us receive a commercial and industrial education... The Native English vernacular papers should preach for the founding of independent Native Banks, Native Companies and Corporations, Native Mills and Factories, the Native Chambers of Commerce in the presidencies. They should denounce the insensate practice of preferring foreign goods to home made manufactures ...They should point out the enormous and increasing drain upon the profit of Indian labour to show that the country is growing poorer year by year and thoroughly exposed to the statistical delusion of the authorities... Let us make use of this potent weapon by resolving to non-consume the goods of England." [7] He then gave the call for boycott to "dethrone King Cotton of Manchester."[8]

It is pertinent to point out here that the two main instances of tariff injustice - the abolition of cotton import duties on Lancashire goods in 1882 and the imposition of the countervailing excise on Indian piece-goods in 1896 - both led to widespread calls for boycott in Bombay, Poona and Bengal.

The boycott movement led to some extreme steps that evoked sharp criticism from some quarters. In some areas, the picketers resorted to the burning of foreign goods, social boycott of indigenous merchants (e.g., the Saha merchants of Barisal) and the forcible prevention of poor people from buying cheap foreign goods. Tagore relates in his novel *Ghare Baire* how the boat of Mirzan - the small Muslim trader - was sunk by the advocates of boycott.[9]

That brings us to Rabindranath Tagore. He was pro-swadeshi, but very much critical of the extreme features of boycott. His Nikhilesh - a character of his novel mentioned above - is out-and-out a swadeshi. He used swadeshi goods himself. In his 'sukh sayarer hat', swadeshi goods were sold. But he was opposed to the policy of boycott and did not forbid the sale of foreign goods there. He was critical of Sandwip - the advocate of boycott in its extreme form. Why should people be forced to boycott foreign goods when these are cheaper than the *deshi* (indigenous) goods in price? The rich people can afford to pay more for swadeshi goods; let them do so. But why should the common people be forced to pay more? Tagore clearly stood against the use of force that threatened the livelihood of the common people. He was opposed to the hegemonic mono-cultural nationalism imposed from above. To him, universalism was more important than nationalism.

There were, however, many advocates of the boycott. They drew attention to the drainage of wealth, de-industrialisation and the general impoverishment and misery suffered by the people of the country. Those who opposed boycott argued that foreign goods could be bought at a price lower than that charged for indigenous goods; so it was not unnatural for the poor people of the country to opt for foreign, instead of swadeshi. In reply, the pro-boycott group argues that the people who had been dying because of undernourishment and poverty caused by colonial rule, could never be able to buy goods even at cheap prices. Moreover, money spent for the purchase of foreign goods are not re-invested in our country, but being systematically siphoned off to Britain and other countries. In order to stop this drainage of wealth, the people should adhere to the call for the boycott of foreign goods. Side by side, this call would also help promote the sale of swadeshi goods whose development would help in the economic uplift of the country as a whole. According to a contemporary journal, during the swadeshi period, a number of swadeshi sugar mills were set up. However, in order to get rid of these indigenous rivals, the foreign companies resorted to the method of rate war and reduced the price of foreign sugar to such an extent that swadeshi mills were finding it difficult to compete with them. Then it stated that once they were able to oust these swadeshi companies, they would again increase the price of sugar to a large extent and establish its monopolistic hold over the market.[10] What is true of sugar companies is also true for other industries such as shipping. In fact, foreign shipping rings resorted to such methods as Rate War, Deferred Rebate System etc.[11] to get rid of indigenous rivals such as the *Bengal Steam Navigation Company, the East Bengal River Steam Service Ltd.*[12] and many others. And when their individual rivals were thus thrown out of competition altogether, they increased their rates again.[13]

One important aspect of our national movement was the cultural transformation of a piece of land called *desh* (country) into a mother figure called Bharatmata (mother India). We get this idea from *Ghare Baire*, Ramendra Sundar Tribedi's *Lakshmir Bratakatha* as also from other sources. This was the image of Lakshmi - the goddess of fortune. Sandwip of *Ghare Baire* spoke of the necessity of creating the image of an ideal woman, while Nikhilesh opposes this concept of a mother-figure. In fact, Tagore himself was aware of the danger inherent in this concept. It was revivalist in nature; it had also an anti-Muslim bias.

Let us now refer to another aspect. From the 19th century writings, we get the picture of an oppressed and dispossessed mother. In the 20th century, this image was transformed into the image of an inspiring mother. Let us reproduce a few lines from a poem entitled 'Bangajanani' (Mother Bengal) by Jogindranath Sarkar.[14]

In this poem, the mother of Bengal comes to the doors of the countrymen with her swadeshi goods to awaken them from their age-old slumber. Wake up, countrymen ! Open your doors ! Welcome her with all your warmth! Do not look towards foreigners. Be self-reliant !

So far, we have attempted to give a very brief idea about swadeshi economic thought that developed in Bengal in the late 19th and early 20th centuries. There were many people who wrote or advocated either swadeshi or boycott or both, but themselves did not become entrepreneurs. There were many others who were entrepreneurs themselves, but themselves did not write down anything. Still there were others who were both entrepreneurs and intellectuals who aired their views through speeches, autobiographies, pamphlets and other writings published in different periodicals such as *Prabasi, Bharatbarsha, Aarthik Unnati, Insurance World, Ayurveda, Advance, Byabosa-o-Banijya, Calcutta Commercial Gazette and Investors' Guide* etc. We propose to pick up some among them e.g., Prafulla Chandra Ray of the *Bengal Chemical & Pharmaceutical Works,* Surendranath Tagore of the *Hindusthan Cooperative Insurance Society Ltd.,* Jogesh Chandra Ghosh of *Sadhana Aushadhalaya,* and Alamohan Das of the *India Machinery Co.,* Gananath Sen of the *Kalpataru Ayurvedic Works* and some others as also the *Bengal National and Chamber of Commerce and Industry* and refer, however briefly, to their swadeshi thinking.

Prafulla Chandra Ray was a Professor of Chemistry, an eminent economic thinker and the founder-proprietor of *Bengal Chemical & Pharmaceutical Works* (BCPW) set up in

1892. He was a pro-swadeshi man; he stood in favour of *khaddar* and *charka* and an admirer of Gandhiji. He strongly held that the Bengalis should cease to take clerical jobs and turn to business and industry. Non-Bengali business communities like the Marwaris and others were draining out all resources from Bengal, and thus reducing this province to a condition of abject poverty and degradation. For views such as these, Ray was accused of parochialism and provincialism.

For the pursuit of economic swadeshi, he adopted the path of self-reliance. He experimented on medicinal plants and herbs to prepare essential chemicals. Then he experimented with *sajimati* and bone-ash and produced phosphate of soda crystals after a long chemical process. He manufactured a large number of drugs, besides other goods, covering a wide range of diseases e.g., malaria, liver troubles, skin diseases, various female diseases connected with pregnancy and child birth, asthma etc. In the face of stiff foreign competition he could push his products with the help of his physician friends such as Nilratan Sarkar, Radha Gobinda Kar and Suresh Prasad Sarbadhikari who started prescribing Bengal Chemical's drugs to their patients. Its *Ext.Khetpapra Liq.* Competed with Wilkinśon's *Sarsaparilla;* its *Ext. Gulanch liquid composita Co.* with Bathgate & Co.'s liver pills etc. Unlike the Indian big bourgeoisie and many among swadeshi bourgeoisie, the BCPW did not use imported machinery; all the machines were designed and constructed in the workshop itself.[15]

The interesting thing is that as an entrepreneur, he was *self-reliant,* and not a collaborator with foreign capitalists, and fought against foreign competition. At the same time, however, there is at least one evidence of a fundamental departure being made by him from such an anti-British attitude. In 1919, Ray was offered the title of 'Knighthood' primarily for his political service to the British raj. He established a sulphuric acid plant for supplying a huge amount of sulphuric acid to the British during World War I.[16] This is in sharp contrast to the attitude of another swadeshi company, namely, *Gopal Hosiery* which, during World War II, refused to supply vests to the British troops even at the risk of suffering not only heavy financial losses, but also political imprisonment.[17]

The next swadeshi entrepreneur-thinker is Surendranath Tagore, the Secretary of *Hindusthan Cooperative Insurance Society Ltd* (1907) which carried out successful insurance business against stiff foreign competition. He described the beginning of the Society in a colourful language:

"We were then (1905-07) in the heyday of the Swadeshi — but where was swadeshi to be had? Stores were necessary to supply would-be consumers. Cottage industries were necessary to supply would-be stores. Money and men were necessary to carry on the would-be industries. Not that our people were unwilling and unfit, but they were overburdened with family worries. How could this man-and-money power be set free, gathered and mobilised? This, in brief, was the chain of needs that led our Founder, Ambica Charan Ukil, to think of an Insurance Organisation on National lines, and to seek some workers who were prepared to give concrete shape to his conclusions."[18]

That brings us to Jogesh Chandra Ghosh, the founder-proprietor of *Sadhana Aushadhalaya,* which produced a large number of ayurvedic drugs. Ghosh, like P.C. Ray, was a Professor of Chemistry; he experimented on ayurvedic medicines for about twenty years before he ventured into this industry. The ideas that were uppermost in his mind were that a national ayurvedic industry such as this would not only open up employment opportunities but would also prevent a huge drainage of national wealth caused by the purchase of foreign drugs. This pro-swadeshi and anti-imperialist attitude was expressed by him quite clearly:

"Every year foreign drugs amounting to Rs.2/Rs.4 crores are imported into India. It is wrong to maintain that everything needs to be discarded. The drugs which are essential for our country and for which money has to be spent should not be considered harmful to the people. However, there is no need to think that all the imported foreign medicines are really necessary for our countrymen. When such ayurvedic ingredients as *Arabic gand, shunthi, sarsap, reuchini* etc. are taken abroad, refined there and then sent to this country in big bottles ...we buy them as 'gum ekesia', 'pulve ginger', mustard and 'pulve beai' by paying thousands of rupees."[19]

He also accused the Indian allopathic physicians of adding to the misery of the people by paying a huge amount of money to foreign merchants. He said: "In reality, the physicians of our country act as agents of the drug-sellers of the world".[20] He made a fervent appeal to the indigenous doctors in the following way: "*Chawanpras, Makaradhwaja* and others are like bright gems in the ayurvedic system of medicine. Lakhs of rupees can be earned by selling those abroad. Every year, the wealth of India is being siphoned off by the introduction of foreign drugs. Is there none among the Indian physicians who can earn money by exporting *makaradhwaja, chawanpras, asokarista* etc. abroad? Will they strive for making our motherland prosperous by propagating Ayurveda in foreign countries?"[21]

One of the most enterprising of the kaviraj - entrepreneurs of Bengal was Gananath Sen. He set up a factory at his own initiative for the manufacture of ayurvedic medicines in Calcutta in 1914, named the *Kalpataru Ayurvedic Works.* At that time, a large number of kavirajas felt the need to oppose the western system; but they were not identical in their response to the challenge. There were purists like Haran Chandra Chakraborty who were opposed to any integration with colonial i.e., the allopathic system.[22] Incidentally, this probably was also the view of Jogesh Chandra Ghosh. Jnanendranath Sen considered the ayurvedic system to be "perfect" and stated that "any mode of unification would be harmful to it"[23]. On the other hand, there were integrationists like Jamini Bhusan Roy and Gananath Sen who believed that both the systems would benefit if the indigenous system adopted modern advances of the European system, and the latter adopted certain invaluable practices and methods of diagnosis and treatment of the former. However, the western system should not be allowed to supersede the eastern system. Gananath Sen was quite categorical on this point when he suggested "the Indianisation of Western scientific knowledge rather than westernising our system". He explained: "...when you teach anatomy, have Indian texts as the basis, using Indian names as far as possible, while the student shall be free to take in anything from Western texts".[24]

Our last personality is Alamohan Das, the founder-proprietor of the *India Machinery Co.,* set up in the 1930s. Hailing from a peasant community of Howrah, he fell on evil days in the early part of his career. He, however, could improve his financial position by the discovery of some gold coins in his ancestral household.[25] According to a government report, this company was one of the four companies that produced machines of grade 1 category.[26] The machines included weighing machine, lathe machine, textile machine, printing machine etc.

The swadeshi movement left an indelible mark on his mind. In his autobiography, he wrote:

"I used to read newspapers, and noticed that trade, commerce, railways and shipping lines were dominated by foreigners. At night, when I was alone, I wondered why should such a vast country like ours, inhabited by crores of people, with a vast coastline nearby, be so poor! While I loitered along the banks of the Ganges, I could see streams of big merchant vessels flying their flags, belching smoke from the chimneys, loading and unloading thousands of tons of cargo, but was sorry to find that there was no Indian vessel around."[27]

It was a period of immense revolutionary-political activity. Acts of revolutionary violence made no particular appeal to him. Instead of indulging in political annihilations, he attempted what he described as the "economic annihilation" of the British. He wrote that one should do something to stop the colonial practice of extraction and subsequent export of raw materials from India to Britain, their conversion into finished products and finally the flooding of the Indian market with those goods. With that end in view, he ventured into the industrial field.[28]

The attitude of the *Bengal National Chamber of Commerce and Industry* was, however, somewhat different; it was more of collaboration with foreign capital than of struggle with it. It was not at all in favour of any boycott of foreign goods; instead, it advocated cooperation with the Europeans. The language was strikingly similar to those used by Rammohan Ray and Dwarkanath Tagore: "...True Swadeshism is always free from hatred of all that is *bideshi;* for a sure and steady growth of swadeshism required the help and cooperation with the European friends. Their ripe business experience and valuable advice are of material assistance to us. Providence has placed our destinies in the hands of the great British nation, and it should be the endeavour of every true swadeshist so to comfort himself as to derive the greatest possible benefit by our association with all that is best and noblest in that great nation"[29] . Rai Sitanath Roy Bahadur remarked: "...We are poor because of the disappearance of our arts and industries...". He, however, hastened to add: "It is from no antipathy against foreign goods but I can say all this from sheer necessity for providing food and subsistence to famished people ...that it has become necessary to revive our decayed industries".[30]

In this paper, I have tried to deal with some features of swadeshi economic thought that had been gaining ground in Bengal from the early 20th century. It started with the consumption of swadeshi and the boycott of foreign goods, and also embraced within its scope Hindu revivalist thinking as also the concept of mother India. Those who were pro--boycott were also quite naturally pro-swadeshi, but all those who were pro-swadeshi were not necessarily pro-boycott. Although entrepreneurial activities along swadeshi lines were determined by social and economic factors, the political movement of 1905 also provided a definite impetus to them. This period witnessed not only a revival of indigenous handicraft industries but also a spurt in the setting up of new industries in diverse fields. These were cotton textile, tannery and leather works, pottery, chemicals and associated industries, match, paper, iron foundries, tobacco, waterproofs, fans and bulbs, glass, shipping, banking, insurance and many other areas. This swadeshi bourgeoisie consisted of the small and medium section of the Indian bourgeoisie. It drew its recruits from the middle-class people (i.e., engineers, doctors, chemists, school teachers, clerks and others); the artisans, and some zamindars. This swadeshi bourgeoisie pursued the policy of self-reliance and opposition to British imperialism.

বঙ্গজননী

(১)

পসরা মাথায় করে ডেকে যায়
দুয়ারে?
খুলে দেরে দ্বার দেখ একবার
উহারে।
দুখের আঁধার রজনী প্রভাতে,
জগৎ ভরেছে কিরণ প্রকাশে
পূরব আকাশে সুমধুর হাসে
উষারে।
পসরা মাথায় করে ডেকে যায়
দুয়ারে?

(২)

ডেকে ডেকে যায়? চেননা উহায়
চেন না?
ওরে ওরে মূঢ় জান নাকি গূঢ়
বেদনা
বাজিছে উহার গভীর মরমে;
ও যে গো জননী ত্যজিয়া সরমে
এসেছে সবার জাগাতে পরাণে
চেতনা,
বিশ্বজয়িনী বঙ্গ মাতারে
চেননা!

(৪)

হের ব্যবসা শিল্পে সাজায়ে পসরা
জননী
ফিরিছে সবার দুয়ারে দুয়ারে
আপনি।
কোরোনাক ওরে অবহেলা আর
বাজিবে সে বাজ হৃদে যে মাতার

হও হোক ধূলি লহ শিরে তুলি
দেখুক নিখিল অবনী।
ধন্য আমরা ধন্য মোদের
জননী।

(৫)

ওরে পরমুখ পানে তৃষিত নয়নে
চেয়োনা।
উঠ সবে লও ধর এই বেলা,
জননীর দান নহে ছলে খেলা,
দেবের প্রসাদী শুভাশীষ (!) ঢালা
দেখনা!
ওরে পরমুখ পানে তৃষিত নয়নে চেয়ো না।

Notes & References:

1. Sakharam Ganesh Deuskar: *Desher Katha* (Story of the country), Calcutta, June 1904, passim.
2. Amit Bhattacharyya: *Swadeshi Enterprise in Bengal 1900-1920,* Calcutta, 1986, passim; Amit Bhattacharyya: *Swadeshi Enterprise in Bengal : The Second Phase 1921--1947,* Calcutta, 1995, passim; Amit Bhattacharyya: *Almanac-maker as Entrepreneur* P M Bagchi & Co. Pvt. Ltd 1883-1947, Calcutta, 1989, passim.
3. Sumit Sarkar: *Swadeshi Movement in Bengal 1903-1908,* PPH, New Delhi, 1973, pp.105-06.
4. *Bengalee,* 19 October 1905.
5. *Swadsehi,* Phalgun 1313 BS (1906).
6. *Swadeshi Movement in Bengal,* p. 106-07.
7. *Mookerje's Magazine,* all the volumes for the years 1873 to 1876.
8. Ibid.
9. Rabindranath Tagore, *Ghare Baire* in *Rabindra Rachanabali* (Collected Works of Tagore), Vol. 9, Government of West Bengal, 25 Baisakh 1368 BS (1961), pp.405-550.
10. 'Bideshi barjan-o-Swadeshi grohon' (Boycott of foreign goods and the consumption of swadeshi goods), *Nabyabharat,* vol.24, No.3, Asad 1313 BS (1906), pp. 139-45.
11. Evidence of Messrs. Bando & Co., Witness No.40 in *Indian Marine Committee Minutes of Evidence,* Calcutta, 1924, pp.391-92.
12. *Swadeshi Enterprise in Bengal 1900-1920, pp.* 145-166.
13. S.N.Haji: *Indian Shipping Series Pamphlet No.3. The Deferred Rebate System,* Delhi, February 1924, pp. 5-7.
14. *Byabosa-o-Banijya,* Vol. 1, No. 5, Bhadra 1319 BS (1912), pp.217-218.
15. *Swadeshi Enterprise in Bengal 1900-1920,* pp. 73-85.
16. *Basumati,* Asad 1332 BS(1925); see also M. Phil dissertation by Nilanjana Sen, entitled *Prafulla*

Chandra Ray: The Thinker, Department of History, Jadavpur University, 1991.

17. Biswakarma: *Lakshmir Kripalabh-o-Bangalir Sadhana* ('The Bengalis' quest for business success'), Calcutta, 1969, p. 104.
18. Speech of Mr. Surendranath Tagore on the occasion of the Silver Jubilee Celebrations of Hindusthan Cooperative Insurance Society Ltd. in *Insurance World,* March 1934, pp.185-201.
19. Jogesh Chandra Ghosh: *Ayurvediya Grihachikitsa,* Sadhana Aushadhalaya, Dacca 1352 BS (1946), pp. 1-9.
20. Ibid.
21. Ibid.
22. Chittabrata Palit, 'Ayurveda in Colonial Bengal: Survival and Revival', *International Seminar on Traditional Medicine Souvenir volume,* Calcutta 1992, pp. 11-21; Poonam Bala: *Imperialism and Medicine in Bengal : A Socio-Historical Perspective,* New Delhi, 1991, passim; Subrata Pahari: *Unish Shataker Banglay Sanatani Chikitsha Byabasthar Swarup* ('Nature of Traditional System of Medicine in 19th century Bengal'), Progressive Publishers, Calcutta, 2nd edition, August 2001, passim.
23. Written Evidence of Kaviraj Jnanendra Nath Sen in *The Report of the Committee on Indigenous Systems of Medicine, Part II, Written and Oral Evidence,* Madras, July 1924, pp.18-19.
24. Written Evidence of Gananath Sen in ibid, p.8.
25. Alamohan Das: *Aamar Jiban* ('My Life'), Howrah, 1 Baisakh 1356 BS (1949), p. 10.
26. *Report of the Indian Tariff Board on the Machine Tools Industry,* GOI, Delhi 1947, Appendix VI.
27. *Aamar Jiban,* pp. 30-31.
28. Ibid, pp. 91-92.
29. See 'Lord Minto and Swadeshism' in Speech of Maharaja Kumar Rishee Case Law, President BNCC, Prgs. of the Annual General Meeting held

on 12 February 1909, *The Annual Report of the BNCC for the year 1908.*

30. Prgs. of the Annual General Meeting held on 2 August 1906, in *The Annual Report of the BNCC for the years 1904 and 1905.*

12

Bengali Business Enterprise and The B N C C I

Chittabrata Palit

The history of Bengali business enterprise is haunted by many shibboleths. One prevailing assumption is that the Bengalis were unfit for business and cut out for clerkdom. The other notion is that the Bengalis preferred landlordism to business when the Permanent Settlement offered opportunities for investment in landed estates. The third fixation is that the Bengalis were genetically prone to litigation and dissipated most of their capital in law-suits. Finally, when they did business, they turned compradorial supplying raw materials to foreign firms and retailing manufactured goods from abroad. They seldom set up their own industries.

It would be my effort to show that most of these assumptions are historically incorrect. These canards were invented by the imperialist historians to prove that British monopoly of business and industry in Bengal was not due to unfair competition between the British and the Bengalis backed by the colonial government.The other critics are the Marxists who insist that Bengali business was by and large compradorial. They are generally hostile to businessmen who are held as class enemies of peasants and workers. They are generally critical of the Bengali middle class and Bengal renaissance for the same reason.

Bengalis can claim their business heritage from the 17th century when the heroes of the Mangal Kavyas, Dhanapati, Chand and Srimanta saudagars scoured the Bay of Bengal on their merchant vessels. After Plassey and before Cornwallis in the 18th century, a number of Bengali businessmen are found in salt, silk and cotton trade. They include Nabakrishna Deb, Krishnakanta Nandi, Darpanarayan Tagore, Lakshmikanta Dhar, Nemai Mallick and others. They did trade with the company and British merchants on equal terms and they were not manufacturers but traders of country produce and handicrafts. All of them made huge fortunes during their careers. The last named, Nemai Mallick was a banker and a millionaire. He can be called the Bengali 'Jagat Seth'. His drafts were honoured all over the country. His total assets at the time of his death amounted to over rupees one crore. There was a succession war among his scions which dissipated this capital in law suits.[1]

We have four major entrepreneurs in the first half of the 19th century. The first and foremost was Ramdulal Dey, another Bengali millionaire who rose from very humble origins to become a formidable business magnate. He was also involved in export-import business and had widespread trade with America and England on the one hand and China and Japan on the other. He had a fleet of ships of his own and was the architect of Indo-American trade which bypassed the inconvenience of British monopoly and allowed Bengalis to come on their own. His was a much adored name among the American business circles. He made it a point in his will that his successors would have to continue in business and not sink money in land. His nephews, Asutosh and Pramathanath Deb continued the tradition after whom the house declined.

Next in importance was the house of Akrur Dutta, a stevedore whose sons Rajendralal Dutta and Kalidas Dutta were also prominent in Indo-American trade. Like Ramdulal Dey, they also ran a parallel trade independent of British monopoly in shipping. They had extensive trade with American houses of Boston, Salem and New Port. Rajendralal was a noted homeopath and a Sanskrit scholar of eminence.

We now turn to one of the greatest Bengali entrepreneurs of all times. It was Prince Dwarkanath Tagore who began as a salt merchant in which he amassed a huge capital. He next floated the Union Bank in 1829 and bought off the assets of Fairlie & Co. and Palmer & Co. He invested in a big way in the Chinakuri Coalmines of Ranigunge. He used to supply coal to British Tug companies. He later established a Tug company himself and his steamer was known as Forbes. He could not survive the competition of British companies for long and had to give it up. As the chairman of the Union Bank, he invested 90% of its capital in indigo trade which was then prosperous and made huge profit for the bank and for himself. Dwarkanath was a land speculator and bought three zamindaries in East Bengal which sustained the Tagore family of Jorasanko. Blair Kling has described him as a partner in empire. But this was an unequal partnership and despite his faith in the empire, all his enterprises were foiled by the British government and its favourites, the British capitalists. During his sojourn in England, the indigo trade suffered from economic depression in Europe and declined. The indigo planters who had heavily borrowed from the Union Bank departed with their capital for England without clearing their debt. As a result, the Union Bank collapsed in 1846-47 and Dwarakanath also passed away in England at the same time.

Another big businessman of the first half of the 19th century was Motilal Seal. He began his business career as a dealer in corks and bottles. Having made a fortune in this trade, he switched over to export-import business. He was hailed as the best judge of country produce of his time. He had both American and British clients and he supplied them with silk and cotton piece-goods, spices and cereals of different kinds. He later switched over to carrying trade and also owned a fleet of ships which travelled to England, Near East and Far East. He invested most of his capital in urban properties owning slums, bazars and mansions in Calcutta. His will shows that he made it binding on his successors not to become landholders and continue in business. Motilal was the last of the four who could maintain independent business without succumbing to colonial stranglehold. But none of the above had able successors to continue the family trade.[2]

From the record, it is clear that these entrepreneurs were businessmen per se and by no means landlords who invested their capital in purchasing zamindaries after the Permanent Settlement. Dwarkanath was also primarily a businessman who also bought some zamindaries as a real estate transaction which was profitable at that time. His case was one of portfolio management of capital and property.

The landmarket that opened up after the Permanent Settlement was also a lucrative field of investment and those who invested money for purchase of estates actually did real estate business. Purchase and sale of estates was part and parcel of this business. As other commercial sectors of business were cornered by the Company and British capitalists, this was found a safe business. Mostly people connected with the Government and Zamindari Collectorates had intimate knowledge of the land market and invested their capital in it. Calcutta businessmen did not make a bee-line for such business. Those who made landed property their sole business naturally had vital stake in it. They would go for utmost litigation to safegaurd it. It was no genetic inclination. It has also been alleged that wealthy Indians squandered their wealth by spending extravagantly on social ceremonies. They did it rather than be fleeced by Government's fiscal policy. They had no trust in Government's benevolence.[3]

In the beginning of the second half of the 19th century we have names of some Bengali entrepreneurs who carried out their one-generation trade successfully and then declined. Ramgopal Ghosh had an extensive rice trade in both Calcutta and Akyab in Arakan. He was a Young Bengal firebrand and known as the demosthenes of Bengal for his oratory. But he could not fight out the shipping monopoly of the Company and unequal tariff of the government favouring British businessmen. Same was the fate of Digambar Mitra, Durgacharan Laha and Bholanath Chandra who also could not withstand the one-way free trade policy of the colonial government. Of them, Bholanath Chandra had written vividly about the colonial repressive policies in the Mukherjee's Magazine in the 1880s. He exhorted his countrymen to establish their own banks and own chamber of commerce to fight the unequal laws.[4]

His suggestion was acted upon in 1887 when the Bengali and Marwari communities together established the Bengal National Chamber of Commerce. Chaturbhuj Narayan of Burrabazar and Sitanath Roy of Kumartuli became the President and the Secretary of this National Chamber with members taken from both Indian Communities and corporate business houses to fight the unjust commercial regulations and practices of the British government and British capitalists.

The National Chamber fought many notable cases against the Government in its long career. In the 1890s, it fought against the unequal tariff on salt trade. The British salt merchants used to bring salt as ballasts in their ships which they would sell duty-free in the Calcutta market. But the local merchants had to pay a duty of 5% of their product. This was extremely unfair but in the end, the National Chamber could not win the battle.[5]

The next important case was regarding the freight and license fees levied on steam navigation on the Bengal rivers. Roys of Bhagyakul had their family business in the Bengal Steam Navigation Company which had its arch rival in the British-owned Indian Steam Navigation Company which was allowed less freight and license fees by the colonial government. Here also, there was a long tug of war but ultimately no concession could be obtained during the second decade of the 20th century.[6]

The remaining two cases to illustrate the contest took place in the 1920s. In the first case, the National Chamber took up the cause of the Bengali colliers. Three such coal magnates were Laik-Banerjee and Company, Gobind Pandit and Company and N. C. Sarkar & Sons who were doing brisk business from the beginning of the 20th century. They successfully competed with the British giant, the Bengal Coal Company run by Andrew Yule & Company. Their combined production went over 40,000 tonnes. The British coal lobby in Calcutta and in England wanted to implement the I. L. O. regulation regarding the use of women and children as labour force in the coalfields. If this regulation was implemented, there would be a total ban on the use of women and children in the pits. Women and children had been working in the mines since the 1880s without a break. The concept of family labour and green and black estates had enabled the owners to get a steady labour supply in this industry. Family labour had been efficient and it had been engaged without complaint all these years. It had been the mainstay of Bengali business. The British lobby envious of the success of Bengali colliers wanted to deprive them of this advantage and mechanism by all means. They had capital - intensive industries and could afford mechanisation. This was not so with Bengali business. They would be crippled if there was a ban on family labour. But the British lobby through its Bengal Chamber of Commerce ultimately won the battle. Family labour was banned in the pits by 1928. As women and children were removed from the pits, there was a shortage of labour supply in the Bengali owned mines. Women labourers became destitutes and prostitutes as many such mines had to be shut down. The National Chamber fought tooth and nail against the Government ban but it was of no avail. Thus, in the name of humanitarianism, the differential advantage of the local colliers in labour supply was knocked out to nock down local competition.

The fourth case of contest was over transportation of goods. The local businessmen usually transported their goods from the godowns to their destination by carts drawn by buffaloes. This was a cheap transport and it could move through lanes and alleys of Calcutta very fast. **The government and the British capitalists conspired to change the mode of transport instead.** This was another scheme to deal a fatal blow to Indian business. To achieve this goal, the Indian Society for the Prevention of Cruelty to Animals (ISPCA) was mobilised. The latter carried out a campaign for cruelty to buffaloes by stipulating their hours of work and rest. The government backed it. This cut across the main hours of business. The National Chamber took up the issue and fought vehemently for its relaxation. As the ban created a commercial deadlock in the city, the government ultimately relented and a compromise was struck.[8]

Though the Bengal National Chamber tried its best to protect Bengali business from unfair regulations, its career was never smooth. There were other sectarian chambers like the Muslim Chamber of Commerce and the Marwari Chamber of Commerce which came into the field and created rift in business and politics. The enlightened Bengali - Marwari combination which was the bed-rock of Bengal National Chamber was also split by 1925 when most Marwaris came out of the National Chamber to form their Indian Chamber of Commerce. Since the First World War, there was an expansion of trade due to war supply and the Marwaris indulged in large scale speculating trade by floating shares which paid off handsomely. The Bengali businessmen did not approve of either. They wanted to do safe business with single proprietorship. They could not also approve of the compradorial nature of Marwari trade consisting in sale of raw material to foreign houses and retailing of their manufactured goods here. Marwaris were dearer to the British and got favourable terms of business from them. Bank loans were easily available to them whereas such opportunities were denied to the Bengali businessmen. There was also a political colour in it. Bengal was at that time in the grip of revolutionary movement and therefore all Bengalies were suspect and kept under surveillance. Marwaris led by G. D. Birla who was the founder and President of the Indian Chamber of Commerce made giant strides in business. Many of them turned into industrialists and set up jute, cotton, paper and cement mills. By 1938, they succeeded to the British companies handed over to them by the owners at throw-away prices before they left for home. By becoming industrialists, the Marwaris shed their compradorial character considerably and also assumed the role of a national bourgeoisie.

The Bengali swadeshi industrialists, despite the negelct of British government and the British capitalists carried on their enterprise in their unique way. They raised their own capital, improvised their own machinery and manufactured their viable indigenous products. They were the national bourgeois per se. Thus Banga Laxshmi Cotton Mill, Mohini Mill, Indian Machinery & Co., Bengal Lamp, Bengal Waterproof, National Tannery, Bengal Pottery, Martin Burn taken over by R. N. Mukherjee, United Bank of India, Bengal Chemical, Ananda Bazar Patrika, Hindustan Insurance - all flourished in the 30s and 40s. Most of them were small and middle scale industries and could not survive for long. Some collapsed after the Partition and some after independence, but a few overcame the trauma of the struggle for independence and Partition and rose to become big concerns. Two of them the United Bank of India and the Hindustan Insurance Company were nationalised in the post-independence period. Bengal Lamp and Bengal Chemical became sick industries and were later taken over by the State Government. But in recent years, Ananda Bazar Patrika, Peerless Group of Companies, Development Consultants and Sahara India are big Bengali Companies which have hit the headlines in Indian business scenario. Many food chains and fabric and saree shops are doing good business in the region at a lower level.[10]

Bengali business heritage therefore spans more than 300 years. This history has been deliberately sidelined in the modern Indian historiography. Bengalis did not wallow in landlordism and clerkdom. It is all the more creditable that Bengalis have maintained a business identity with their high cultural profile. Now even Bengali NRIs like Purnendu Chatterjee and Bikram Dasgupta have started investing in Petro-chemicals and I.T. industries. Time has come for the Bengalis to turn the corner in business. Historians beware of it !

Notes and References

1. C. Palit : Growth of Commerce and Industry in Bengal, BNCCI, Kolkata,1991, pp. 9-18.
2. Ibid.
3. Ibid.
4. Ibid, pp. 18-26.
5. Ibid.
6. Ibid, pp. 26-37.
7. Ibid, pp. 58-67.
8. Ibid, pp. 67-83.
9. Ibid, pp. 98-104.
10. Ibid, pp. 138-160.

13

The Marwaris : Transition from Trader to Industrialist

Pranjal Kumar Bhattacharyya

The present paper seeks to trace how from traders the Marwaris eventually shot into prominence in modern industries in colonial India during and after World War I. After a very brief resume of their role as traders, an attempt has been made to identify the different modern industries where they ventured till 1947, highlighting the diverse viewpoints of business historians regarding the reasons for this significant shift from trade and its nature. The paper, it is hoped, would show that the pre-eminence of the Marwaris as industrialists today has its roots in the colonial period, especially because of the outbreak of World War I which created a situation that was conducive to their venture into industries.

The Marwaris had been primarily traders till the outbreak of World War I and all scholars agree that their ties with British rule and British capital during this period were compradorial in character. 'The establishment of British power furnished the conditions of their migration from different parts of Rajasthan. There was a gradual decline in their traditional activities like 'financing the warring princely states and trading along Rajasthan's caravan routes'. New opportunities 'to serve as intermediaries in the foreign oriented commerce' developed by the British presented themselves before the Marwaris and they successfully availed themselves of these opportunities. The British adopted a discriminatory policy 'against businesses based in the princely states of Rajasthan' and 'provided relative security of property to those based in British India'.[1]

The Marwaris used to sell in the domestic markets goods imported through British firms and procured raw produce from the hinterland through their correspondents for the same firms for export.[2] They were initially employed as brokers and agents under the European Agency Houses which had controlled trades in Eastern India and had consolidated their position during 1860-1914.[3]

A number of Marwari traders also served as banians and brokers of British merchants and industrialists. Ghanashyam Das Birla wrote to Ambalal Sarabhai on 30 April, 1930 : "You know Marwaris are mainly responsible for the establishment of the Manchester market in Calcutta".[4] They also acted as leading speculators. In fact, the Marwaris made fortunes by speculating on raw jute, gunny and hessian, imported cement and sugar, cotton, grains as well as on company shares.[5] The firm of 'Baldeodas Jugal Kishor', so called after Ghanashyam Das Birla's father and elder brother, traded in wheat, silver, oilseeds, etc. and was one of the leading exporters of opium to China.[6] The Birlas started procuring raw jute for British industry and established contacts with Mitsui and other Japanese trading firms. They were supposed to have been the first Calcutta firm to import Japanese cloth in 1911. The house of Keshoram Poddar was among the first to deal with Japan which had at that time become one of the important cloth exporting countries. The Japanese managers like R.N.D. Senda from Mitsui 'seem to have been far more accessible to the Marwaris than the British'.[7]

A Marwari group was enlisted as banians when the Bird and Co. opened its piece-goods department as an agency in Calcutta. Sir Hari Ram Goenka was the guaranteed broker to Ralli Bros., the largest of the cloth importers by the time of World War I and one of the leading exporters of raw jute and hessians. Kettlewell Bullen, another European Managing Agency, had the Goenkas as banians. Besides, they procured and supplied raw jute to local mills and to Dundee and Germany.[8] Sir Omkarmal Jatia was the banian of Andrew Yule and Company, Lakshmi Narain Kanoria of Mcleod and Company, and Rameshwar Nathani of Jardine Skinner. By 1913 the firm of Bacchraj Jamnalal Bajaj had reaped a profit of Rs.75 lakhs by shipping out 40,000 bales of cotton a year to the Japanese.[9]

The Marwaris, however, began to shift from trade to modern industry during and especially after World War I and eventually shot into prominence as industrialists. Many examples may be cited to show their emergence as industrialists in this period. From control of the raw jute market they first entered into jute baling and then into jute manufacturing which till then was dominated by the Scots. To Omkar Goswami, perhaps the most significant index of Marwari presence in the jute trade was the phenomenal growth of *fatka* or speculation in raw jute as well as gunny. The *fatka* was 'exclusively' a Marwari institution and introduced by the Marwari traders as early as the beginning of the 20th century. The European controlled Indian Jute Mills' Association (IJMA) had already 'begged the Government to ban *fatka* which was apparently making legitimate trade something of a huge gamble'.[10] The Birlas, who had entered the cotton business, invested in a ginning press and purchased two mills in Bombay, one in 1917 and the other in 1919.[11] Ghanashyam Das Birla assisted the Marwari traders of Calcutta in making direct contact with the jute market in Europe and founded the first Indian Office in London in 1917 for jute export. The office was, however, not admitted to the 'official' Baltic Exchange for many years.[12] In 1919 he had the first jute mill constructed near Calcutta.[13] Sir Sarupchand Hukumchand, a Marwari banker of Indore, built a large scale jute mill named after him in the same year also near Calcutta, followed by an insurance company and a large steel processing mill. He competed with the Birlas in jute manufacturing till 1939 when he sold out his mills to them. His firm also acted as banians to the Bird and Co. since 1920 when it took out an agency of a Manchester firm, Ledward and Taylor, for their piece-goods.[14] Keshoram Poddar bought a cotton mill from Andrew Yule in 1918. Hargovindas Dalmia of Calcutta bought the Mathuradas Mills for Rs. 5 lakhs in 1921.[15] Surajmal Jalan, a founder of Surajmal Nagarmal, a very large Marwari firm, founded the Hanuman Jute Mill in Calcutta in 1928.[16] The family of Harduttrai Chamaria, a great opium speculator, and a very wealthy Marwari, built two jute mills in the early 1930s, one in Katihara, (Purnea), and the other near Jogvani Station.[17] The firm of Kanoria founded their first jute mill in 1935.[18] These jute mills are significant from the point of view of India's industrialization because they represented the first large jute mills owned by the Indians in the colonial era.

The Birlas floated a Rs. 18 lakh equity textile mill in Gwalior in 1921. The shift of its site from Delhi, where they had already built a mill, to Gwalior was prompted by concessions or loans from the Maharaja.[19] The Singhanias were major financiers of the early British-owned mills in Kanpur and, in return, received sole selling agencies for them. The war time profits enabled them to set up in 1921 their first cotton mill in Kanpur. More cotton mills, one jute factory and two sugar mills followed .[20] The Singhanias also had heavy investments in the European controlled mills of Kanpur, especially the Atherton West Mill.[21] By 1916 Sir Sarupchand Hukumchand had set up three cotton mills and took over the management of another in 1918.[22] In Indore the Bhandari family built their first cotton textile mill in 1922. Other Marwari-owned cotton textile mills were located through Central India as well as in the major industrial centres.[23] Birla's 'encouragement' of any venture into industry and its 'profitability' in the 1920s contributed to the establishment of six Indian and one Armenian mill in Calcutta.[24]

The firm of Anandilal Poddar, a broker to other Bombay firms, dealt in cotton, grain, etc. In 1919 Poddar became chief broker to Toyo Menka Kaisha Ltd., a subsidiary of Mitsui. An old cotton mill of Bombay was purchased in 1926 by a Japanese Syndicate which included Poddar as one of its members and was renamed Toyo Poddar Cotton Mills Ltd. The managing director, the general manager and the technical adviser were all Japanese.[25]

Though a few pioneering Marwari firms had owned marginal coal mines and tea gardens in the period before World War I, several Marwari firms bought major collieries and a few tea gardens during the 1920s.[26] In fact, the business of trading in coal throughout the sub-continent was very much in Marwari hands. There were thirteen Marwari directors in the eighty-two collieries listed in the

Investors' India Year Book, 1930-31 which were under European managing agencies. The Jatias completely took over the Parasea colliery whose board now had three Marwaris and only one European.[27] The Aggarwal brothers and Sukhlal Karnani took over the collieries under H.V.Low and Company, a leading European managing agency in the coal industry.[28] The Marwaris also controlled the Stock Exchange of Calcutta. The protective tariff for sugar in 1932 led to the construction of a large number of sugar mills in eastern UP and western Bihar. Government encouragement helped the cement industry. Ghanashyam Das Birla built three 'giant sugar mills' and Dalmia built one. The Seksarias, already prominent in Bombay textiles, and the Khaitans were involved in some others.[29] In the paper industry the Marwaris accounted for 29% of the capacity available in the Eastern region and were setting up mills in other regions as well.[30] Ramkrishen Dalmia became 'a major factor' in the cement industry.[31] The Goenkas first entered into industry in 1934 when they purchased the Kamala Mill in Bombay. They also owned a number of tea gardens and many power companies in Patna, Saharanpur and Bangalore.[32] The Ruias were managing agents of cotton textile mills in 1934 and one of the leading Marwari industrial firms of Bombay.[33] The Bangurs owned two cotton mills, one in Bombay and one in Rajasthan. They also had a cement company in Saurashtra.[34] The Marwaris also were buyers of shares sold by the European agency firms. R.N. Jaju, the biographer of Birla writes: "By 1935-36 the Birlas had ten big industries : four (cotton) textile mills, five sugar mills and a jute mill. First the boom in the speculation market and then the (second world) war gave a boost to their activities and they acquired twenty-two big factories for an investment of only rupees twenty crores."[35]

Economists and economic historians differ in their explanations of the reasons for the shift of the Marwaris from trade to industry. First, it is agreed that the Marwaris had accumulated enough capital as traders and speculators and liquid assets from the war boom to invest into industries. Second, it has been suggested that the Marwaris had a long history of business heritage as a 'resource group' for upcoming entrepreneurs within the caste providing experience, connection and finance. As Timberg writes : "They did not sink too much of their capital inland but preferred more risky and perhaps more profitable pursuits. It was partly because they had relatively easy access to credit, information, and man power from their organization as a commercial community. A historical explanation is that their circumstances and connections enabled them to migrate throughout India, and enter several profitable commercial lines opened up by the British."[36] Timberg further points out that as the Marwaris moved into industry, other transformations occurred among them. They were very much influenced by the movements for nationalism, social reform, and "modernization". "In part these movements helped put the Marwaris into industry, because industry was felt to be more productive than trade. Industry decreased dependence on England while trade was the substance of that dependence. Industry was a modern activity; trade a traditional one." Industry was also 'profitable' as 'it enabled its owners to contribute to political movements, to aspire to higher social levels, even to abandon industry' and plough back the profits earned in other fields.[37]

Third, as suggested by V.I. Pavlov, a Soviet theoretician, there was a decreased demand in the export market, especially after the Great Depression of 1929-1933. This led the Marwaris to look for new investment opportunities in industry. He points out that industries developed in the 1930s, high grade cotton textiles, sugar and cement were all oriented to the internal market, as compared to the external orientation of the older jute and cotton textile industries.[38] Another Soviet interpretation looks on this shift as 'the essence of the transmutation of the Indian capitalist class, from one of compradors, ancillary to foreign business, to an independent factor in the country's development'.[39] Fourth, S.K.Ghosh is strongly of the opinion that the shift of the Marwaris from trade to industry was influenced by a change in the industrial policy of the Government since World War I.[40] The same opinion is shared by B. R. Tomlinson and Timberg. With World War I industrialization was officially proclaimed as the aim in the economic field. The reasons for the proclaimed change in policy arose from the conditions of war. Three main groups of reasons may be distinguished — military strategic reasons, competitive economic reasons, and inner political reasons. The war conditions, the breakdown of communications and supplies exposed the weakness of the old-style Indian Empire and of the whole British strategic position in the East. This was due to the failure to develop the most elementary basis of modern industry in India and the consequent dependence for vital military needs on long distance overseas supplies. Foreign competitors like the Japanese and the Americans were beginning to break down the British monopoly in the Indian market and the weakening of the British industrial position because of war needs threatened to open the way to a rapid foreign advance after World War I and the loss of the Indian market. The danger, as Viceroy Lord Hardinge explained in his despatch to the Secretary of State for India on 26 November, 1915, was that India would become 'the dumping ground for the manufacture of foreign nations'. Viceroy Lord Chelmsford wrote to King George V on 21 July 1917: "We are of course handicapped by our inability to procure machinery and by the necessity we are of under establishing industries which should have been set up in pre-war days."[41] The Indian Industrial Commission set up in 1916 under the Chairmanship of Sir Thomas Holland of the Munitions Board indicated a major change in the industrial policy of the Government of India.[42] Its report of 1918 pointed out that the list of industries which were lacking in India was 'lengthy and ominous'. It made 'a clear exposition of a detailed and subtle plan for Indian industrial development', advocated that Central Government 'play a major role' in industrialization 'by the investment of social overhead capital, the promotion of technical education and research, the provision of industrial banks and the supply of direct financial and entrepreneurial assistance to private industry where necessary'.[43] The Indian Fiscal Commission was appointed in 1921 and Tariff Boards for selected industries in subsequent years. Finally, to maintain control of India during World War I and in the disturbed period after the War, it was imperative to secure the co-operation of the Indian bourgeoisie. It was necessary to make certain concessions and promise of concessions, economic and political, to win their support. Concessions were granted, as Judith Brown says, 'to contain growing public discontent and to attract collaborators who would form a stable foundation for their rule'.[44] Timberg adds, 'the growing clamours of the Indian nationalist movement, the demise of *laissez faire* ideology at home, and the general recession of Imperialist self-confidence' were also among the causes of the change in the industrial policy of the Government. The feeling developed that 'the colonizer had an obligation to actively assist the economic growth of the colony'. Consequently, the Government of India after the War undertook a series of programmes to encourage selected Indian industries. There was resistance to the industrial drive but the large Marwari houses were economically strong enough to overcome it.[45] Their enterprise and efficiency also helped them. But they were abused and blamed for all the woes of industries. *Capital* called them 'mugs with money'. Ghanashyam Das Birla was singled out as `the villain of the peace.[46] He was `the mammon of unrighteousness' as Sir James Grigg, Finance Member of the Government of India, commented in 1939. He complained that expatriate businessmen were 'making friends' with the 'mammon'.[47]

Amiya Kumar Bagchi and Rajat Kanta Ray have attempted to explain the shift of the Marwaris from trade to industry 'in terms of a dichotomy' between the export and the import sectors. The implicit hypothesis is that the Europeans, with their substantial knowledge of foreign markets controlled or monopolised the export oriented sectors while the Indians with their knowledge of local markets moved into the domestic sectors.[48] Omkar Goswami has, however, dubbed it as an 'expatriate-centric view', a view which asserts that 'under colonialism natives had access only to residual areas'. The Marwaris not only entered into 'activities catering to the domestic market but had firmly entrenched themselves in traditional European enclaves such as jute and coal'. Even in an European-industry as jute, the powers of the Europeans were weaker than what one generally believed. "They could not effectively penalise Indian interlopers for not adhering to the European rules of the game".[49]

Different viewpoints about the reasons for the shift of the Marwaris from trade to industry notwithstanding, their dominant role as industrialists continued unabated . By the time of India's independence they not only moved into new industrial activities but were poised to take over industries which were the exclusive preserves of the expatriates. They also developed all linkages of business amongst the business communities of India. In 1925 Ghanashyam Das Birla formed the Indian Chamber of Commerce (ICC), Calcutta, to represent new capital and industry. It laid stress on raising larger resources and encouraging a professional secretariat. It was the ICC which would acquire importance on the national scene and joined with its counterparts in Bombay to form the Federation of Indian Chambers of Commerce and Industry (FICCI) in 1927 - the major business organization of India. Ghanashyam Das Birla, President of the ICC, was the first Vice President of the FICCI and later was elected President in 1930.

The 1940s witnessed the gradual decline of British political domination in India and the growing entry of American capital. It was during this period that the Birlas ventured into the automobile industry. In 1942 Birla with a paid-up capital of Rs. 4.96 crores set up the Hindusthan Motors Ltd. It was a major industrial enterprise. Birla also moved into engineering industry and set up the Textile Machinery Corporation (TEXMACO) with a capital of Rs. 1 crore. It performed remarkably well during the period of World War II because of 'the fall in machinery imports from Britain and Northern Ireland'.[50] Hind Cycles started functioning since 1940 and the United Commercial Bank was set up in 1943. In June 1945 an agreement was concluded between the Birla Bros. Ltd. and the Nuffield Organization in England for the manufacture of motor cars - Morris cars - in India. It was reported in a section of the press that the agreement would provide for the establishment of a joint company in India. The Nuffields would have a share in the capital to the tune of 25 to 30%, royalties for patents, etc. The Nuffields would manufacture and supply the technical parts which could not be economically made in India and the technicians of the Nuffields were to decide which components should be made in Britain and which in India. As reported by the Birlas' *Eastern Economist*, there was 'a merger of financial interests between Nuffield and Birla' which formed 'the basis of the new enterprise'.[51] The Managing Director of the Nuffield Organization, Miles Thomas came to India to finalize the deal.[52] The first car was produced in 1950 with the brand name of Hindustan. Incidentally the House of Tata also made similar agreements with the Imperial Chemical Industries of Britain.

The agreements between the Indian big capital and the foreign big capital were, however, opposed by the small industrialists and merchants who wanted to get rid of foreign capital and thereby promote indigenous industries. The difference of opinion between the two sections of the Indian bourgeoisie came to a head in 1944 when the Indian big capital led by Ghanashyam Das Birla, J.R.D. Tata, Sri Purshotamdas Thakurdas and others sponsored the so-called Bombay Plan. It was called 'A Brief Memorandum Outlining a Plan of Economic Development for India'. It provided for foreign loans of Rs.700 crores to finance the Rs.10,000 crores plan. The publication of the plan was followed by the visit of Ghanashyam Das Birla, J.R.D. Tata and other top business magnates to the U.S.A. and the U.K. and invitation to foreign capital to invest in India.[53] Manu Subedar, the representative from Bombay to the Indian Merchants' Chamber, denounced in 1945 that an 'illegitimate marriage' of Indian and foreign big businesses was being celebrated.[54]

By 1945 British firms feeling 'insecure' because of sweeping nationalism began to sell out to their older Indian associates. Many Marwari firms bought European managing agencies. Dalmia bought Govan Brothers and Bennett Coleman which owned *The Times of India*. Bangur bought Kettlewell Bullen, Surajmal Nagarmal bought Davenport and Mcleods in jute and many other lines. Badridas Goenka bought Octavius Steel and Duncan Brothers. Kanoi bought Anderson Wright. The Birlas bought Sirpur Paper and Sirsilks from the Hyderabad princely state Government and acquired other Hyderabad firms from other groups. 66 European firms have been transferred to Indian ownership by 1952.[55]

The shift of the Marwaris from trade to industry during and after World War I has prompted scholars like V.I. Pavlov, A.I. Levkovsky and Rajat Kanta Ray to suggest that from being comprador bourgeoisie the Marwaris became national bourgeoisie. Bipan Chandra has also suggested that the capitalist class that developed after 1914 'did not develop an organic link with British capitalism: it was not integrated with foreign capital in India'.[56] These suggestions have been contradicted by other scholars. M. Kidron holds that in the period before World War II, the Indian big bourgeoisie was eager more for collaboration with the British than hostility. The foreigners had shares in Indian companies, the managing agents were foreigners, the indigenous companies had to depend on foreign experts for their proper functioning and on foreign machinery. It was these colonial constraints that have led Amiya Kumar Bagchi and Paresh Chattopadhyay to describe Indian capitalism as 'dependent capitalism'. This aspect of collaboration was discernible in the 1940s when various agreements were made with foreign companies.

Nevertheless, it is undeniable that the Marwaris had to work in a given situation. As entrepreneurs they indeed played a vital role in India's industrialization, albeit limited, in the colonial era and succeeded in establishing an identity as an Indian business community. Their ties with British rule and British capital till the outbreak of World War I were no doubt compradorial in character and there were also many instances of collaboration with the foreigners for the industrial development of India in the post-war period. A question, however, might be put : was there any viable alternative route available to the Marwari community or, for that matter, to any business community bent on industrializing India in the colonial period? In proper historical perspectives the Marwaris should not be denied the epithet of national bourgeoisie.

Notes and References

1. Thomas A. Timberg, *The Marwaris : From Traders to Industrialists*, New Delhi, 1978, p. 97
2. S.K. Ghosh, *The Indian Big Bourgeoisie : Its Genesis, Growth and Character* (Second Edition), Calcutta, 2000, p. 200.
3. Timberg, op.cit., p. 56.
4. Cited in Ghosh, op.cit., p. 201.
5. Ibid.
6. Ibid.
7. Timberg, op.cit., p. 63.
8. Ghosh, op.cit., p. 204.
9. Timberg, op cit., p.155, p. 220.
10. Omkar Goswami, "Then came the Marwaris: Some aspects of the changes in the pattern of industrial control in Eastern India" in *The Indian Economic and Social History Review*, XXI, No. 3, July-September, 1985, p. 231.
11. Ghosh, op.cit., p. 201.
12. Timberg, op.cit., p. 62, p. 171.
13. Ibid, p. 64.
14. *A History of Bird and Company 1864 - 1929*, II, Calcutta, 1929, p. 319.
15. Timberg, op.cit., p. 64, p. 171.
16. Ibid, p. 228.
17. *Ibid*, p. 64, p. 228.
18. Ghosh, op.cit., p. 204.
19. Timberg, op.cit., p. 171; Ghosh, op.cit., p. 202.
20. Ghosh, op.cit., p. 203.
21. Ibid, p. 204; Timberg, op.cit., p. 228.
22. Timberg, op.cit., p. 228.
23. Ibid, p. 64.
24. Goswami, op.cit., pp. 234-35.
25. Timberg, op.cit., pp. 183-184; S.M. Rutnagar,

Bombay Industries : The Cotton Mills, Bombay, 1927, p. 721.

26. Timberg, op.cit., p. 64.
27. Goswami, op.cit., p. 233.
28. Ibid.
29. Timberg, op.cit., p. 64.
30. Goswami, op.cit., p, 243.
31. Timberg, op.cit., p. 64.
32. Ghosh, op.cit., pp. 204-205.
33. Ibid, p. 205.
34. Ibid.
35. R.N. Jaju, *G.D. Birla : A Biography*, New Delhi, 1985, p. 75, p.77, p.130.
36. Timberg, op.cit., p. 175.
37. Ibid, pp. 67-68.
38. Timberg,op.cit., pp. 64-65; A. Bagchi, "Entrepreneurship in India, 1900-1930" in S.Mukherjee and E. Leach (Eds.), *Elites in South Asia*, Cambridge, England, pp. 243-244.
39. Timberg, op.cit., p. 65.
40. Ghosh, op.cit., p. 189.
41. Cited in Ghosh, op.cit., pp. 189-190.
42. B.R. Tomlinson, *The Political Economy of the Raj 1914-1947*, London, 1979, p. 58.
43. Ibid, pp. 58-59.
44. Judith Brown, *Gandhi's Rise to Power*, Cambridge, 1972, p. 123.
45. Timberg, op.cit., p. 65.
46. Goswami, op.cit., p. 234.
47. Tomlinson, op.cit., p. 53.
48. A.K. Bagchi, *Private Investment in India, 1900-1939*, Cambridge, 1970, p. 195.
49. Goswami, op.cit., p. 244.
50. *Ibid*, p. 246.
51. Cited in Ghosh, op.cit., p. 248.
52. Ghosh, op.cit., p. 248.

53. Ibid, p. 247.
54. Ibid, p. XXIII.
55. Timberg, op.cit., p. 78.
56. Bipan Chandra, "The Indian Capitalist Class and British Imperialism" in R. S. Sharma (Ed.), *Indian Society: Historical Probings*, p. 391.

14

Caste, Religious Traditions, Society and Business Network : A Case Study of the Marwari Community of North Bengal

The Composition of every society and its ethos are largely determined by religion, caste, tradition and customs. In a changing world, the characteristics of any society are bound to undergo gradual change under the impact of progress in science and technology as well as some changes in the religious outlook of the people. In our country too, changes have occurred over the decades, in our plural society with six major religious communities (Hindus, Muslims, Sikhs, Buddhists, Jains and Christians) and numerous caste and linguistic groups.

The Community :

In the present paper, attention has been focussed on the Marwari community with its religions, rutials, tradition and its distinctive characteristics. Here I propose to dwell on how the Marwaris, a 'baniya' ('trading') class, moved to the North Bengal region and established themselves as a dominant business community in the area.

Strictly speaking, the inhabitants of Marwar should be termed as Marwaris. But it is a common practice to term the inhabitants hailing from the State of Rajasthan and its adjoining places, as Marwaris, though Marwar was technically only an old State of Jodhpur in Rajasthan. Thomas A. Timberg, an expert on the Marwaris writers, "Since significant groups of traders and industrialist come from the Shekhawati region of the neighbouring states of Jaipur and Biakner and other areas of Rajasthan, there has been a tendency to join all these Rajasthani emigrants under the rubric of Marwar. In colloquial usage, outside of Rajasthan, Marwari is used to refer to emigrant businessmen from the vicinity of Rajasthan".[1] A recent researcher on the Mawaris, Dr. D.K. Taknet says, "Marwar is confined to the geographical and cultural aspects of Rajasthan. In fact, three factors: language, geography and the exclusive social caste phenomena constitute the Marwaris who use dialects spoken all over Rajasthan except for Bharatpur, Dholpur and Karauli regions. Some people living in Rajasthan, Haryana, Punjab and a few parts of Madhya Pradesh have their origin in Marwar and have similar lifestyles and traditions."[2] According to All India Marwari Yuba Manch, all persons having adopted the lifestyle, language or culture of Rajasthan, Haryana, Malwa in Madhya Pradesh or nearby regions and who themselves or whose forefathers living whether in India or any part of the world, would be identified as the 'Marwaris'.[3]

Religion and Caste :

The Marwaris are a community by themselves in India and they are separated by caste, religion, ritual, regional and economic differences and like all the communities living in India, the Marwari community, as we all know, is divided by several castes or jatis. Like the Rig Vedic Aryans, this community was divided into four castes ('Chatur Varnas'), viz., the Brahmanas, the Kashatriyas, the Vaishyas and the Sudras. The Brahmanas were at the top of the society, having taught the Kshatriyas and Vaishyas, observed religious customs and rituals, and worshipped gods and goddesses. They mostly lived by remuneration or lands provided either by the State or by royal families.

The Kshatriyas were the protectors of the societies and their social status was next to that of the Brahmanas. Members of this caste were known as the Rajputs who had a glorious past.

Bravery, self-sacrifice and chivalry were invariably associated with the Rajputs. The Rajput women once glorified their womenhood by performing the horrible rite 'Jauhar' ('Jawaharbrata') to preserve their chastity from invading Muslim miscreants. This practice proved their bravery, devotion, patriotism and heroism and this heroic posture of the Rajputs helped them in later years to take part in the bold venture of trade and commerce which is full of risk and adventure. Dr. Taknet truly writes, "A glorious tradition of gallantry has been set by the martial castes of Shekhawati like the Rajputs, the Jats, the Yadavas, the Kayamkhanis and the Gujars. The Kshatriyas have continued the tradition till date, though other castes have also not lagged behind."[4]

The Vaishyas had been ranked third in the social hierarchy. Later, they became Mahajans or money-lenders. But basically, they were traders and were connected with both export and import business and to some extent with retail and wholesale trade too and that is why they are often called 'baniyas'. Among the four castes of the Marwaris, they were the pioneers who have migrated to every nook and corner of India in quest of career in the 19th century. Perhaps there is no periphery in India where they did not migrate. The discomfiture of the geographical conditions had created in them, since their birth, the spirit of enterprise, adventure, hard work, fortitude, frugality, adjustment, moneysaving habit and it admits of no doubt that all these human qualities are essentially required for a man or a community to achieve success in trade and commerce.

The Vaishyas are sub-divided into a few categories, such as Agarwals, Maheshwaris, Oswals, Khandelwals, Porwals and so on. Of them Oswals and Jains and the rest are Hindus. The Agarwals are the followers of Raja Agrasena of Agroa which is situated in Haryana and that is why their surname is 'Agarwal'. At first, Agrasena was a Khsatriya but for some reason or the other, he gave up 'Khsatra Achara' and became a Vaishya. The Maheshwaris are the devotees of god Maheshwara (Shiva) and for this reason, they commemorate the day 'Mahesh Navami' of every year as the inaugural date of their society. According to a legend, they were transformed from Rajputs to Vaishyas by the grace of god 'Mahesh' (Shiva).

The Jains are sub-divided into two sects — Oswals and Saraogis and of them again some belong to Shuetamber and some to Digambar sects. Though by religion they are Jains, by practice, they are, to some extent, Hindus. Among the Marwaris in general, the folk-god 'Hanumanji' has been very popular.[5]

The Sudras were the last in social ranking. They were the backward class people in the society and their major duty was to serve the other communities.

However, the traditional or ancient caste – composition did not remain un-altered in modern times and a kind of inter-castes toleration among the various castes, and sub-castes of the Mariwaris grew up with the passage of time. There are instances of taking to money-lending as a profession by the Brahmanas. So also the Kshatriyas were taking up business as an occupation. Generally speaking, there are at present only two wings of the Marwari Community as a whole — the Brahmanas and the Vaishyas. The Brahmanas generally perform religious duties and rituals, though again many of them are inclined to seek employment and some also do business, specially hotel business by opening 'dhabas' (wayside eateries).[6]

Incentive to business

One may be curious to know why the Marwaris took to business as their occupation. Socio-economic compulsions such as the barrennees of the soil of Rajputana, increased population pressure, bad or oppressive law, heavy taxation, religious bondage, natural calamities like scanty rainfall, famine and plagues, no doubt, provided an inducement to go into business.[7] But perhaps a positive inducement also came from their religion. Jainism preached non-violence (ahimsa) according to which, the killing of any creature is a great sin. The vow of non-violence was so rigid that even an unconscious killing of an ant, while walking, was regarded as a sin. Non-violence was an obsession with the Jains, and the wore a muslin mask which covered the mouth and nose to prevent the involuntary inhalation of even microscopic insects. So agriculturists could not opt for Jainism as cultivation involved killing insects and pests. Jainism also denied crafts as a profession, for it endangered the life of other creatures, which meant committing of vice. Even ownership of land was very much limited within the fold of Jainism. So with the prohibition on farming, craftsmanship and restriction on ownership of land, trade and commerce were the only possible occupation open to the Jains and the encouragement of frugality prescribed by Jainism also coincided with a proclivity to take up commerce as an occupation. For these reasons, Jainism spread rapidly among the trading community to which the Marwaris belonged.[8]

The discovery of new routes and the revival of the old were further incentives to trade.[8] The Jains became gradually experts in the purchase and sale of manufactured goods as bankers and in the job as middlemen. Thus Jainism became interlinked with the spread of city culture. The prospect of maritime commerce was bright on the west coast of India, where the Jains became the money-lenders while others sailed overseas with their merchandise.[9] The Marwari Community initially was of Jain faith, though caste division has been a later development. Naturally, they opted for trade and commerce, the only possible occupation open to them.[10]

These religious factors also coincided with the non-existence of any business community in the North-Bengal region. W.W. Hunter writes, "There seems to be no tendency on the part of the people to gather into towns, or into seats of commerce and industry. The population is a purely agricultural one, and Deputy-Commissioner estimates that forty nine out of every fifty persons live more or less by cultivation".[11]

Migration to North Bengal – a Zone with Considerable Business Potential :

The North Bengal zone has a great commercial prospect which had been a point of attraction to any migrant merchant community. The three basic components of its economy were tea, timber and trade. The cultivation of various cash crops like jute, tobacco, tea, coffee, orange, cardamom and preservation of forests for good quality of timber, etc. had greatly enriched the commercial heritage of this region. The Cooch Behar state was famous for its tobacco cultivation in addition to jute and paddy. Jalpaiguri and Darjeeling won world-wide renown for plantation of tea and tea industries in addition to tobacco, jute, paddy, timber, etc. However, the impetus to cultivation of various cash crops came from the British. The princely state of Coach Behar came under British tutelage in the second half of the 18th century. Jalpàiguri had been brought under British revenue administration earlier as it was once a part of British India. So the traditional mode of cultivation of this region had been superseded by advanced and scientific methods of cultivation. Darjeeling was handed over to the British by the Raja of Sikkim in 1835. Immediately after its cessation, various development projects had been initiated by the British to make Darjeeling a trade center in connection with frontier trade among the Himalayan and Sub-Himalayan countries like Nepal, Sikkim, Bhutan and Tibet. The Britishers had also a great ambition to open up a trade link between Calcutta and China, even with central Asia through the trans-Himalayan mountainous trade routes.[12]

Kinship and Fellow-Feeling:

The kinship, caste and religious systems of a region also produce an inducement to human or community migration. The Marwari migration, to some extent, was influenced by these factors, though other commercial groups in Bengal took this hypothesis from the social point of view. These groups had a heterogeneous character, unlike the professional commercial groups from outside Bengal – the Oswals, the Agarwals, the Khetris, etc. The Marwari migrants, once established their business in a particular place, would always lend a helping hand to a person of their own community, caste and religion, coming from their own native places, by making arrangements for his food and lodging at their own 'basas or goddis' (dwelling places or business–cum–residential establishments). Sometimes they would even provide a temporary job to their fellow migrant so that he could initially start his career there. This kinship bondage or community feeling facilitated further migration. Dr. Taknet truly writes: "This is a well-known fact that early migrants attracted large groups from Rajasthan mainly by virtue of the ties of religion and kinship."[13] The Marwaris expert Thomas A. Timberg also expresses the same view by stating that sometimes the presence of one big firm owned by a fellow of his community, as in the case of Jagat Seth of Mushidabad, would attract immigrants. Marwari traders also set up shops in new areas because their friends and family wanted agents there.[14]

To these were added the militarism of Rajputs and the predatory hordes of Mairs who perhaps pushed the Marwari migrants in the same direction and persuaded the enterprising class to move out in quest of fresh woods and pastures new.[15]

However, a few deviations could be marked in connection with Marwari migration in the districts under study – a contrast indeed to the general theory of migration. The marriage of females had been a factor in the process of human migration. But this cause was not a potent factor in the case of Marwari migration to the region under study. Here, the female migrant came, not by virtue of marriage from her paternal house to her in-laws, but by virtue of husband-wife relationship or family ties and that again, after her husband or her family members here settled well. That is why the female migration at the initial stage of migration was conspicuous by its absence. Prof. Haraprasad Chattopadhyaya who has made a special study of internal migration in India has stated that the normal practice of the Marwaris had been, however, to migrate, unaccompanied by the womenfolk.[16] But things changed during the last decade of the nineteenth century. The number of females in relation to males in the Marwari community in Darjeeling, Jalpaiguri and Cooch-Behar began to increase remarkably. The following table will make the point clear:

Marwari Migrants in the three districts

	1881-91		1891-1901		1901-11		1911-21		1921-31	
Darjeeling	74	6	501	146	753	102	808	117	612	189
Jalpaiguri	45	11	592	265	1007	182	948	524	2201	1132
Cooch-Behar	-	-	689	50	884	64	899	101	627	44

The above table clearly indicates an unprecedented upward trend of female migration in the districts under study. This trend supports the postulate that the Marwari families in those districts had been settled more or less permanently.

Another unusual aspect of Marwari migration into the North Bengal is that the Marwaris did not migrate here as landless agricultural workers as it usually happened in the case of rural to urban migration in quest of employment in factories or industries as wage earners. Here they migrated exclusively as money-lenders or traders. Prof. Chattopadhyaya has noticed that migration between Rajputana and Bengal (which obviously covers the North Bengal region), or, broadly speaking, between Rajputana and the rest of India is essentially understood as a movement of the Marwari community, in search of opportunities for industry, trade and commerce. During the decade 1891-1901, 40,572 persons emigrated from Rajputana to the then Bengal, almost all of whom were traders.[17] This goes contrary to the general theory of human migration.

Another exception could still to be discerned between the general theory of human migration and the Marwari migration in the North-Eastern Region. According to accepted theory, migration usually takes place from the periphery to the centre. But in the North Bengal Zone, Marwari migration took place from the centre to the periphery in the sense that there was, indeed, hardly a remote corner in this zone where they did not migrate. Perhaps the Marwaris could settle in any place or region, be it a remote village or a backward area. This is a rare quality of human beings, which a Marwari possesses.

Specific Factors:

These are the forces and factors behind Marwari migration anywhere in India. But as the present study ventures to focus on the North Bengal syndrome, it is relevant to pinpoint the specific forces and factors which caused the Marwari migration to this region.

(1) North Bengal from time immemorial, had been a purely agricultural tract and the development of its economy was mostly agriculture-based. As most of the people of this region earned their subsistence from agriculture, they took to agriculture rather than commerce as their profession.

W.W. Hunter writes "There seems to be no tendency on the part of the people to gather into towns, or into seats of industry or commerce. The population is a purely agricultural one, and .... that forty-nine out of every fifty persons live more or less by cultivation.[18] The same view, Mr Hunter expresses about Darjeeling and says, "The population of the district is entirely rural .... and live solely by agriculture.[19] The same picture could be found in the district of Cooch-Behar too.[20] Naturally, no business community could emerge from among native inhabitants of this region. So this somewhat rare situation was a positive inducement behind Marwari migration to the districts under study.

(2) Again non-existence of any business community in this zone meant non-competition in the business arena. When the region became extremely viable in respect of its economic potentiality under the aegis of British administration and when commercial agriculture had become a grand success with cultivation of various cash crops, like paddy, jute, tobacco, cotton, cardamom, etc., and plantation of tea, coffee, cinchona, oranges, etc., there was none, to compete with the Marwari traders in the arena of commercial entrepreneurship. In Bombay, there was competition as there existed Gujarati and Parsee merchants, in Calcutta, there were the Bengalees, Europeans, Punjabis, Kashmiris, Beharis, in East Bengal there were the Bengalees, i.e., Subarna Baniks, Gandha Baniks, Vaishya Sahas along with the Marwaris. But in the north-eastern India and more specifically in North Bengal, there had always been a commercial vacuum which the Marwaris filled in. That is why the Marwaris from the very beginning exerted a monopoly control over all kinds of trade and commerce in this region.

(3) Money-lending had been the traditional or rather ancestral profession of the Marwaris and the highlight of their banking business was that, in order to make money-lending exclusively as a monopoly business of their own community, they favoured their own-caste fellows and did not put their money in bank stocks where it could serve the general trading interest. This professional attitude

otherwise helped them to establish their monopoly control over trade and commerce. T.A. Timberg has quoted a Soviet scholar who writes, 'those narrow boundaries within which they contain their banking activities must be to a significant degree correlated with their monopoly position in the trade of Bengal.[21] Fortunately for them, the North Bengal region was a virgin soil of money-lending or banking or Mahajani Business. In the Cooch-Behar State the native people of the State did not come forward to introduce systematic banking establishments in order to lend money to the people who were mostly agriculturists. Only a few 'Bairagi and to some extent some company officers would lend money to the peasants at an exorbitant rate of interest upto 72 per cent. The Commissioner of Cooch Behar, H. Douglus informed the Governor-General in a letter, dated 19 May 1990, that 72 per cent (of interest on money) is considered as very moderate interest and what almost exceeds belief is that in many instances which came to immediate knowledge, 360 per cent has been exacted.[22] There had been no State or government provision for granting agricultural loans to the peasants. So the Dadni Mahajans fully utilized this opportunity in their favour. Ananda Chandra Ghosh, a member of 'the Cooch Behar Hitaishani Sabha' in his historic lecture on the 'History of Cooch Behar' in 1872, had mentioned that in the absence of any strong State economic support base, the money-lender's role in building the agricultural economy was significant.[23] It was only during the reign of Maharaja Nripendra Narayan that the State Co-operative Financing Society was established for providing financial assistance to the peasants.[24] Favourable conditions for the money-lending business prevailed in the district of Jalpaiguri too, for the obvious reason that once upon a time, it was the Baikunthapur Zamindari Estate of Cooch Behar. Still the prospect of the money-lending business had been greater here than in Cooch Behar in view of the fact that the district's economic vitality had increased with the growth of tea plantations and the tea industry since 1874 when a tea garden was opened by Richard Haughton, the pioneer of the tea industry in the Jalpaiguri district. This tea garden was owned by Dr Brougham.[25] So also the growth of tea plantation and the tea industry, attracting an enormous inflow of population, in the district of Darjeeling since its session in 1835 and subsequent additions in 1850 and 1864, made the tract extremely profitable in the money-lending business and since the original inhabitants were averse to this type of economic ventures, the tract had always been left open for any foreign migrant community to start this type of enterprise. So the money-lending profession was a point of attraction of the this region to any migrant community like the Marwaris, the forerunners of India's indigenous system of banking.

(4) Sometimes, the religious identity and caste of a particular community of a region attracts men of the same religion and castes of different regions. The religion and culture of the North-Bengal region are mainly based on Hinduism. Hunter writes, "divided according to religion, the majority of the population of the district of Darjeeling are Hindus whose total number was 69,831 or 73.7 per cent of the district's total population, according to Census Report of 1872'.[26] In the district of Jalpaiguri too, the Hindus occupied the majority position and according to the Census Report of 1872, the Hindus, as loosely grouped together for religious purposes, numbered 1,82,353 or 55.6 percent of the total population of the district.[27] J.F. Gruning has also given a statistical report on the total Hindu population according to the Census of 1801.[28] The same position was maintained in the district of Cooch Behar where the number of the Hindus was 1,27,928 or 72 per cent of the total population according to the Census of 1872.[29]

(5) The Hindu based society of the North Bengal region was another factor of inducement to the migration for the Jain Marwaris whose religion, i.e. Jainism, though it rose as a protest against confused Vedic practices of religion, made a compromise with Hinduism in respect of observance of rituals, customs, etc., and it is due to its affiliation to Hinduism that Jainism could survive in India. Jainism really settled with the Vedic caste system and outwardly showing Vedic rituals.

Apparently, although Jainism seems to be a great impediment to Hinduism, there are many resemblances between the two:

(i) The rise of Jainism mentioned by some scholars as 'Protestant Hinduism', is itself indicative of some kind of assimilation between the two.

(ii) The theory of 'trans-migration of soul' (Janmantaravada)', the doctrine of 'Karma' ('Karmaphalavada') or action and the doctrine of 'non-violence' ('ahimsa') of the Vedas and Upanishadas were borrowed by the Jain preachers.

(iii) Mahavirs, a great religious teacher is supposed to be the prophet and reformer, but not the originator of Jainism. Parsvanatha preached the four vows, viz. ahimsa (non-injury), satya (truth), asteya (abstinence from stealing) and 'aparigraha' (non-attachment to worldly things). To the four, Mahavira added a fifth, i.e. 'Brahmacharya' (Chastity).[30]

(iv) In respect of image workshop, the two religious came close to each other's thoughts and practices. The workshop of Jain image was in vogue as early as the 4th century B.C. This concept of image-workshop became very popular among the Jains and this practice was borrowed from the Brahmanical Hindus first by the Jains and later on by the Buddhists.[31] The Jains pay homage to a class of divinities called Vidyadevi. These goddesses, headed by Sarasvati (goddess of learning), are 16 in number. An epigraphic record reveals the dedication of a statue of Sarasvati by a Jain lay disciple.[32] The Jains also worship other two deities, Ganesh and Laksmi. So it is found that in many respects relating to religion, the Marwaris, the followers of Jainism, were very close to the Hindus in the observance of rites and customs. In this context, one more point to be emphasized is that the Maheswaris, Agarwals Brahmanas, of the Marwari community are the followers of Hinduism. Naturally, the Marwaris with their, to some extent, Hindu outlook did not hesitate, to migrate to a region where the absolute majority population were the exponents of the Hindu faith.[33]

(6) Rajasthan has an affinity with Cooch Behar in another respect. This affinity grew up through the establishment of a

matrimonial relation between Rajasthan and the Cooch Behar State. In 1956, Prabhabati Devi, sister of Maharaja Lakshminarayan of Cooch Behar was given in marriage to Mansing, King of Amber.[34] So also in 1940, Gayatri Devi, the second sister of Maharaja Jagatdipendra Narayan of Cooch Behar was wedded to Mansingji of Jaipur according to Hindu rituals.[35] This feeling of affinity might have enhanced Marwari migration in this region.

After their migration to North Bengal, the Marwaris took up all kinds of business activity. They would first make a modest beginning as money-lenders and retail traders. Sometimes they would also hawk goods, toiling long hours all day to collect small amounts of capital for investment in other ventures.

Those who came almost empty handed with no money to start even a small business, would hawk goods, taken on contract or for sale on a commission basis, from the few fellow Marwaris already settled in the region. Nathmal Lakhotia, for instance, who came to Dimla in Rangpur (now in Bangladesh) in 1870, started his career as a hawker of textile goods.[36] Others who came with some capital usually took to money-lending as the starting enterprise.

Eventually, however, the Marwaris took to all kinds of trade and invested their capital in industrial ventures too. Their enterprises included money-lending, 'Jotedari' (Purchase of 'Jotes' and cultivation with hired labour), 'aratdari' (stock business — maintaining stocks of various goods for sale), import and export business, and wholesale and retail trade. They embarked upon industrial ventures, particularly in tea plantations, at a later stage.

Money-lending :

The Marwaris, as the forerunners of an indigenous banking system in colonial India, had always clung to their traditional business of usury and banking. So when they migrated to North-Bengal, their role as money-lenders remained as important as before. In the district of Malda, silk and cotton weavers obtained their finance from Marwari mahajans. The trade of silk cloths of Murshidabad and Malda also used to be transacted with advances from marwari money-lenders.

In the princely state of Cooch Behar the Marwaris were the leading money-lenders.[37] As there was no landed aristocracy in the State as in rural Bengal and also no state provision to advance agricultural loans to peasants, the Marwaris took advantage of the situation by becoming 'mahajans' providing loans to distressed peasants. But the rate of interest was usually very high – 6 pies per rupees a month or 37.5 percent per annum. The Marwari money-lending system thus proved ruinous for cultivators. An administrative report stated: "A ruinous practice widely prevails here, viz. the system of making advances to the cultivators for their crops. While the crops are still green in the fields, the cultivators take advances or undersell them at wretchedly low rates, while the inability to satisfy the Mahajans brings about suits for the value of crops at rates ruinously exorbitant and the so-called high prices, therefore, inevitably benefit the merchants and impoverish the people. A single season of poor crops and high prices plunges the defaulting cultivator deep into debt, from which years of plenty and prosperity cannot rescue him.[38]

The mode of Marwari money-lending had been so disastrous and slow-poisonous that the State had to think of rescuing the debtors from the clutches of the 'mahajans'. And the Cooch Behar Banking Corporation Ltd. came into existence in 1913. This was the first time that a regular banking business had been started in Cooch Behar.

In the district of Jalpaiguri which was once a part of Cooch Behar State, the nature and scope of money-lending was more or less the same. There was no banking establishment to provide loans. The money-lending business was in the hands of 'Jotedars', shop-keepers, Marwari traders and some others. The business of money-lending to cultivators was almost entirely in the hands of Marwari 'mahajans' who were only a few in number but were bent on making the business a monopoly one exclusively for their community.

When petty loans were advanced by a Marwari 'mahajan' to a borrower pawning ornaments or household goods, the rate of interest varied from 24 to 60 percent according to circumstances. When the loan was large, a mortgage was required by the money-lender on immovable property such as houses or lands and the rate of interest in such cases varied from 18 to 36 per cent.

The money-lending business of the Marwaris had been rather comprehensive and striking in the district of Darjeeling. The increasing importance of the district as a trading zone after its all-round development attempted by the British made the area a suitable place for the money-lending business. The Marwaris with their business acumen were quick to grab this opportunity. They started advancing loans to traders, cultivators and even coolies in distress. Advances were also given to contractors working in tea plantations. The rates of interest were pretty high and exploitative, providing ruinous for many a borrower.

Trade and Commerce :

After they settled in the three northern districts of Cooch Behar, Jalpaiguri and Derjeeling, the Marwaris began to dominate over the Districts' trade and Commerce. In the district of Cooch Behar, they were engaged in all sorts of economic enterprises such as money-lending, 'Jotedari', 'aratdari' (stock business), export and import business and wholesale and retail-trade. Bhagavati Charan Banerjee, Sub-Deputy Superintendent of schools in Cooch Behar, stated in his book "History of Cooch Behar" in 1884 that trade and commerce of this district was mainly controlled by the foreign merchants, most of whom were the 'Kainya' (Marwari) 'mahajana' who came from Jodhpur, Bikaner, Murshidabad and other places. Their main activities centred round the Capital city. Cooch-Behar but they also had their branches in some mofussil towns.[39] According to W.W. Hunter's observation, "Nearly all the Commerce of the State except such as is carried on at the weekly markets is in the hands of foreign merchants, chiefly the Marwaris from Bikaner who bring more energy and enterprise to the work than the Cooch-Behar is usually possess."[40] The Capital city was well-fed by bunders like Haldibari, Mekhligunj, Changrabandha, Mathabhanga, Dinhata, Dewanhat, Shitai, Balarampur, Law Kuthi, Moranga etc.[41] The commodities marketed were tobacco, jute, rice, pulses and mustard seeds.[42] The chief items of exports were tobacco, jute, mustard oil and rice; and the chief items of imports were cloths, salt, utensils, sugar and spices.

Harendra Narayan Chaudhury speaks of the Cooch Behar town : "A bazaar containing a large number of shops of Marwari and Bengali merchants furnishes articles of local and foreign production of every description and variety."[43] The Marwari traders also established 'basas' (business establishments) or shops at every important bundar or trade centre, market, haat or 'ganj' of the district. Haldibari was known for its jute traffic. A contemporary administrative report points out: "Here the Marwari Mahajans used to board jute in abundance to earn a huge amount of profit ranging from Rs. 70,000 to Rs. 80,000 in 1891-92. Similar is the case with the business of tobacco and foodgrains.[44] The stocking of jute was mainly intended as a wait for higher prices and thereby to make large profits. Thus, one well-known Marwari merchant made profits even to the extent of Rs. 80,000 in a single year. However, the Haldibari mahajans did not usually keep jute in stock for long periods. In a rough estimate, the total quantity of jute brought to Haldibari was about 3,50,000 maunds in the single year of 1891-92.[45] The number of jute carts coming to the Haldibari bundar showed an appreciable increase of 1959 in a single year from 65,583 in 1900-01 to 67,542 in 1901-02. The tolls collected from these carts also increased from Rs. 8,197 to Rs. 8,442.12. Here also many Marwari merchants used to even take the risk of stocking large qunatities of jute remaining unsold.[46] Even now a few Marwari Jute Firms exist there though at present trade is limited to traffic with Jalpaiguri.[47]

Chowrahat was another principal seat of commerce in the state. Here also some Marwari merchants had set shops and used to exchange commercial goods. They annually purchased large quantities of jute and exported them to Sirajganj and other places.[48] Babu Hukum Chand Oswal was a notable Marwari merchant of Chowrahat. He imported large quantities of rice to Chowrahat during the bad harvest of 1891-92.[49] He also made a huge purchase of 30,000 maunds of jute. Babu Taktamal did the same of 20,000 maunds of Jute in the single financial year of 1899-1900. There was a dull season for the jute market around 1897-

98. Still Hukum Chand could maintain a stock of about 8,000 maunds of Jute while Kheturam Misser had 25,000 maunds of Jute at his disposal. Other Marwari merchants could stock 5,000 maunds of Jute. Most of the Marwari merchants of Chowrahat used to make annual purchases of large quantities of Jute for export to Sirajganj and other places.[50]

The Mekhligunj bundar was important for its tobacco traffic in addition to rice. Naturally the Marwari merchants had their big shops here. Tobacco was exported to Rangoon and other Burmese ports by boat via Kaliganj in Rangpur and Chittagong.[51] Babu Johermal brought to Mekhliganj and Jamalda large quantities of rice in 1891-92 when the state became badly a victim to natural calamities. Babu Aidam Oswal had a large stock of Jute in that year. He also imported rice in boats from Sirajganj and exported jute in those very boats.[52]

Changrabandha was also a centre of export trade in jute and tobacco. Here the Marwaris had their big shops and were connected with the stock business (aratdari) in tobacco and jute. Now Changrabandha has lost its comemrcial importance. So some Marwari families left this bundar and settled at the nearby town of Jamaldaha where a good business is carried on in jute, tobacco, rice and vegetables.[53]

By far the most important of the bundars in the district is Mathabhanga. The bundar and the haat ground are situated in the northern part of the town wherein were located several big shops of Marwari merchants who traded with the parts of Brahmaputra, Mekhligunj and Narayanganj.[54]

The Dinhata bundar had a long tradition of jute and tobacco trade which undoubtedly, were controlled by the Marwari merchants whose shops grew, centred round the haat.[55] Dewanhat was famous as a tobacco trade centre while Balarampur was an excellent jute centre in addition to being a good mustard oil centre too. Some big Marwari merchants had their business firm there.[56] Lawkuthi was otherwise called Buxiganj. There were some big shops of Marwari merchants. Moranga was a frontier bundar which contain shops of Marwari and Bengali merchants.[57] Bakshirhat and Tufanganj were also other two important commercial seats wherein the Marwari merchants had business firms.

In the district of Jalpiguri, the Marwari predominance over trade and commerce had been more prominent than in Cooch Behar as is evident from the fact that 82 percent of the total commercial organisations in the district had been in the grip of the Marwaris.[58] Although the trading commodities of the district did not differ much from those of the district of Cooch-Behar, the sole exception, of course, was tea. Apart from tea, the district had a number of important items of export, such as rice, paddy, jute, mustard seed, betel-nuts, cotton, lac, sal timber, tobacco, till seed, Bhutia ponies, Bhutia blankets, Yak's tails, ghi, wax, musk, etc. Against those the district had to import the items like brass utensils, salt, oil, cloth, spices, coconuts, cotton, piece goods, machinery, corrugated iron, kerosene oil, and coal and coke.[59] A number of factors such as the tea industry, the influx of population to the western Duars and opening up of the Eastern Bengal State Railway, the Bengal Duars Railway and the Cooch Behar State Railway, provided an impetus to the growth of the district's trade. The principal seats of commerce were Jalpaiguri, Titalya, Rajnagar, Saldanga, Deviganj, Baura, Jorpakri, Mainaguri, Falakata and Alipurduar.

In this district, the Marwaris started their business in cloths at the initial stage. But gradually they entered into business in tobacco, tea, wood, jute, paddy, rice, foodgrains, etc.[60] At the later period, petrol pumps, motor parts, electrical goods, office furniture, jewellery, Courier Service, also entered into their commercial venture. At present most of the tea gardens are owned by the Marwaris. The Daga and Kalyani groups are now the pioneers in tea plantation industries.[61] The overwhelming Marwari predominance over the trade and commerce of the district has been varified by statistics furnished by the Merchant's Association of Jalpaiguri. According to these statistics, 82 persent of the membership of the Association are kept by the Marwaris. In 1987, out of a total of 384 business concerns, the number of Marwaris concerns was 321; in 1988, out of 376, 330; in 1989, out of 387, 318; in 1990, out of 370, 301; and in 1991, out of 371, 302 concerns belonged to the Marwaris.[62]

Likewise, in the district of Darjeeling, the Marwaris, since their emergence, played a very dominating role in trade and commerce and there had been hardly any avenue of trade and commerce which the Marwaris did not explore. For a pretty long time, they had been directly or indirectly connected with all kinds of enterprises, such as money-lending, 'Jotedaris' (Holding of 'Jotes'), aratdari (stock business), Commission agency, wholesale and retail trade, export and import business, ownership of hotels, restaurants, godowns, and lately tea plantations and tea factories. Though many merchant communities other than the Marwaris, had been engaged in the district's trade and commerce for a pretty long time, the Marwaris were the pioneers and maintained a dominating role, both in volume and category of all trade and commerce, carried on in the said district. A contemporary District Gazetteer truly observes, "....... the Marwari dominates most of the exporting trades, viz., cardamom, oranges and potatoes and practically all the import trade of consumption goods. In addition, he has an almost complete control of the retail sale of consumption goods too and of the purchase of produce from the small consumer and producer. It cannot be denied that the Marwari has played an important part in the development of the district" ..... He still plays a most important part in the economic life of the district and his dominating position is due to his efficiency, hardiness and assiduity.[63]

Concluding Remarks :

The Marwari community, having settled themselves in this region, more or less on a permanent basis did not keep them apart from the mainstream society, culture and religion. Their coolheaded and amiable temperament, their power of adaptability and adjustability to any kind of circumstances, environment, whether regional or local, their exceptional sense of conciliation and assimilation, above all their' philanthropic outlook — all these traits of their character helped them considerably in doing business in distant and unknown places, far away from their native land. They are aware that good public relations are a requisite for business transactions and that a rapport with the general public can best be established by making cordial gesture. Their quick adoption of the local language helps them immensely in establishing this rapport. Initially, they used to migrate to a place in search of subsistence alone, keeping their womenfolk at home. So there had always been an identity crisis which they suffered from at the place of migration and to overcome this crisis they thought it wise to mingle with the local people by participating in local festivals and attending social gatherings of other communities who lived there. Thereby they tried to join the mainstream of the Society.[64]

However, after they consolidated their position in, business, and became acquainted with the new socio-economic environments they began to live with their families at the places of their migration. At this stage, their relation with the native place was just mental and a matter of formality. Sometimes, it was confined to one or two fugitive visits annually. This long absence from the native land largely increased their affinity to the place and society they migrated to and through long associations with the alien folk, both came nearer to each other and began to imbibe each others' thoughts and customs. They brought in their trail their rich culture, customs, social habits, religion and a glorious heritage which came into confrontation with a local or a regional culture, the consequence of which has been a synthesis. This assimilation was spontaneous and came through a give and take process. The policy of toleration is the basis of this assimilation as well as synthesis which is still on in a society where the Marwaris migrated and came in close contact with the masses of that society. The process is on as is evidence in different fields of social reforms and welfare, different cultural programmes, establishment of academic institutions, cultural clubs, 'Dharmasalas' (Wayside inns) publication of magazines or patrikas, little magazines, even newspapers and participation in politics, both local and national.[65]

The Marwaris of the present generation though still

predominantly a 'Bania' class (traders) are fanning out into other occupations too. There was a time, not very long ago, when no Marwari would think of any occupation other than business. But now there are Marwaris in the legal and medical professions as well as in schools, and colleges as teachers. The accountant's job is another vocation for which the Manwari seems to have a special aptitude. Although members of the Marwari community have a strong inclination to earn their livelihood by working independently as doctors, lawyers and accountants. One does come across these days a small number of job-hunters among them. The job-hunters are mostly absorbed in business and industrial establishments owned by the Marwaris themselves.[66]

The interaction between the Marwari culture and other community cultures through long associations have brought about a significant change in the Marwari orthodox culture, religious practices and social habits or customs. The spread of education among the Marwaris and their contacts with different communities, castes, social practices or customs, and religious rituals have largely contributed to broaden their outlook. Their rigid social and religious customs, traditions and habits are now on the brink of slackness. The practices of inter-dinning, intercaste marriage even inter-community marriage and widow remarriage are knocking heavily and repeatedly at the door of Marwari conservatism. The dowry system, practice of vegetarianism, divorce, etc., are now on their last legs. Marwari children are exchanging Rakhi-Bandhan with other community mates. Bengali girls are wearing clothes and garments in Rajasthani fashions and using 'Mahendi' on their palms. Marwari girls are also imitating Bengali styles and fashions in their dress, etiquettes, foods habits, etc. The Marwaris are now well conversant with the local languages or rather local colloquial languages. Thus they have partly submerged their culture in the mainstream culture of the district under review.

The Marwaris have no doubt carved out for themselves an important place in the area under study. They are now a substantive segment of society in each of the districts of

Darjeeling, Jalpaiguri and Cooch Behar. By dint of hard labour and with perseverance and tenacity, the Marwaris have risen from a modest beginning, sometimes even starting from scratch, to their present day position of importance and pre-eminence. Like the Jews of Europe and later of Americans coming from almost nowhere with a towel and a tooth brush and succeeding in his commercial venture within an unbelievably short period, the Marwari too coming from his far off homeland with a 'lota' (Vessel made of brass or copper) and a 'Kambal' (Blanket) has achieved spectacular success on the business front. The Marwaris are today unmistakably among the captains of trade and commerce in North Bengal.

Notes and References

1. Thomas A. Timberg, The Marwaris (from Traders to Industrialists), 1979, p. 10.
2. D.K. Taknet, Industrial Entrepreneurship of Shekhawati Marwaris, 1906, p. 24.
3. A1l India Marwari Yuba Manch : A brief introduction, p. 1.
4. D.K. Taknet, op.cit, p. 26.
5. Rajkumar Jajodia, "Uttar Banger Marwari Samaj" vide Kaliyaganj Barta, Sarodia Sankhya. pp. 2-3.
6. Ibid, pp. 2-3.
7. Narayan Chandra Saha, The Marwari Community in Eastern India, 2003, pp. 53-54.
8. Romila Thapar, Ancient Indian Social History : Some Interpretations, 1978, p. 44.
9. Romila Thapar, A Hstory of India, Vol. I. 1982, p. 65.
10. Narayan Chandra Saha, op.cit., p. 37.
11. W.W. Hunter, A Statistical Account of Bengal, Vol. X, 1974, p. 261.
12. Narayan Chandra Saha, op-cit, pp. 67-68.
13. D. K. Taknet, op-cit, p. 55.
14. Thomas A. Timberg, op-cit., p. 102.
15. B.B. Mishra, The Indian Middle Class, 1978, p. 32.
16. Haraprosad Chattopadhyay, Internal Migration in

India : A case study of Bengal, Calcutta, 1987, p. 338.
17. Ibid, pp. 336-338.
18. W.W. Hunter, op-cit., p. 261.
19. Ibid, p. 87.
20. Narayan Chandra Saha, 'Kuchbeharer Marwari Samaj', 'Madhu Parni', a special issue on the district of Cooch-Behar, BS 1396, p. 147.
21. Thomas A. Timberg, op-cit., p. 58.
22. Krishnendu Dey, 'Madhuparni', op-cit., p. 176.
23. Ananda Chandra Ghosh, Lecture on the History of Cooch-Behar, BS 1272 , p. 158.
24. Asruman Dasgupta, "Krishak Samaj O Riner Dai", Cooch Behar, Darpan, 1st year, 1st edn., C.S.P., BS 1345, p.15.
25. J.F. Gruning, op-cit., p.130.
26. W.W. Hunter, op-cit., p. 85.
27. Ibid, p. 260.
28. J.F. Gruning, Eastern Bengal & Assam District Gazetteers, Jalpaiguri, 1911, p. 42.
29. W.W. Hunter, op-cit., p. 358.
30. Kalyani Bajpeyi, "Jainism in Early Inscriptions of Mathura", Religion and Culture of the Jains, 1973, p. 38.
31. Kalyani Bajpeyi, op.cit., p. 39.
32. Ibid, p. 41.
33. Narayan Chandra Saha, op.ct., p. 65-66.
34. Khan Chaudhury Amanatullah Khan, Cooch-Behar Itihas, 1936, pp. 137-138.
35. Bhagabati Charan Bandopadhyay, Cooch Beharer Itihas, (ed.) Dr. Nripendra Nath Paul, 1987, p. 177.
36. Interview with Punam Chand Lakhotia, Cooch-Behar.
37. Harendra Narayan Chaudhury, The Cooch Behar State and its Land Revenue Settlements, Cooch Behar, 1903, p. 195.
38. Judub Chandra Chuckerbutty, Civil Judge, Cooch-

Behar, The Annual Administrative Report of the Cooch-Behar State for the year 1891-92 , 1892, p. 3.

39. Bhagavati Charan Banerjee, Cooch-Beharer Itihas, (ed.) Dr. Nripendra Nath Paul, 1987, pp. 20-21.
40. W.W. Hunter, Vol. X, op.cit., p. 398.
41. Krishnendu Dey, op.cit., pp. 178-179.
42. Bisweswar Ray, District Census Handbook, Cooch-Behar, 1966, p. 123.
43. Harendra Narayan Chaudhury, op.cit., p. 53.
44. The Annual Administrative Report of the Cooch Behar State for the year 1891-92, 1892, p. 10.
45. Ibid, p. 23.
46. The Annual Administrative Report of the Cooch Behar State for the year 1897-98, 1898, Sec. VI, p. 82.
47. Durgadas Majumder, West Bengal District Gazetteers, Cooch Behar, 1977, p. 211.
48. The Annual Administrative Report of the Cooch Behar State for the year 1892-93, 1893, p. 21.
49. The Annual Administrative Report for the year 1891-92, 1892, Sec. I, p. 9.
50. The Annual Administrative Report for the year 1892-93, 1893, p. 21.
51. Harendra Narayan Chaudhury, op.cit., p. 63.
52. The Annual Administrative Report of the Cooch Behar State for the year 1891-92, 1892, p. 9.
53. Interview with Bachhraj Chowdhury, Changrabandha, 13.10.1992.
54. Harendra Narayan Chaudhury, op.cit., p. 64.
55. Ibid, p. 50.
56. Ibid, pp. 67-69.
57. Ibid, p. 69.
58. Records and Registers of the Merchants Association, District of Jalpaiguri.
60. Kalyan Das, Jalpaiguri.
61. Interview with Madan Lal Lakhotia, Jalpaiguri, 28.7.91.
62. Records and Registers, Jalpaiguri Merchants' Associations, Jalpaiguri.

63. A.J. Dash, Gazetteer of Darjeeling District, Alipur, 1945, p. 174.
64. Narayan Chandra Saha, op.cit., p. 269.
65. Ibid, p. 270-271.
66. Ibid, p. 305-306.

INDEX